Energy and Form

The MIT Press

Cambridge, Massachusetts,
and London, England

Energy and Form

An Ecological Approach
to Urban Growth

Ralph L. Knowles

This book was set in IBM Composer Univers
by The MIT Press Media Department,
printed on Mead Moistrite Matte
by Halliday Lithograph Corporation
and bound in Columbia Milbank Linen
by Wm. F. Zahrndt & Son Inc.
in the United States of America.

Library of Congress Cataloging in Publi-
cation Data

Knowles, Ralph L.
    Energy and form.

Bibliography: p.
    1. Architectural design. 2. Energy
        conservation.
I. Title.
NA2750.K56   711'.55   74-3003
ISBN 0-262-11050-4

Contents

Preface

The work presented here spans a decade, from 1962 to 1972. The projects that form its nucleus resulted from studio work undertaken with architecture students, first at Auburn University, Auburn, Alabama, and later at the University of Southern California. The teaching methods and projects were influenced by work done much earlier under the direction of Eduardo Catalano at North Carolina State University in 1953-54. Catalano encouraged his students to see and to measure the impact of natural forces on buildings. The experience revealed for me, and for many others, a realistic architectural path into the future. Catalano's message was that construction could take place in a rational way.

Not until almost ten years later, in 1962, at Auburn University, did I have an opportunity to personally develop the theme of environmental impact on buildings. This effort was supported by the Graham Foundation for Advanced Studies in the Fine Arts, then under the direction of John D. Entenza.

The original intent of the study was not to involve natural forces but rather to improve the quality of the urban environment by designing buildings that offered clues to orientation. The impetus came from Kevin Lynch's book, *The Image of the City,* published two years before, in 1960. In Lynch's study, which he states was strongly influenced by the painter Gyorgy Kepes, he raised the issue of man's dependence upon perceiving the city as a set of associations. He did not provide a framework within which such perceived associations might be generated.

William K. Turner, who was also teaching architecture at Auburn, and who has since become Dean of Architecture at Tulane University, undertook with me the search for rational design criteria that would provide clues to orientation in the urban environment. This search eventually led to James Marston Fitch's book, *American Building,* which had been published in 1948. In it, Fitch posited that the ultimate task of architecture is to interpose itself between man and the natural environment. Furthermore, he criticized the overreliance upon mechanical systems as means of response.

The work at Auburn resulted in the development of systems comprised of structural planes that were sized, shaped, and oriented to control wind and sun, while carrying the weight of the building. These planar structures were applied to an array of basic building shapes. The surface structures, in responding to natural forces, became differentiated in a way that provided clues to orientation, just as differentiated structures in nature offer clues to orientation. Near the end of the project, in 1963, I began to speculate on the possibility of generating building shapes with special adaptive properties so that shape as well as structure combined to provide a form response to natural forces—or what Sir D'Arcy Thompson called in his 1917 work, *On Growth and Form,* "a diagram of forces."

In the fall of 1963 I joined the architecture faculty at the University of Southern California in Los Angeles. Preoccupation with the development of teaching methods delayed further work on form response for three years. Then in 1966 a study of form response to natural forces was begun under a grant from the National Endowment for the Arts. Working with me in the third-year undergraduate studio were architect Pierre Koenig and landscape architect Emmet Wemple. From 1966 to 1968 we undertook both historical and laboratory studies to investigate the correlation of building form with variation in the forces of sun, wind, and water. For these studies, Koenig dealt primarily with the impact of wind, Wemple with water, and I with the sun. Each of us, working with third-year undergraduate architecture students, developed equipment and simulation techniques to evaluate historical building forms and to generate new ones using modern building technology.

In 1968, with a second grant from the National Endowment for the Arts, I undertook a large-scale case study of diversified settlement in Owens Valley, California. This work was done with graduate urban design students and a group of professional consultants including architect-planner Richard D. Berry and biologist Robert M. Chew, both of the University of Southern California, and meteorologist James Edinger of the University of California at Los Angeles. The purpose of this case study was to develop ecological frameworks within which buildings could be formed and located to minimize the energy cost of maintaining their equilibrium in a natural environment of cyclic forces.

While this theme had generally run through all my work since 1962, new meaning had been lent to it by a growing national recognition of what has come to be called the "energy crisis." The term is appropriate and describes a state resulting from the rapid, worldwide development of natural resources. When I was an architecture student in the 1950s, Buckminster Fuller was teaching at North Carolina State University and prophetically warned us of the consequences of such rapid development. At the time, we heard him only faintly.

Owens Valley Study, a documentation of the work, was printed in 1969 with the additional support of the Architectural Guild, a professional support group for the Department of Architecture, at the University of Southern California.

It was also in 1969 that Ian McHarg published his brilliant study, *Design With Nature,* making any future pleas redundant and, at the same time, charging the rest of us with the responsibility to further develop needed design tools. Finally, in 1970, support was given by the Los Angeles Department of Water and Power to continue the study of Owens Valley, and three students, Alan E. Gatzke, Gary S. Shigemura, and Gilbert A. Stayner, who had all participated in the original study, after their graduation undertook with me a continuation of the Owens Valley study, which brings it to its present state.

This work of ten years has been influenced by my teachers and teaching colleagues. It has been supported and encouraged by architect Sam T. Hurst, who was dean of the schools of architecture at Auburn University and at USC. Beyond that, I wish to express my thanks to Inez Riley, who spent many weekends typing the manuscript, and to the several people who provided editorial assistance: my wife, Mer, biologist Robert Chew, and biology student James Nelson of USC.

Perhaps most important, I thank the students of Auburn and the University of Southern California for their help and their enthusiasm. There is no way this work could have been undertaken without them.

Funding has come from various sources and is gratefully acknowledged:

1962-63:
The Graham Foundation for Advanced Studies in the Fine Arts, Chicago, Ill.
1967-70:
National Endowment for the Arts, Washington, D. C.
1969-70:
Architectural Guild, Los Angeles, California.
1970-71:
Department of Water and Power, Los Angeles, California.

Ralph L. Knowles
School of Architecture and Fine Arts
University of Southern California
Los Angeles, California

January 1974

Student Credits

1962-63:

Building-surface responses.
Auburn University, Auburn, Alabama—
fourth-year architecture students.

S. P. Acton, J. H. Ballard, R. R. Biggers,
A. L. Binkley, C. A. Boutwell, J. W. Bowden,
J. H. Brady, W. W. Brown, J. I. Carrera,
J. K. J. Colman, J. B. Coykendall, R. M.
Cugowski, D. E. Egger, R. M. Freeman,
B. L. Hagler, H. S. Hill, B. D. Knodel,
L. M. Leeger, B. F. Love, D. L. Meador,
G. H. Oldham, J. T. Regan, W. L. Richmond,
W. T. Savage, J. M. Smith, C. J. Snook,
S. B. Todd, J. B. Williams, C. D. Woodfin.

1965-66:

Building-form responses. University
of Southern California, Los Angeles,
California—third-year architecture
students.

J. D. Black, S. L. Blair, A. Bruno, M. Chen,
S. Dent, G. Getchel, R. Hippenhammer,
R. Holz, V. Inoshita, D. B. Kilman, A. Kuro-
kawa, R. K. Lashier, D. Malone, S. A.
Nicholson, A. Stewart, H. Tracy, R. Wer-
ner, R. York, D. Zimbaldi.

1966-67:

Building-form responses. University of
Southern California—third-year architecture students.

C. Chern, G. E. Freedman, M. C. Klinger-
man, J. D. Meisenhelder, D. C. Moser,
P. B. Ohannesian, S. Panja, M. A. Pearce,
A. Sakamoto, R. S. Selvidge, D. J. Shonk-
wiler, A. B. Susser, J. N. Talsky, G. N.
Togawa, S. A. Woolley, R. I. Yanagawa.

1967-68:

Historical studies. University of Southern
California—third-year architecture students.

G. Anderson, P. Canelo, R. Davidson, R.
Dewar, M. Dubin, R. Gallagher, T. Jacob-
son, S. Jhono, R. G. Kaufman, R. Mac-
Donald, R. McMahon, R. Nickum, J.
Parkin, G. Talmadge, D. Williamson.

1968-70:

Owens Valley study. University of
Southern California—graduate urban
design students.

S. Burton, A. E. Gatzke, R. Linnell, J.
Meisenhelder, C. Okumura, M. Pearce,
G. S. Shigemura, D. Shonkwiler, G. A.
Stayner, A. B. Susser.

Introduction

The subject of this book is energy conservation through design. Its scope is the form of our built environment. Its method is deductive and rests on the premise that human survival depends on our willingness to consciously direct urban growth.

Design implies planned direction. For the built environment, the end is generally a project consisting of a single building or a number of buildings arranged as a group to satisfy some purpose related to economics, community need, and aesthetics. Unfortunately, the economics are often viewed in the short run, the community at too small a scale, and the aesthetics in fashionable terms.

Such views of the purposes for design are inadequate for our time and must be replaced. This book advocates three new purposes for design: First, an economic purpose for urban growth that stresses the long-term costs of maintaining equilibrium in the built environment over the short-term costs of development; second, a large-scale view of a community as a set of associations in which the diversity of community needs is met not by supplying ever increased mobility but by building closer contact diversity into the arrangement; and third, an aesthetic based on form as a natural adaptation for survival.

Each of these three purposes requires some change of attitude on the part of industrialized nations. The first of these, a revised economic attitude, seems to fly in the face of all our established notions about supporting urban growth, whether held by a capitalist or a socialist society. But attitudes can change rapidly in time of crisis, and an energy crisis is with us now. Its beginnings go far back in time but its accumulated impact has recently hit us full-blown and is going to be long-lived. An unfortunate, short-term solution

to this problem would hold to the old attitudes and continue the old methods of supplying increasing demand with more oil drilling, more strip mining, more nuclear plants and so on in a desperate attempt to keep a wasteful system running. A new attitude is required that will make long-term conservation of our natural resources a governing purpose for design.

The second purpose requires a change in the way we achieve the associations that make up a community. The basic components of any association of buildings are those that allow us to be housed, to work, and to shop in some balanced combination. The automobile has allowed the past two decades of urban growth to space these three basic functions very far apart. The great new cities of the southwestern United States are spectacular examples of arrangements comprised of large and specialized segments of housing, commerce, and industry. Access to all three functions requires that people migrate daily, often over great distances. The development of rapid, public transportation promises only to maintain the segregation of activities and people that now characterizes our sprawling cities. An attitude is now called for that allows diversity of activity in near proximity to become a governing purpose for new growth.

The third purpose requires that we change our prevalent attitudes about what constitutes good building design. Fashion can play a part, but the governing criteria must include response to the cyclic forces of nature. The forms of buildings and groups of buildings must, themselves, be adaptive. The cyclic variations of nature must be specifically recognized as a governing purpose for the design of an adaptive architecture that will embody a new aesthetic.

If each of the three design purposes of economics, community, and aesthetics were restated in terms responsive to the natural environment, the result would be a transformation of our existing cities and a different mode of new growth resulting in the conservation of energy and of our natural environment.

The underlying premise of this book is that urban growth, consciously directed and based on principles that correlate building form with natural variation for purposes of energy conservation, will exhibit a diversity of built forms that, when transferred into functional terms, will usually produce the close-contact diversity essential for a rich and humane community life without overreliance on mobility.

The approach taken in this book is a three-part investigation of built form. The first part is historical. It analyzes indigenous buildings of the southwestern United States and derives from them principles of form that correlate with natural variation. The second part moves to the present and uses modern techniques for measuring natural variation in a large valley region as a basis for matching general descriptions of building form to environmental conditions. The third part moves into the future to suggest the general character of individual buildings and building/groups as they might be sequentially built using energy conservation as a criterion.

Over the past two decades, urban development has been characterized by millions of acres of detached single-family houses, as in the rapidly growing southwest of the United States. The resulting arrangement requires great mobility to sustain the daily contacts for living, working, and shopping. In addition, the low diversity of the arrangement does not reflect the variety of environmental conditions that result from the cyclic forces of nature.

Such natural variation should inspire a rich variety of building shapes and structures.

Most of the projects described in this book specifically concentrate on reducing the susceptibility of individual buildings and groups of buildings to environmental perturbation as a way to conserve energy. The object is to use the shape and structure, the geometry and scale of buildings to help maintain equilibrium within a building under the stress of multiple cyclic forces in nature.

The energy required to maintain equilibrium within a building is a function of its susceptibility to the stresses of environmental variation. Susceptibility, in turn, can generally be expressed as a ratio between exposed surface and contained volume. This ratio (S/V) is relatively high for the detached single-family dwelling that comprises the majority of our housing.

Variations in the amounts of maintenance energy result from the fact that the building forms are not differentiated in order to reduce the effects of such important variations as seasonal insolation. The failure to differentiate is paid for with the high cost of controlling variations in the demand for energy. The energy input is differentiated continuously over the life of the building, with virtually no differentiation of building form as a supporting mode of response. An important step would be to shape buildings to reduce seasonal variations in sun energy to equalize insolation from summer to winter.

Because the susceptibility of the building envelope is not usually considered, great amounts of energy are needed for maintenance. The failure to take daily and seasonal variations into account, particularly with reference to sun energy, produces high maintenance costs over the life of the building and increases the need for control. This problem of control is the result of what is generally described in terms of "peak loading."

Stated simply, we grow cheaply and maintain expensively. But the energy-resource condition today requires that we consider alternative modes of growth with more initial control and higher growth costs but also with the promise of longer range stability, lower maintenance costs, and a lessening of control over the life of the system. Such alternatives would exhibit higher diversity than we now see. Modern societies possess the technological ability to go beyond the primitive industrial phase of multifolding as the primary means of production; they can infinitely diversify their industrial output. This has provided an unprecedented opportunity to build urban arrangements at a large scale that are vastly more responsive to variations in the natural environment.

Although it might appear that ongoing internal activity, rather than reaction to environmental stimuli, is fundamental to existing urban systems, the laws of dynamic balance cannot forever be ignored. In respecting them lies the possbility of generating large urban arrangements that are purposefully differentiated in terms that complement nature and are comprehensible to man. Only then will it be possible to build an artificial environment in which the forms of the built arrangements respond to the same rhythms that have guided men's steps from the beginning.

Of course, energy conservation cannot be the sole criterion for the design of our urban environments and built form is not the only mode of response to cyclic forces in nature. To be sure, the immediate needs of people must be considered, but those who would take a more directly social approach to community development still need a physical framework which, if sufficiently diversified, can meet an array of human needs now and in the future. An energy-conserving approach to urban design would provide such diversity. Those who would respond to the cycles of nature by, as one stoic has said, "simply putting on and taking off one's sweater," have not yet recognized the enormity of the problem or the full potential of built form at the twentieth-century urban scale.

While this book states all the evidence I have collected to this point on the potential of built form to mitigate the effects of cyclic natural forces, and while it does show frameworks for community development and even some examples of isolated building forms, it does not show examples of a fully developed range of diversified buildings comprising a community. There are two reasons for this. The first is that there are, quite obviously, other criteria to be considered. This book does take a singular approach that provides a framework for developing many specific design options while meeting the limited criteria for energy conservation. The second reason is time. Specific images *do* need developing. They must be new images, based on a new approach to building by a new generation of builders. It is hoped that this work may offer some guidance to those builders.

Part One   Adaptation to the Environment

1
Adaptive Behavior in Nature

All things in nature respond to change and to transitions from one state of the environment to another. The environment changes when the natural forces of sun, wind, and water interact with each other and with the earth. Differing lengths of grass in a field or shifts in the pitch of a cricket's song correlate with variations in their surroundings. Changes in the color and condition of a bird's feathers announce the seasons. The sun's daily cycle can be read in the flower's rotation. Such phenomena are generally attributed to the necessity for natural systems to exchange material, information, and energy with their environments in a manner favorable to their survival and, during a certain period, to their growth. In this exchange, nothing escapes exposure to natural variation, and survival depends upon a wide range of adaptive behavior. The response may be relocation, as with migrating birds; transformation of skin pigment, as with some fish; or variations in the rate of energy transfer, as with the reduced metabolism of some hibernating animals. Such techniques are part of an inherent capability that is unique and characteristic of that system.

Natural systems do not adapt equally well to all kinds of change. Exceptional occurrences in nature evidently do not result in adaptive behavior, although the displacement that results from exceptional pressures may lie within a system's existing capacity. Such occurrences, however, do not apparently determine the system's limits of response. A system's capacity to act in a favorable way must evolve in response to insistent and approximate repetition of similar sets of conditions in the environment. The changes must be recurrent.

The result of adaptation in recurring conditions in nature is a remarkable array of forms that can be characterized in both static and dynamic terms. Static or spatial manifestations are observed at an instant in time as differences in any selected condition from one point in an adapting system to another. Such differences occur in the dimension, temperature, mass, or salinity, for example, of parts being compared. Dynamic or temporal manifestations may be observed as differences that occur over time in the condition of a system as a whole or in the condition of a selected part or combination of parts. A continuity of instantaneously observed differences in the condition of related parts or differences recognized in the same part or arrangement of parts over time is generally called *differentiation*.

Differentiation corresponds with directional variations in the influence of natural forces. The vertical separation of color in algae growth, for example, correlates with the penetration to different ocean depths of various parts of the sunlight spectrum. The result is a differentiated response with green algae in shallow water and red algae further down, since the red end of the spectrum penetrates least and the green end of the spectrum continues to greater depths.

The biologist Marston Bates has drawn an interesting analogy between the forest and the sea and, in the process, has transferred to the forest a vocabulary more often used to describe life in the sea.[1]

1. See Marston Bates, *The Forest and the Sea* (New York: Random House, 1960), p. 19.

While studying jungle yellow fever, in the Amazon forest, he recognized a vertical distribution of insect life that could be correlated with the differential penetration of light. He described a "pelagic zone" of active photosynthesis and, below that, a "benthos zone" where organisms live entirely on second-hand materials that drift down from above. With such terminology, he compared the vertical differentiation of two diverse realms.

Although Bates's observations were made in a Brazilian rain forest where the trees close in overhead and the forest floor remains a "damp gloom," the basic fact of vertical differentiation can also be observed in the more familiar scene of the rural wood or neighborhood park (fig. 1.1). Vertical changes occur here, too, in response to heat, gravity, and water, as well as light, and the activity cycles of insects, birds, and animals are structured in the time intervals of day and season.

In addition to the vertical changes that occur so obviously in the forest and the sea, a great range of horizontal variation takes place, but seems less evident because of the greater dimensions involved. The shape of the ocean floor produces variations of water depth that result in remarkable differences in fishing conditions from one location to another. The great riverlike currents of the world's oceans enrich their paths, while often leaving the regions between diminished of warmth and life.

Temporal, as well as spatial, aspects of differentiated natural responses have been reported by Karl von Frisch in his famous studies of bees.[2] Frisch reported on the honeybee's ability to orient itself in relation to the food source and the hive and, beyond that, to communicate the information to other bees (fig. 1.2). The honeybee apparently orients itself in relation to the food source and the hive by using the sun, which the bee's particular seeing equipment allows it to locate, even on cloudy days. By means of a little "dance," the bee then communicates this information to the others.

The migration of birds provides another example of temporal differentiation. Recent observations indicate that newborn chicks operate on a twenty-four-hour oxygen consumption and activity cycle, independent of exposure to the cyclical movement of the sun. They have a built-in biological clock. Using this clock in combination with the ability to see and to fly, a bird apparently uses the sun to orient itself in the north-south migration. The sun orientation has long been suspected, but researchers were at a loss to explain why the bird did not fly off course as the sun moved through its daily cycle. It is now clear that a bird reorients itself over time. It will also fly in a false direction if the sun is artificially repositioned by the use of a mirror. But short of this kind of mischief and by virtue of his internal clock the bird seems to know what to do when flying long distances over time.

2. Karl von Frisch, *Dance Language and Orientation of Bees* (Cambridge, Mass.: Harvard University Press, 1967); and von Frisch, *Man and the Living World* (New York: Time, Inc., 1962).

Feeding territories offer another example of adaptation to spatial and temporal influences. By studying the Scottish red grouse during successive springs, V. C. Wynne-Edwards was able to describe changes in the size of land areas controlled by male grouse.[3] He found that such individual territories change in size from season to season (fig. 1.3). This is a temporal change, which results from variations in rainfall, humidity, and the amount of sunlight. The territories are not the same size upon the same site within any given season. Wynne-Edwards correlated the size of individual territories with feeding conditions. He observed that territory size was smaller where the feeding conditions were good than where they were poor. The result would be a kind of vertical differentiation, with large feeding territories on the tops of hills and small ones in the valleys if, for example, the heather grew very well in the damp valleys and poorly on the dry uplands (fig. 1.4, *top*). If heather grows well on the sunny, south slopes, the result would be generally smaller territories, while the larger territories would occur on shady, north slopes (fig. 1.4, *bottom*). A combination of moisture and sun would produce changes of territory size from top to bottom of slope and from one orientation to another that could be related to a stable grouse population.

3. V. C. Wynne-Edwards, "Population Control in Animals," *Scientific American,* 211 (1964), 68-74.

In the example of the grouse, once the word *territory* is replaced with the more generally useful term *increment,* states and events affecting the general welfare of the grouse may be viewed in the more general terms of functional differentiation. Then the natural world can be seen to abound with examples. The paths trodden by grazing animals often indicate that because of ground slope, incrementation resulting from the intersection of paths does not look alike in all directions (fig. 1.5). The increments appear to be polarized so that their dimension is consistently smaller down the slope from what it is across. The feathers of a bird or scales on a fish are obvious displays of variation in size and shape as well as color. These and countless other examples fill and enrich our world. They are enjoyed by men but are often taken for granted because of their inevitability, their "naturalness." Under some circumstances, similar examples of functional differentiation become apparent in man's own arrangements. Such examples also seem to be inevitable and "natural."

Fig. 1.1.
Vertical differentiation can
be observed in the familiar
scene of the rural wood or
neighborhood park.

Fig. 1.2.
The honeybee apparently orients himself in relation to the food source and the hive by using the sun, which his particular seeing equipment allows him to locate even on cloudy days. Then, by means of a little "dance," he communicates this information to other bees. Based on the drawing by Henri A. Fluchere in *Man and the Living World* by Karl von Frisch (New York: Time Reading Program Special Edition, 1965), p. 160.

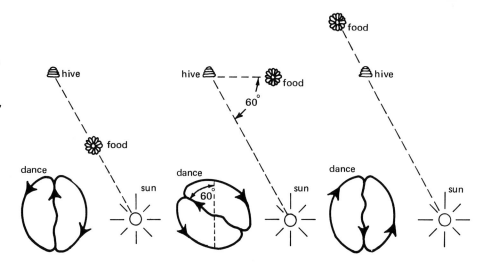

Fig. 1.3.
The feeding territories of the Scottish red grouse change in size from season to season. This is a temporal change resulting from variations in rainfall, humidity, and the amount of sunlight. This and fig. 1.4 based on the drawing by Thomas Prentiss in an article "Population Control in Animals" by V. C. Wynne-Edwards, *Scientific American*, 211 (August 1964), 73.

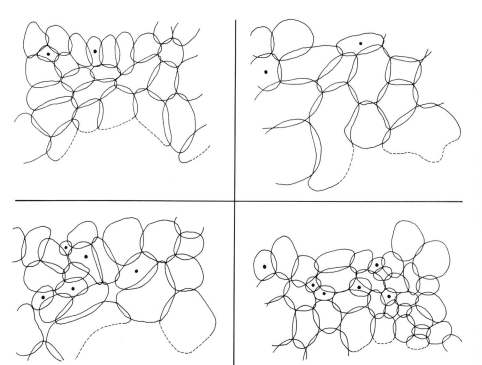

Fig. 1.4
(a) The grouse territories are not the same size upon the same site within any given season. A kind of vertical differentiation, with large territories on the tops of hills and small ones in the valleys, would result if the heather grew well in the damp valleys and poorly on the dry uplands. Where the feeding is better, the territories are smaller. (b) If the heather grows well on the sunny, south slopes, the result would be generally smaller grouse territories, while the larger territories would occur on shady, north slopes.

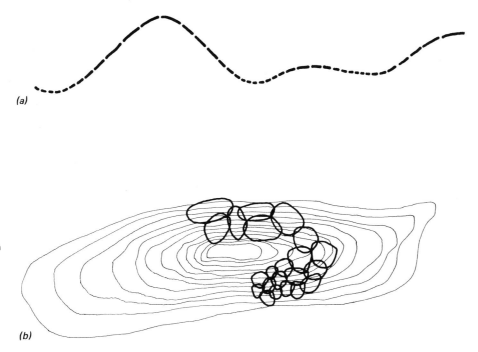

(a)

(b)

Fig. 1.5
The paths trod by grazing animals often indicate that because of ground slope, incrementation resulting from the intersection of paths does not look alike in all directions. The increments appear to be polarized so that their dimension is consistently smaller down the slope than across. Based on a photograph by Edward P. Lanning in his article "Early Man in Peru," *Scientific American*, 213, (October 1965), 73.

Adaptive Behavior in Man

In primitive situations men's marks upon the land exhibit some of the same characteristics as those of other free-moving forms of life. In simple conditions where they do not have the machine ability to carry out grand and purposeful arrangements, men proceed in response to forces beyond their control, through unselfconscious processes rather than by design. With feet, hands, and simple tools of stick and stone, they acted in ways that were little more than slight modifications of the techniques of creatures far below them on the evolutionary scale. Their behavior was adaptive and displayed itself through characteristic modifications upon the land, such as paths to follow game and stones to mark special places. Primitive man's own territories and paths could be directly correlated with the recurring and insistent effects of environment. Along with the other creatures, he was susceptible and almost immediately responsive to variations in a world that pressed insistently upon him.

Under these circumstances, man's will to survive was probably not unique. What set him apart must certainly have been a gradually developing awareness that guided his anticipation of recurrences for which he might consciously plan and consider alternative modes of response. While the extent to which he could modify his environment was not dimensionally great, his situation was obviously improved by the awareness of recurrence; he might consciously prepare for the next event which he understood would be only slightly modified from the last. The phenomenon repeated itself; only by degree did it vary. The snows fell every winter but some winters made walking more difficult and the game more vulnerable. The rivers wrenched at their banks every spring, but some springs saw the banks give way and the river change course, leaving oxbow-shaped lakes behind.

Based upon the knowledge of what had gone before, primitive men could, for instance, dig holes in the hillside to collect rain water from seasonal storms. In itself this is a purposeful thing to do, an effort that is the result of conscious planning and choice; some other course of action, such as migration, might have been selected. On the other hand, once the decision was made to modify the land, the particular form taken by this response lay outside his ability to affect. Instead, the form was subject to minor variations in the shape and structure of the site and must be described as adaptive. It could hardly be described as planned. Its limits and internal structure must have evolved from topography, geology, and orientation to sun, wind and water, not from a specific image held beforehand.

Examples of primitive agriculture still exist in some parts of the world, looking very much like other efforts found in nature. Some African peoples still terrace the ground, collect rainwater in small pools, and then plant seeds upon the containing earth walls.

Although such water systems are purposefully derived in order to supply food for the community, the major forces at work are still those of natural selection, and any purpose beyond basic survival is not much evident in the marks left upon the ground by these laboring farmers. What is evident in their marks, is a functional differentiation very much like that already described in animal territories. Simple farming techniques anywhere in the world and at all times seem to exhibit similar attributes, which can be directly correlated with the effects of environmental force action. The distinction between adaptive behavior and purposeful action is an important one. The functional differentiation of such early farming cannot be described as purposeful in the sense of being a willful imposition at every productive step along the way.

At this adaptive stage of development, men cannot choose to overcome nature by some splendid expenditure of energy, and they must content themselves with what is available through the relatively meager and direct action of their own bodies. Although the environment has been modified through some transformation of the shape and structure of the earth, its scale is only a slight multiplication of the fox's den or the beaver's pond. Up to this point men have not fundamentally altered the environment to suit their purpose of survival. Variations in each environmental factor can still be easily and directly correlated with variations in the physical arrangement. Even though men might have considered their purpose beforehand, they could not operationally overcome primitive technological abilities.

Primitive men must have felt keenly the impress of environment. Under the constraints of natural recurrence, their essential exchange of material, information, and energy was very much in the manner of all mobile life, and this exchange left them open and susceptible. The harder the environment thrust itself upon them, the more immediate and characteristic became men's responses. They could not escape the recurrence of winter snow or the oppressive heat of midsummer except by modifying their activities to a considerable degree. The recurrence of seasons had its counterpart in the rhythm of those activities.

One means of response used by early men derived from their mobility. They were free to get up and move when they became uncomfortable. Before men learned to improve a fixed location by physically transforming it or by radically modifying the rate of energy exchange through the controlled use of fire, men could only reduce environmental stress by moving from place to place. This movement could be directly correlated with variations in the environment. As winter approached, they migrated to a warmer location or found shelter at the forest's edge or in the lee of a hill. As the hot sun of August dried up the watering holes, they sought new sources in cooler and wetter terrain. As conditions recurred with the seasons they traced their steps, cycle upon cycle, until the lines they trod became paths. The paths met and crossed. This tangible network established spatial limits upon their domain and its internal structuring.

A temporal as well as spatial aspect to this arrangement existed. Some parts were regularly inhabited at one season and not at another. The intensity of the activities rose and fell according to daily cycles of heat and wind and in conformity with the longer, seasonal cycles affecting food and water. Under these circumstances, the intervals marking activities, as well as the variations in those activities, were essentially tied to the cycles of nature.

One clear example of a spatial-temporal structure achieved by the cyclical process of relocation can be recognized in the territories of Piute Indians who once inhabited California's Owens Valley.[4] Their settlements were strung out in a north-south direction at the base of the Sierra Nevada Mountains. The Sierras rim the western edge of the valley and from them flows virtually all of the surface water entering the basin. Villages were located beside streams that dropped quickly from the mountain crest to the valley floor and on to join the Owens River (fig. 1.6).

From these permanent settlements, generally located in the most favorable microclimate, including a good water supply, the Piutes made seasonal migrations as village groups (fig. 1.7). Each summer, as the days began to lengthen and the temperature began to climb, the group moved west into the higher meadows of the Sierras. Here they enjoyed the coolness of an increased elevation. As the fall approached and passed into early winter they migrated ten to fifteen miles across the valley to the east, where they gathered pine nuts at the base of the Inyo and White Mountains. Here they were at a lower elevation and had a west and somewhat south exposure adding to their comfort as the winter days approached. The seasonal cycle was finally completed when they returned to their permanent campsite at the base of the Sierras to live out the winter in the relative comfort of primitive enclosures that could be heated

in a reasonably effective way. At each stopping point along this seasonal migration they made daily forays for water, game, and any vegetable material to supplement their diet.

The long orientation of twenty miles from the crest of the Sierras to the crest of the Inyos lay in an east-west direction. It established the magnitude and direction of seasonal migrations. The north-south dimension of a territory was about two to four miles and established similar limits upon the daily foray. This description is typical, with a few notable exceptions. The shape and internal structuring of the greatest number of Piute territories is strong and evident as a set of related natural domains. It is essentially a highly differentiated structure in which location becomes a function of time, with the interval being marked by a recurrence of natural events.

No doubt it took the Piutes a long time to put their mark upon the land and, when they had finished, their efforts were hardly discernible among the grasses and rocks and trees. There is no regular imprint of geometry here, no apparently self-conscious arrangements. The marks signaled a cumulative fit—the result of a slow process and not a planned arrangement.

4. W. A. Chalfant, *The Story of Inyo* (Stanford, Calif: Stanford University Press, 1933); Neil M. Judd, *The Material Culture of Pueblo Bonito* (Washington, D.C.: Smithsonian Institution, 1954); and J. H. Steward, *Ethnography of the Owens Valley Piute* (Berkeley, Calif.: University of California Press, 1933).

Fig. 1.6
A typical site for permanent settlement of Piute Indians. The site was usually in a meadow area adjacent to a stream.

(a)

(b)

Fig. 1.7
(a) An example of a spatial-temporal structure achieved by the cyclical process of relocation can be recognized in the territories of Piute Indians who once inhabited California's Owens Valley. From their permanent settlements, located in the generally most favorable microclimate, which included a good water supply, the Piutes made seasonal migrations as village groups. (b) The Piute territories did not function in precisely the same way to support the village groups living within their limits. Variation of site produced three different kinds of territory that can be characterized by the structure of seasonal migrations.

linguistic barrier
pine forests
marsh
rivers
band territories
○ permanent villages

Through a process of slow growth, the Piutes generated what appears to have been a stable system until the westward migrations of hunters, trappers, miners, and farmers during the eighteenth and nineteenth centuries. It is quite unlikely that all their original settlements were made simultaneously; not all the territories would have come into use at once. Rather, there was probably a slow growth of the valley's population over a period of time through migration and reproduction.

The convenient instrument for systematically generating settlement in the valley would appear to be the territory of a village group. It comprised an increment for bringing about the original change in number and distribution of people; it then continued as a mechanism for maintaining a stable population. Each Piute territory comprising an increment-of-change appears to have been self-sufficient insofar as food, water, fuel, and building materials were concerned. Each territory appears to have maintained a constant size after it was established. Within this territory they relocated to satisfy their needs as the seasons changed. The main relocation took place as an east-west migration. In that direction the valley is most highly differentiated, allowing the greatest diversification and consequently the greatest choice of conditions in the shortest dimension.

Throughout the entire valley, down the cool and well-watered Sierra slopes to the western edge of the basin, across the marshy land that then formed the valley's floor, and finally up the gentle, arid slopes of the Inyos on the east, ecological domains were extremely narrow compared to their north-south dimension. While there were seasonal variations in that structure, the picture of a rather broad range of ecological domains comprising the territory generally holds true. This array of conditions afforded the Indians all their needs and, with the exception of a communal hunt for which all groups gathered in the fall, there was no reason to move in the north-south direction; to move that way would not increase choice for the village group unless they were willing to migrate many times the distance required along the east-west axis. Besides, to move in the north-south direction brought one quickly to his neighbor's territory and invited retaliation, sometimes involving death for the offender.

All territories did not function in precisely the same way to support the village groups living within their limits. Three basic types have been distinguished, all having in common a higher degree of ecological structuring in the east-west than in the north-south direction, but differing in the particular combination of domains comprising that structure.

The central, shank portion of the valley provides the most typical arrangement and has been previously described. It was generally the exclusive holding of a single village group and could be characterized as migratory. Access across the valley was clear in this area and the paths for seasonal migration could easily stay within and parallel to the long boundaries of the territory. There was essentially no reason for the group to trespass across its boundaries on the north or south.

The second type of territory lies in the southern part of the valley and may be characterized as both communal and migratory. It fell within the region of a granite formation called the Alabama Hills, which blocked the east-west seasonal migration of several groups (fig. 1.8). In this situation the Piutes could choose to migrate around the hills, to the north and south, or through a single pass at their midsection. In any case, these groups could not afford the luxury of exclusive territories with inviolate boundaries. To enjoy the full range of choice necessary for life required that they merge their lines of communication. It demanded that they share paths with neighboring villagers to their north and south; and this they apparently agreed to do for the maximum use of their resources.

At the northern end of the valley are a few settlements representing the third type. It may be characterized as agricultural. These territories do not bear the marks of seasonal migration. They are as large in their north-south dimension as in the east-west and do not extend across the width of the valley, which suggests that these groups did not make the seasonal migration to harvest pine nuts. For two reasons such a migration was neither essential nor desirable. The dimension across the northern part of the valley is almost double the fifteen miles of the southern section. In addition, water resources are nearly twice as plentiful as in the south, allowing the possibility of primitive agriculture that is more controlled and regular than foraging for nuts.

These northern territories of the Piutes, like the water tables of Africa, suggest a second major device for adaptation: transforming the environment to allow men some freedom from their forced travels. A meager ability to shape the land and to restructure it, by loosening, packing, fertilizing, or watering, allowed these Piutes to remain localized. The total extent of that part of the world that could be touched and affected was small, and its limits hardly out of reach or beyond understanding.

With this tool of *transformation* as with the other one of *relocation,* strong and recurring force action still required an immediate response. Shape and structure were no longer established by a network of paths for migration. Instead, territories were established by the group's primitive techniques for structuring the land, and as those techniques improved, the territory sometimes was drastically reduced in size. This took time and care and required a permanent place to live.

The provision of such places often made a strong impact upon the land. Their form seemed to derive either from the adaptive processes allowed by time or, in certain cases, through an apparently conscious reconciliation with nature. In the second situation there often appears to have been an awareness of the functional implications of form itself and the intent to build toward it. In both cases, the form of the constructions tended to take on symbolic meaning for the builders.

Fig. 1.8
The metavolcanic Alabama Hills rise sharply from the valley floor to present a forbidding obstacle to east-west movement. The migration of several Piute villages was restricted to passes that were shared, and therefore did not provide the exclusive migratory paths of territories further north.

As the processes of relocation gradually gave way to those of transformation, forms made by men left their mark on the land. The migratory animal was becoming a sower and a reaper. Men were still immediately susceptible to nature and their efforts still required great amounts of time but they needed less space. They had found it possible to satisfy their needs by modifying a limited territory, reducing their environment without critical loss of diversity and choice. This smaller area was more intensively used. A more constant application of tools and a higher density of effort gave the land men touched a different look—agriculture was responsible for part of the change; the greater permanence of construction that such an agricultural life allowed was responsible for the rest.

Agriculture and permanent construction represented men's newest and strongest efforts to deal with natural recurrence, and yet they were still susceptible and necessarily responsive. Men continued to adapt to the world, and not it to them. Their relative weakness during early attempts to transform the land through agriculture and permanent construction locked men into an incremental process that met with only occasional success. Stone was added to stone, and one planting hill followed another. In most cases, the stone or the seed was handled by an individual. As the parts of a larger arrangement accumulated, whether it completed itself as a building or a field of grain, the builder or farmer could see and have some appreciation for the process as one part fit with another.

The possibility of self-correction is one of the advantages that must accrue from such a slow process. In nature, a slow process of self-correction takes place when parts of a system may make attempts to locate themselves. Sometimes the position turns out to be advantageous and at other times it does not. The spread of ground plants is an example. Their distribution may occur upon the wind or water or by clinging to the fur of a passing animal. In any case, the seed survives some locations and not others. Where it survives, it may become dominant. Where it cannot grow, it may be replaced by a different species with perhaps a better chance of survival. This process of trial and error seems bound to produce irregular results, but over time the effect is actually a highly organized arrangement within which the environmental stress upon individual plants is minimized through a process of location and relocation.

If the manifestations of adapting systems can be viewed as representative of the formal structure of natural phenomena, perhaps this view can be extended to man-made arrangements. If the differentiation in man's arrangements can be compared to that in natural systems, it is possible that man-made arrangements exhibit differentiation as a manifestation of adaptive behavior. The arrangement as a whole attempts to match or become compatible with its environment. Under these circumstances, primitive constructions would be expected to behave as natural systems, exhibiting variations in states and continuities of events that invariably accompany natural phenomena. The kind of arrangement that could be expected to demonstrate such behavior most clearly would be one that has been slow in building over a small ground area. Under such circumstances, its structure would be compact rather than spread out and should be most evident to an observer.

For men, as for plants and other animals, the process of building would have been one of trial and error. Every decision would have to refer to natural recurrence: flood stage might discourage a second man from locating where the first settler's house had washed away the spring before; several attempts to place the fire too near the cave opening might discourage the primitive cook who had to deal with a flickering and uneven heat. Each of these observations might also lead to a minor discovery. Step by step, as seeds take root or as birds claim territory, the parts of a man-made arrangement could fall into place, producing not a haphazard or random arrangement, but a structure in which modifications occurred between the placement of one generative increment and the next. A difference of location was accompanied by a working difference among related parts. In this way, one part of an adaptive response became functionally differentiated from another by trial and error.

When the differentiation of an arrangement occurs in an unselfconscious way over a long period of time and is accompanied by an apparently decreased susceptibility of the arrangement to environmental stress, it may be described as self-organizing. This term may be equally applied to systems in nature and to those made by men under the most primitive circumstances. As long as men remain unaware of a larger purpose, submerged within a continuous environment where the events of nature comprise variation and that variation can only be answered piecemeal, then men remain part of the system; they live "inside" without a really good view of the world beyond. Under these circumstances, it takes a long time to develop an evident direction. Each corrective step along the way is guided by a sense of purpose, but at the same time, each step is discrete and not necessarily related to a general direction in the minds of the builders. They do not initially work from an image of ultimate form. Then, over time, form does emerge and with it the possibility of a correlation with some purpose, seen dimly at first, but nonetheless one that will allow a plan of action. From that point on, men may build purpose into their systems; they may build machines.

It is difficult to determine the beginning step of very early or primitive developments that have since come to be regarded as purposeful, but in all likelihood the emergence of purpose in man-made arrangements must have been gradual. It emerged as form emerged; as stones accumulated and as the earth was scooped out, some purpose arose beyond the single act. It is not likely that the builders began with an image of ultimate form. Through their tenacious and prolonged efforts to shape and structure an immediate response to environment, form and purpose blended to become inseparable in the mind of the builder.

As long as men remained unable to anticipate ultimate form, their actions must be described as adaptive. Beyond that they must be considered to be part of the self-organizing system in which they may act purposefully in relation to each corrective step along the way while lacking an overall sense of organization. As soon as an apparently useful system emerges from the trial and error of self-correction and self-organization, and as soon as the correlation between form and purpose becomes evident, men may possibly anticipate such a correlation in the future and go on to build a mental image of a machine before construction takes place. Then they can hold an image of form that anticipates construction, viewing the system from outside. Their actions may still be described as adaptive but the arrangements that deal with the environment are preorganized.

At this point, men have learned to make a plan of action and their actions have become fully purposeful, although the purpose may be only indirectly related to the accomplished fact of adaptation to nature. They may give a significance to their action that is higher than mere survival or earthly comfort. In addition, while the initial purpose for preorganization might be the same equilibrium with nature that was attempted through earlier, self-organizing processes, the advantage of self-correction over long periods of time has been lost. Lost, too, might be the clear correlation between natural phenomena and specific form. Through a process of cultural attrition, the form becomes transmitted from one place to another and from one generation to the next with the possibility of being used inappropriately and ineffectively. In spite of this possibility, early examples of man-made construction seem remarkably free of debilitating preconceptions. If prior images of form were held by those early builders, they were not so rigid that the special conditions of site could not usually be recognized. Men could and did initially perceive a correlation between form and function, and, regardless of the terms they applied to it, they were able to use this knowledge. With a sense of purpose and a plan of action, men could build more complex arrangements, but, although complex, they remained essentially based in nature and determined by nature's recurring events.

As long as it was nature to which men were susceptible, the only variations to be handled by machines were recurring ones. The sun was expected to rise, and its regularity confirmed men's images

with each day and season. Confirmation led to reinforcement and on to institutionalization. It is not difficult to imagine a situation in which social gatherings and certain legal observances evolved from the annual kill of seasonally migrating animals; nor does it seem at all unusual to think of morning and evening religious rites that accompany and reinforce the daily cycle. Within such a framework, men could feel secure in their long-range decisions.

Whether the early systems were self-organizing or preorganized, and whether they emerged over a long time or short, equilibrium with the main recurrences of nature was fundamental. Whatever else men accomplished in the way of defense or trade, enclosure or exposure, their systems must have contended with nature. The clue to this lies in their limits and internal differentiation, in their shape and structure; in short, it lies in their form. When nature presses hard, the response must be equivalent. When the pressure is more gentle, the response may be less distinctive, the correlation less clear; but nature is insistent and no exposed system may totally escape. Some response is demanded, and is displayed as form.

If form can be generally accepted as a manifestation of adaptive behavior in systems, its careful consideration should give clues to the particular technique a system employs. More specifically, this would involve the means by which the system is generated, i.e., its growth, and the special way in which it operates to gain and sustain its purpose. The principal question is whether purpose and the technique of growth can be surmised by studying man's past efforts.

A first step in such a study can usefully reduce natural phenomena to simple descriptions of relationships. Such contrasts as wet-to-dry, hot-to-cold, or dark-to-light may seem to be oversimplifications of a complex situation, but they describe diverse states in nature without having to initially commit the quantity or degree of those states. As a preliminary expression of phenomena, such descriptions recognize the fact of a change in state and establish *variation* as fundamental. Since the usually desirable state of the system is steady, any variation of environment tends to induce a response in the system. Consequently, such a minimal structural description of variation would link two environmental states in a fundamental relationship and simultaneously signal an imminent system response. If the response depends upon the adaptive use of form, the result should correlate directly with natural variation.

In 1967-68 an effort was made at the University of Southern California to test the correlation between form and natural variation. Using the techniques of on-site inspection and laboratory simulation, a group of architecture students working under the author's direction studied the relation between sun action and historical building forms. The modern observer enjoys an advantage in this kind of study because he can view the historical, man-made arrangements from outside their time. Unlike the original builders who participated directly in the building process, sometimes without a clear idea of its structure or limits in space and time, the modern observer can often see the whole along with its internal relationships at their final development. Such an external view allows a convenient classification of systems based upon their form attributes and apparent mode of organization; specifically this means the variability of the limits of the system over

time and the mechanism for incrementally generating a change in those limits. Such a classification can be made for both self-organized and preorganized systems (fig. 2.1). Using sun simulator techniques, three building arrangements were studied in detail. Each had the ability to mitigate seasonal variations in the thermal environment. They were analyzed in terms of that purpose but their relative attributes of form and modes of organization lay in sharp distinction. As all three developed over time, their forms changed, but their increments for generating that change, the rate at which change occurred, and the direction taken by the evolving form are unique in each case and significantly related to the fulfillment of purpose.

Fig. 2.1
The classification of three selected pueblos among eight theoretically possible modes of generating form toward some purpose.

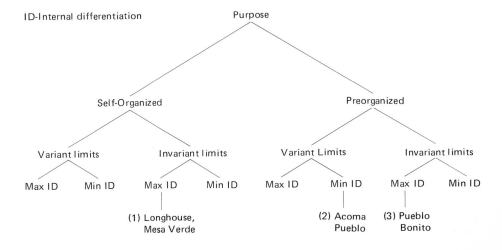

Fig. 2.2
Longhouse Pueblo at Mesa
Verde, Colorado.

Longhouse Pueblo, Mesa Verde, Colorado

In the extreme southwestern corner of Colorado lies a deeply eroded tableland called Mesa Verde. Its geological formations consist of deep layers of sandstone on a slate base. Over millennia, stream action has cut deep fingerlike ravines into the sandstone, exposing vertical faces to the further effects of sun, wind, and water. Together those elements have shaped and textured the malleable cliffs into astonishing features.

In addition to its role as a major force in eroding valleys, the water has worked its way through the sandstone from the mesa above, settling upon the slate base and flowing outward toward the cliff faces. When it reached the sheer surface it softened the sandstone and carried it out and down over the harder edge of the slate. Where the layers of sandstone and slate met the cliff face, the continuous water action produced shallow caves with broad openings under the mesa (figs. 2.2, 2.3). The caves have sloping floors of slate; the sandstone overhead rises steeply to the cliff edge. In the bright summer sun of the region these edges cast deep and mobile shadows, leaving the impression of a furled brow on the remains of some ancient cyclops.

There is evidence that men have inhabited the region of these caves for twelve to fourteen thousand years, often taking refuge in them for defense from invaders. Even when farming was first begun on the mesa above, the caves were used at night for refuge. Between A.D. 750-1100 men apparently felt secure enough to build permanently on the mesa where they worked the fields. Their houses were mostly one story, built side by side in crescent-shaped rows opening to the south. Around A.D. 1100 the region fell under attack from marauding nomads.

The inhabitants returned to the caves, where they built extensive and permanent dwellings while continuing to farm the mesa. By A.D. 1500 an extensive drought had diminished their ability to withstand further attack and the culture died. An impressive record remains today behind the stone prosceniums of the caves.

From the beginning, the people of Mesa Verde took refuge in these caves. In spite of some dampness and danger from falling sandstone, the caves had the advantage of being highly defensible. They were exposed on only one side and were often located several hundred feet above the valley floor. In addition to offering a good defense, they gave some protection from the weather. When permanent dwellings were finally built into the caves, the slate floors acted as a good foundation, and the years of flaking had produced something of a natural quarry. With small stones from the cave, larger stones and short timbers from the mesa, and clay from the river below, living spaces were enclosed in a terraced arrangement in which the roof of one space became the terrace of the one above and further to the rear of the cave (fig. 2.4). The terraces were generally at a lower elevation at the cliff face and rose step by step until they met the sandstone overhead at the rear.

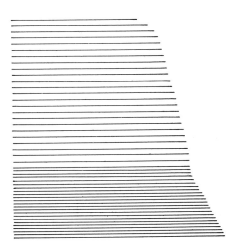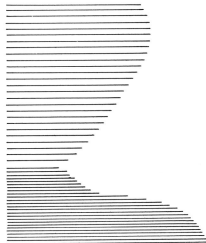

Fig. 2.3
Continuous water action where the layers of sandstone and slate met the cliff face produced shallow caves with broad openings under the mesa.

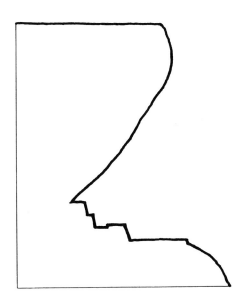

Fig. 2.4
With stone from the cave, short timbers from the mesa, and clay from the river below, living spaces were enclosed in a terraced arrangement wherein the roof of one space became the terrace of the one above and further to the rear of the cave.

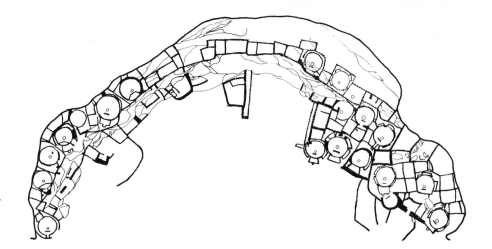

Fig. 2.5
Composite plan of long-house, Mesa Verde. Plans of Longhouse prepared in 1967 at the University of Southern California by S. Jhono, R. MacDonald and R. McMahon and based on a reconstruction by anthropologist Douglas Osborne, California State College, Long Beach, California.

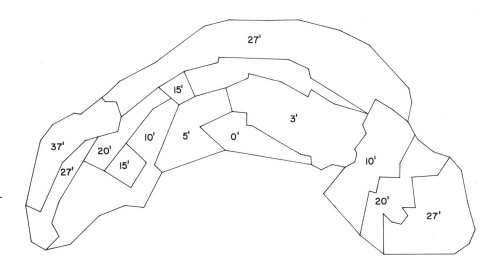

Fig. 2.6
Contours of the Long-house plan showing levels of major terraces and building groups; the elevation numbers relate to an arbitrary reference (0') at the cave front.

The anthropologist Douglas Osborne has carefully examined several such cave settlements, with particular attention to the one called Longhouse (figs. 2.5-2.6). This settlement occupies a cave 500 feet across and 130 feet deep. At the face of the cliff the cave rises 200 feet in a long vaulting arch. These large dimensions provide ample space for a settlement of considerable size. There are other large caves among the hundreds in the Mesa Verde area. Many of them have access to the agricultural land on the top of the mesa and are defensible by virtue of difficult access. Most of them, along with the Longhouse cave, are subject to water action and flaking from above; but while those showing signs of past settlement are numerous, on-site observations indicate that most other caves at Mesa Verde have an east or west orientation and do not feel as comfortable throughout the year as Longhouse. Those facing east tend to feel too cold in winter. Others opening to the west seem too hot in summer.

A southern exposure distinguishes Longhouse from most other caves in the area.

Its particular proportions, with broad opening and a relatively shallow depth, combine with the sun's geometry at a latitude of $37°$ north to produce an interesting phenomenon, and one that would have increased the desirability of the Longhouse cave as a place to live throughout most of the year. The advantages of Longhouse result from a seasonal difference of insolation. Summer sun first appears on the horizon at about $30°$ to the north of east. It rises to a high noontime altitude of $78°$, and when it disappears at sunset its path has taken it $30°$ to the north of west. By contrast, the winter sun appears at 30° south of east. Its noontime altitude is only slightly over 30° above the horizon and sunset occurs 30° to the south of west (fig. 2.7). This means that the summer sun does not fully strike the sheer south faces of the cliff until midmorning and disappears from those faces at midafternoon. In the interim, its angle of incidence upon the face is very small in contrast to the winter sun, which stays continuously on the cliff faces at an angle of incidence never less than 30°.

A patient observer viewing the cave from the south would notice summer light first strike the easternmost building at about one hour after dawn. Its roof would remain half-dark, half-light until another hour had passed. Then the southern projection of those buildings at the west edge of the cave would balance the composition with an accent at each extreme edge on the east and west.

From 6:30 a.m. the western area of light spreads east across the inside surfaces of the cave, never engaging more than one-quarter of those areas and leaving the eastern three-quarters dark. Then at 10:00 a.m. the eastern part of the cave shares the spotlight and by midafternoon monopolizes the light over a quarter of its area. By 4:00 p.m. all the major work areas are in shadow, and by 5:00 p.m. all light has disappeared from the interior cave surfaces. Twilight arrives at 5:30 p.m. when constrasts subside. It is still one hour and forty minutes before the sun sets.

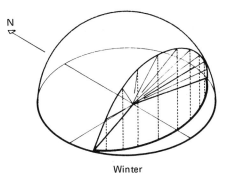

N

Winter

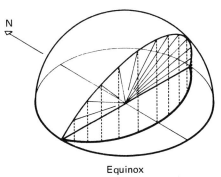

N

Equinox

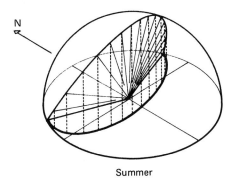

N

Summer

Fig. 2.7
The advantages of Longhouse result from a seasonal difference in the dynamic relationship between sun and cave. A construct of the earth-sun geometry shows the winter sun rising and setting south of an east-west axis. The summer sun rises and sets to the north. Equinox is the only time when the sun rises and sets directly on the east-west axis. In the construct, the sun's path is taken to lie on the surface of a hemisphere and is shown projected down onto a horizontal plane.

Fig. 2.8
Buildings were placed inside the cave in such a way that their vertical stone walls and horizontal terraces received great benefit from the low winter sun while being protected during the summer by shadows cast from the upper edge of the cave opening and by the high summer altitude of the sun.

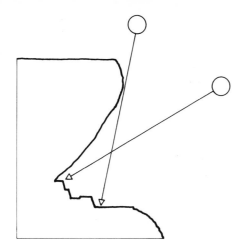

Fig. 2.9
The projected area of a form upon a plane normal to the sun's rays gives a comparative measure of what is "seen" by the sun.

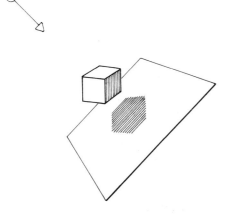

Winter provides an entirely different picture. While never more than a quarter of the cave's inner surfaces are lighted in summer, only a quarter remains dark through the winter day. First light of the winter solstice floods the cave, with the exception of a small area in the eastern extremity. By 9:00 a.m., virtually all cave surfaces are lighted, and no building is shadowed by the cave roof. This situation is maintained until 2:00 p.m., when shadows first appear on the westernmost surfaces of the cave. From there they spread east to cover a quarter of the cave and buildings; but even at sunset, the eastern two-thirds of the cave and buildings remains in bright light, with the sharp contrasts of late afternoon that are common to a high, desert-like region.

The cave thus offers a high degree of protection from the summer sun, compared to a deep penetration of light during the winter. Still more careful observations show that buildings were placed inside the cave in such a way that their vertical stone walls and horizontal terraces received great benefit from the low winter sun, while being protected during the summer by shadows cast from the upper edge of the cave opening and by the high summer altitude of the sun (fig. 2.8).

Seasonal differences in the way the sun acts upon all surfaces, whether building or cave, become significant in such a partial enclosure. There is an advantage in having surfaces lighted during winter so they may absorb and re-radiate energy. Surfaces should be shaded in summer if the desirable internal state of the cave is thermally steady. An accurate measurement of the higher degree to which this happens in the winter indicates the significance of the effect cave surfaces must have had upon the comfort of the people living there.

The techniques employed to measure the insolation performance of Longhouse and the other pueblos in this study were based on projecting the shadow area of the form by means of a heliodon, in which a camera replaced the sun. An accurate model of Longhouse, based on Douglas Osborne's reconstruction of the pueblo (see fig. 2.5), was placed on the heliodon in the Architecture Department at the University of Southern California, and photographed at hourly intervals. From these films a measure of seasonal insolation was made.

A comparative measure of the areas "seen" by the sun can be made by projecting the films onto a calibrated surface. After the areas have been determined, they are modified by the sine function of the sun's altitude to approximate the effect of atmosphere. A final expression of incident energy in units of projected area is the following:

$E_i = (\sin a) A'$; where
E_i = incident energy in units of area.
$(\sin a)$ = sine of sun's altitude angle to correct for atmosphere.
A' = projected area of form as seen by the camera (or as a shadow is cast upon a plane set behind the form and normal to the sun's rays) (fig. 2.9).

A graph of comparative energy-profiles for summer and winter indicates two significant facts. First, incident energy is higher on a summer morning than on a winter morning while just the reverse is true for the afternoon. Since ambient air temperature tends to be higher in the summer, especially in the afternoon, there would be an advantage in reducing incident energy between noon and sunset (fig. 2.10). Second, a comparison of the total amount of energy received directly from the sun in summer and winter indicates that the energy total in the winter is only 12 percent less than that for summer, despite the fact that the summer sun stays in the sky 30 percent longer, with an average of 50 percent less reduction per hour due to atmosphere.

The arrangement of cave and buildings provides for more efficient energy collection in the winter when such efficiency is of great advantage (fig. 2.11). The degree of efficiency can be plotted by comparing the actual amount of energy received per hour (E_i), with the amount that might be received if all surfaces acting within the perimeter of the cave opening were totally effective (E_m), as if they all lay normal to the sun's rays (fig. 2.12). Efficiency is expressed as a percentage by the following:

Percent efficiency = E_i/E_m; where

E_i = incident energy in units of projected area (previously derived), and

E_m = (sin a) A; where

E_m = incident energy in units of projected area if all surfaces of the form were normal to the sun's rays and parallel to the plane of projection.

(sin a) = sine of sun's altitude angle to correct for atmosphere.

A = maximum projected area of all exposed surfaces of the form.

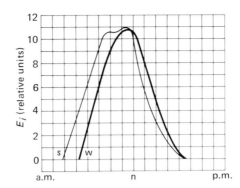

Fig. 2.10
Incident energy is higher on a summer morning than on a winter morning while just the reverse is true for the afternoon. Since ambient air temperature tends to be higher in the summer, especially in the afternoon, there would be an advantage in reducing incident energy between noon and sunset.

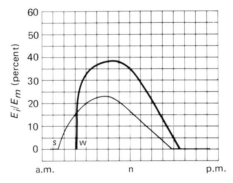

Fig. 2.11
The arrangement of cave and buildings is a more efficient energy collector in the winter when such efficiency is of great advantage.

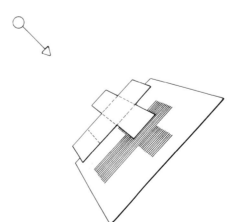

Fig. 2.12
The projected area of a form, if all its surfaces were normal to the sun's rays and parallel to the plan of projection, provides a reference to measure efficiency of the form as a receptor of insolation.

A situation in which all surfaces can be exposed and remain normal to the sun's rays would be impossible to attain in any multidimensional relationship, but it serves as a useful base to compare the way in which surfaces are used during each season. Such a plot indicates that the building and cave arrangement is 56 percent more efficient as an energy collector in the winter than it is in the summer, which raises the question of purpose and how these builders went about realizing such an efficient energy system. It is difficult to believe that they worked from a plan. The arrangement is too complex and the buildings too specialized in their siting. On the other hand, it is unreasonable to believe that they were not somewhat aware of the potential for shelter from rain and wind or that they did not hold some general notion of the advantages to be gained from a southern exposure. After all, they had previously grouped their one-story, mesa houses in a crescent shape, opening to the south.

The question must finally be resolved in relation to a possible mental image of ultimate form. Purpose, vaguely defined in the mind of the builder, is not a plan of action. Longhouse does not manifest the regular geometry that seems often to accompany such an image. Instead, the plan is irregular. The diversity of internal relationships is rich and would be difficult to preconceive. The high degree of internal differentiation lies beyond the ability of the individual or group to determine beforehand. Relationships do not repeat themselves precisely in dimension. While the terraces display a general tendency to rise one above another in an incremental way, the modifications upon that theme have few close repetitions.

Such diversity suggests a relatively slow growth and a rate of change that would have allowed time to consider the array of details apparent in the construction. Each building fits with another, and every stone matches the next in such a diversity of special ways that the beginning point and the direction of generation are difficult to determine from the plan. There are no straight lines or simple patterns to act as a guide for change in the form of the system.

While this situation would seem to lead to visual chaos, such is not the case, principally because the construction is contained within the unifying limits of the cave. These limits are both spatial and temporal, in the sense that they are established by the physical dimensions of the cave on the north and by the seasonal shift of protective shadow on the south. There was no great advantage in building outside this protected domain and several advantages were gained by staying within it. The system is maintained, and can be recognized as a whole, by the way its invariant limits were recognized.

If the builders of Longhouse did not make a plan and did not perceive ultimate form as a basis for organization, then they worked within the constraints of site and main recurrence in nature. These early builders were part of a self-organizing process from which purpose emerged slowly with the construction. Regardless of their degree of awareness at the time, the result can be defined and measured today: it provided people living so long ago with a more desirable set of living conditions than similar groups living nearby. The proof of this can be taken by comparing Longhouse with other less desirable cave constructions.

Longhouse appears to have been a self-organizing system with invariant limits and a high degree of internal differentiation of the form. While the plan clearly demonstrates spatial organization, the natural recurrences of day and season structured activities in time, gave life to the settlement as a whole, and probably structured its institutions. As seasons changed, the depth of sun penetration into the cave must have shifted the work areas from inside to outside and back again. As the sun rose and set in a diurnal cycle, the intensity of activity must have varied from one part of the cave to another in the east-west direction. In such a restricted space, with the contrasts of light and dark, warm and cool so sharply drawn, the changes that occurred with time and place must have been obvious in the organization of daily life of the whole community. The pulse of such a system and the distinctions among its parts must have been sensitively tuned to the cyclical variations of nature.

Acoma Pueblo, New Mexico

Acoma pueblo, a second example of man-made arrangements, lies about fifty miles west of Albuquerque, New Mexico, at 35° north latitude (fig. 2.13). For defense it was placed atop a flat and nearly inaccessible mesa that rises 400 feet from the plain below. The climate is generally desertlike, but ambient air temperatures are modified by the mile-high altitude.

The pueblo appears to have been continuously occupied for over a thousand years.[1] It was first described by a chronicler of Francisco Coronado's expedition in 1540 and the form of the present pueblo coincides in its essentials with the descriptions of early observers. They record two-hundred houses of two-to-four stories each—a greater number of houses than exists today. This may be explained by an attack in 1599, when Spanish soldiers killed many Indians and burned some of their houses. Later, in 1629, a Spanish mission was built on land that prior to the attack had probably contained houses. The mission and much of the original pueblo remains in use today. With the exception of some additional door and window openings, especially at the ground floor level where there had probably been none, and some modifications in the buildings themselves, such as an occasional metal shed roof, the pueblo remains essentially as it was when the Spanish first located and climbed the single and difficult path to the mesa.

1. See Mrs. William T. Sedgwick, *Acoma, The Sky City* (Cambridge, Mass.: Harvard University Press, 1926); J. H. Steward, *Ethnography of the Owens Valley Piute* (Berkeley, Calif.: University of California Press, 1933); and U.S. Bureau of American Ethnology, *Annual Report No. 47* (Washington, D.C., 1930).

Fig. 2.13
Acoma pueblo, New Mexico, looking northeast.

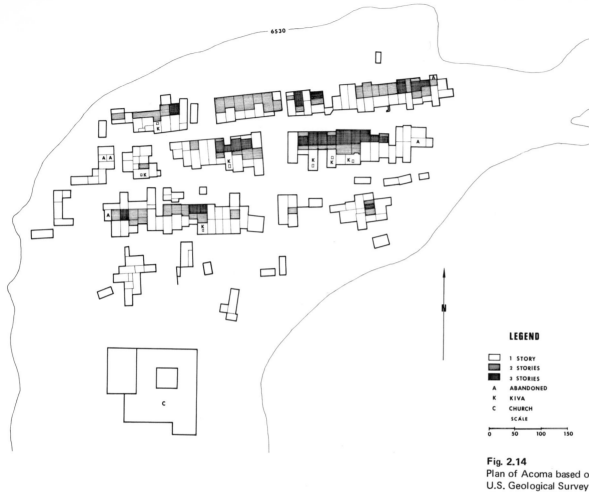

6530

N

LEGEND

▢ 1 STORY
▨ 2 STORIES
▣ 3 STORIES
A ABANDONED
K KIVA
C CHURCH

SCALE

0   50   100   150

Fig. 2.14
Plan of Acoma based on
U.S. Geological Survey
photograph (1956). Map
prepared at the University
of Southern California by
P. Canelo, R. Gallagher, R.
Kauffman and R. Nickum
(1967).

A plan of the pueblo shows three nearly parallel rows of buildings extending for about a thousand feet at just a few degrees off an east-west axis and terminating at the steep slopes of the mesa (fig. 2.14). Each row consists of several groups of houses separated by gaps that vary in width from minor walkways to major spaces. One major space occurs halfway along the length of the center row, adjacent to and west of what was the original block of the city. Construction was first begun here; this easternmost block of the middle row became the most important group, containing the houses of the chiefs. Following its completion, the north row was begun and remains today in a fairly regular and unmodified condition. The south row is the latest addition to the existing pueblo and has evidently been influenced by the placement of the Spanish mission. Several isolated buildings between the south row and the mission have a relation to both. It is likely that this southern row suffered under the Spanish attacks and was rebuilt with reference to the Spanish buildings.

The blocks of which the rows are comprised generally contain many individual houses that share a common wall on the east and west. Their width is quite uniform, suggesting a modular construction in which units were regularly added in a line using common walls to extend in the east-west direction. Groups were then multiplied to generate rows. Rows were laid down parallel to each other, defining streets that extended to the east and west. Such an arrangement seems to favor a regular process of growth that might theoretically have extended itself indefinitely.

The typical Acoma house is generally tiered, as is the row itself (fig. 2.15). It steps down, exposing broad areas of roof and vertical wall to the south. In this arrangement, the ground floor was always used for storage and was the largest space in the house to provide the necessary reserves in case of crop failure or sustained attack. It extends its greatest length in a north-south direction of the plan, and is generally twelve to fifteen feet high. A second story averages eight to nine feet in height, and in the most typical three-tiered sections this second floor is stepped back. It originally contained spaces for sleeping and some storage in addition to a terrace upon the roof of the space below. The third story has a slightly smaller vertical dimension of about eight feet. It contained the main living area, including cooking facilities.

Generally, the houses contain the larger spaces below and smaller ones above. This is true of the vertical dimensions and it is true of the north-south dimensions in plan, with the differences occurring as open terraces adjacent to the second and third floors. In order to accommodate this arrangement structurally, the walls are generally sloped from a fifteen inch thickness at the base to ten inches at the top. They are composed of adobe-covered rubble for the first story and adobe-covered brick for the stories above. Floors and roofs are adobe packed on grass or sticks that are laid over small wood members that span timbers. The vertical dividing walls between units are slightly extended two to four feet above the terraces to give some separation between individual work areas and to provide a small amount of shade when the sun is in the east or west. All doors and windows originally opened off these south-facing terraces. The ground floor, used for storage, was entered through its roof, permitting easy access from the living spaces above and affording protection for the stored food.

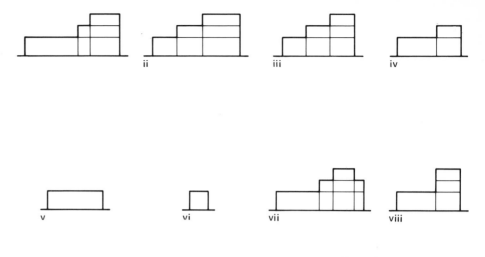

ii iii iv

v vi vii viii

N ⟶

Fig. 2.15
Typical building sections found in the Acoma pueblo. The tiered section usually contains six rooms separated by bearing walls (vertical lines) and floors (horizontal lines). North is to the right thus exposing tiers to the south.

While there are modifications upon this three-tiered arrangement, it is typical, and its six units of volume provide a useful basis for study.

Both the regularity of the plan and the southerly orientation of the sections suggest a significant relation between the building arrangement and the sun. Heliodon studies using a model of Acoma reconstructed by architecture students from aerial photographs prove this to be true and demonstrate an interaction that is dynamic and complex and that occurs on two levels.[2]

First, consider the interaction between the sun and the typical unit. The terraces and south walls of a unit generally receive the first light of morning and the last at evening during most of the year. Upon the roofs and terraces the summer sun is more direct, while the winter sun favors the vertical south-facing walls. Careful observation reveals a second and more subtle level of interaction characterized by almost shadow-free work areas from sunrise to sunset during all seasons. It is possible to imagine that a people for whom the sun is so important might achieve such a delicate interaction among the parts of their building arrangement that no vertical portion of one building ever shades the work areas of surrounding buildings. A general lowering of building heights from the high and central group of the chiefs to the low, peripheral buildings toward the mesa's edge facilitates this condition and suggests such an intention by the Acomas.

2. Olgyay, Victor, *Design with Climate* (Princeton, N. J.: Princeton University Press, 1963); and Sir D'Arcy Wentworth Thompson, *On Growth and Form* (London: Cambridge University Press, 1961).

Observations made over day and season suggest the dynamics of possible interaction at both levels. Summer sunrise strikes north and east walls, and by 5:15 a.m. all such faces of the upper two stories are light. By 7:00 a.m. the light is directed down the streets from the east and is just beginning to select details from the south walls, still leaving doors and windows in deep relief. Because of the extreme height of the summer sun, no light penetrates to the interior, and the openings remain in shadow until 4:00 p.m. when all light disappears from the south walls. From that time, when only west and north walls are lighted, until 6:30 p.m. shadows quickly subdue the streets and alleys leaving only the upper stories to punctuate the evening with their brightness.

The south walls, obliquely lighted in the summer, are more directly served by the winter sun. By 8:15 a.m., in spite of the apparently random placement of the upper stories in relation to each other, some light falls directly on every south-facing surface above the first floor. By 9:30 a.m. even the south faces of the ground floors are in the light and remain so until 3:00 p.m. when shadows begin to rise up from the darkened street below. Even then, and until sunset, the upper two floors and their adjacent work surfaces remain in bright sun.

The existence of such particular relationships over time is principally due to the three-tiered building section and its arrangement in parallel rows, with sufficient separation to avoid critical shading on the north. To test the specific attributes of this section with terraces to the south, a unit length (ignoring east-west walls) of a generalized version containing six identical volumes was employed. A comparison of seasonal energy profiles showed a summer increase of 187 percent over the winter (fig. 2.16a).

If investigation stops at this point, the conclusion must be that no particular advantage has been gained insofar as equalizing energy profiles between summer and winter. But if the question is raised as to the possibility of other combinations of six volumes, it becomes clear that the Acomas' choice was not so unreasonable. Consider a situation in which the tiered section is reversed so that all work surfaces face north (fig. 2.16b). If a higher energy profile for winter is considered desirable, the results are disappointing, with a 33.3 percent loss for the winter energy profile. When this northern orientation is compared to the original section during the summer, the loss is only about 4.5 percent. This means that while a reversal of the section has decreased the winter energy profile, it has maintained virtually the same incident energy during the hot months of the summer. There is no evident advantage in such a reversal. A third alternative would have been to lay all six volumes down on the ground. Such a solution would theoretically have been possible for the Acomas but its vast horizontal exposure results in an 88.4 percent increase in the summer profile over the original section while the winter gain is only 26.7 percent. In addition, a comparison of the summer and winter profiles in this horizontal arrangement indicates a summer increase of 327 percent over the winter, hardly an equalization of seasons (fig. 2.16c).

An arrangement that does equalize the seasonal energy profiles is one that stacks all six volumes vertically, exposing a large surface to the south. It offers a 52 percent reduction in the summer energy profile when compared with the original section and a 17 percent increase in the winter profile. The result is a near coincidence of the two curves. This solution, however, was technically difficult, if not impssible, for the Acoma culture to attain (fig. 2.16d).

Such a comparison of possible combinations of six volumes suggests that the Acomas' choice was the best under the circumstances. A further investigation of the section they used reveals additional support for their choice. If the efficiency of the form is plotted for summer and winter, the two curves come still closer together. As in the Longhouse study, efficiency is taken to be a ratio between the energy received by the form (E_i) and the energy that could be received by all exposed surfaces if the sun were normal to them (E_m). The ratio E_i / E_m is expressed as percent efficiency. Generally the study indicates that the form is 32.5 percent less efficient in the way surfaces are exposed to incident energy during the winter compared to summer (fig. 2.17).

Since the summer sun is more direct upon horizontal surfaces and the winter sun is more direct upon the south-facing walls of the tiered section, it would have been most reasonable if the vertical walls receiving winter sun had a high transmission coefficient and a high heat storage capacity (fig. 2.18). Conversely, the horizontals receiving their maximum energy in the summer should exhibit a low thermal transmission coefficient and a low heat storage capacity. A comparison of the materials used by the Indians reveals this to be the case.

In a desert climate where the extremes of temperature are great from day to night, a wall's ability to store heat is critical. For an arrangement like that of the Acoma Pueblo, in which the wall receives a high percentage of the winter energy, thick masonry would help to maintain an internally steady state by virtue of the time lag required for heat transfer. Once a steady state is achieved, the critical factor becomes the transmission coefficient of the material, which describes the rate of energy transfer. A comparison of the winter and summer profiles of energy reaching the interior shows a tendency for the two curves to coincide (fig. 2.19), with a 43 percent increase in the summer rather than the 187 percent summer increase of incident energy upon the outside surfaces of the form (fig. 2.16a). Finally, if the form's efficiency in transmitting energy from outside to inside is plotted for summer and winter, a revealing picture emerges in which the winter profile shows a 50 percent increase over the summer (fig. 2.20). Here, efficiency is taken to be a ratio between the sum of energies transferred through the verticals and horizontals compared to what might be transmitted if the sun were constantly normal to all surfaces. It is expressed as a percentage by the following:

Percent efficiency = $(E_{vt} + E_{ht})/E_{mt}$; where
E_{vt} = energy transmitted through walls
  = $U_v(E_v)$; in which
U_v = transmission coefficient of (0.4) for walls,
E_v = incident energy upon vertical walls.
E_{ht} = energy transmitted through roofs
  = $U_h(E_h)$; in which
U_h = transmission coefficient of (0.1) for roofs,
E_h = incident energy upon horizontal roofs.
E_{mt} = transmitted energy if all surfaces of the form were normal to the sun's rays.

The study reveals what the Indians must have understood for the past thousand years: the pueblo is an efficient energy system that tends to equalize internal energy profiles over the extremes of season and day. By its shape and materials, it provides an internal consistency, a steady state. As with Longhouse, the study raises a question of the Acomas' purpose, their conscious intentions. Were they aware of what they did? Did they build a purposeful system, a machine for equalizing seasonal extremes?

The nature of the house would suggest that they were aware and did act purposefully. The house is a preorganized and generative increment. When houses are placed beside one another so that their east and west walls are covered, each individual house tends to act in very much the same way as a group comprised of ten or fifteen houses. Even if the end walls are considered to affect the arrangement as a whole (which might be the case if the interior volumes were continuous rather than segmented), their influence soon drops off. After eight houses

Fig. 2.16
A comparison of seasonal energy profiles for various arrangements of the six volumes comprising a house. While stacking all six volumes vertically tends to equalize seasonal insolation, such an arrangement was technologically difficult. The next best arrangement, which is tiered on the south, could be more easily built.

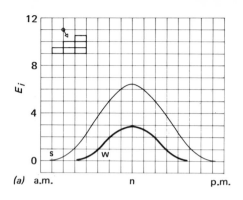

(a) a.m.   n   p.m.

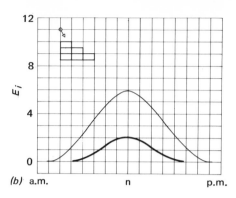

(b) a.m.   n   p.m.

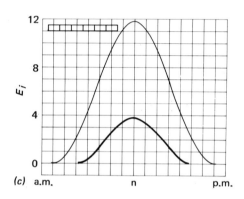

(c) a.m.   n   p.m.

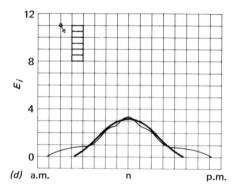

(d) a.m.   n   p.m.

Fig. 2.17
Efficiency of the form; a comparison of the actual amount of energy received per hour (E_i) with the amount that might be received if all surfaces were totally effective (E_m).

Fig. 2.18
Percent of incident energy received by vertical and horizontal surfaces.

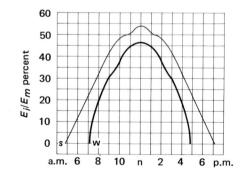

a.m. 6   8   10   n   2   4   6 p.m.

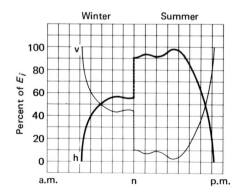

have been lined up, i.e., incrementally added along an east-west line, the end walls' share of total incident energy has dropped to 5 percent. After that, the decline continues at a decreasing rate. At the same time, as increments are added, the combination of all north, south, and horizontal surfaces accounts for a percentage of incident energy that is increasing at a decreasing rate. The leveling off of these percentages is due to the diminishing effect of the east-west walls (fig. 2.21).

When the first tiered section is completed, it has essentially all the attributes that can be described for tiered sections anywhere on the site, so that the system maintains approximately the same attributes whether it is comprised of one set of houses or many. This would seem to be true independently of the overall dimensions of the settlement and results from the repetitive nature of the increment.

The basic increment for generating change in the form of Acoma is the house. The direction in which the house generates a change of form is either to the east or west to complete a second order of increment—the line. Lines are then repeated in a north-south direction producing streets. While other factors might limit growth, such an arrangement would not seem to suggest inevitable limits in and of itself.

Acoma pueblo can be characterized as a preorganized arrangement since the initial increment is obviously preorganized in relation to the sun. The increment is then

simply allowed to generate itself in a logical way with no subsequent decisions
having to be made; but while this system
could theoretically provide a rapid growth
rate, its undifferentiated expansion does
not seem to evoke inevitable limits, and
the limits must be considered variant.
At least, they are indeterminate in relation to the criteria upon which the initial
increment is established.

The result of growth based upon a simple, repeated relationship cannot display
the overall diversity of Longhouse, where
each part lies in unique relation to all
other parts and to the whole. In fact, the
tiered unit at Acoma exhibits a higher
level of differentiation than seems to be
attained by the arrangement as a whole.
Differentiation correlates with function,
in that activities seem to be more clearly
structured at the level of house than at
the larger level of the whole settlement.

The distinctions between horizontal and
vertical, inside and outside, and upper and
lower floors find a parallel in the differentiation of individual family function
with reference to the dynamics of sun
action. It is not difficult to imagine a life
in which people moved outside or inside,
to the left of their work terrace or to the
right (following the slight shadows of the
vertical dividing walls), to the large lower
work surfaces or the small upper ones
in regular cycles directly related to the
intervals of day and season that affect
variations of light and heat. Such cycles
would doubtless have become institution-
alized; but it seems likely in the case of
the Acomas that this would have occurred
at the level of the house and the individual family rather than at the less clearly
structured level of settlement and group,
as must have been the case in the Longhouse enclosure.

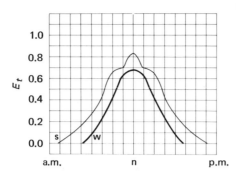

Fig. 2.19
Energy transmitted to in-
terior spaces through building surfaces.

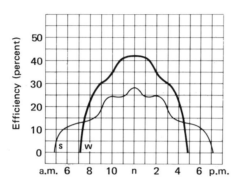

Fig. 2.20
Efficiency of the pueblo
in transmitting energy
through all roofs and walls
to the interior spaces.

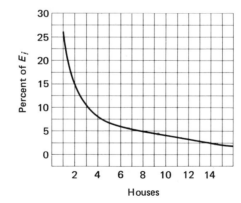

Fig. 2.21
The influences of end walls
(east and west facing) diminishes as the size of a
group of houses increases.
There is an advantage in
such a grouping because of
the detrimental effects of
east-west surfaces on the
energy profile. However,
beyond a certain point the
advantage of grouping di-
minishes. There is some
indication that the Acomas
treated the last house in
each row somewhat differ-
ently to make up for its
poor exposure. Further
study is required to determine the significance of
the differentiated ends of
the rows.

Fig. 2.22
Pueblo Bonito in Chaco
Canyon, New Mexico, as
it was unearthed by N. M.
Judd during seven Nation-
al Geographic Society ex-
peditions, 1921-1927.

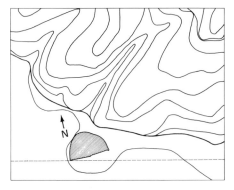

Fig. 2.23
Site plan of Pueblo Bonito
in Chaco Canyon showing
special orientation.

Pueblo Bonito, Chaco Canyon, New Mexico

If the tiered rows of Acoma had been curved so that they opened to the south, the result would approximate Pueblo Bonito (fig. 2.22). Unlike Acoma, which could have generated easily in all directions, the curved plan of Pueblo Bonito closed the arrangement to the possibility of unlimited expansion. A semicircular plan resulted, and further growth would apparently have required the duplication of this closed arrangement.

The remains of this once impressive settlement are located about one hundred miles south of Mesa Verde at 36° north latitude in the middle northwest section of New Mexico. The pueblo lies about 100 feet south of the sheer rock cliffs of Chaco Canyon (fig. 2.23). The mile-high elevation modifies a generally hot and arid climate so that the winters are cool and extended.

The history of the pueblo can be read in its changes of plan as interpreted and recorded by archeologist N. M. Judd over a period from 1921-27.[3] The Chaco Canyon area had been occupied long before the pueblo was begun. During this early time the occupants lived in small huts, isolated from one another. For some reason, perhaps for protection, they later decided to group their houses into a simple arrangement with common walls. Thus the old pueblo was literally a curved version of Acoma. It had three tiers and opened to the southeast (fig. 2.24).

3. Neil M. Judd, *The Architecture of Pueblo Bonito* (Washington, D.C.: Smithsonian Institution, 1964), and *The Material Culture of Pueblo Bonito* (Washington, D.C.: Smithsonian Institution, 1954).

This simple combination of small houses built together in a crescent made use of relatively primitive methods of construction. The walls were made of single blocks of sandstone ranging to a thickness of three feet. The outside walls were almost twice as thick at their base as they were at the top. Roofs and floors consisted of crude assemblages of cottonwood, pine, or juniper logs covered with a mud or adobe. This early construction has been dated at A.D. 919.

Like Acoma, the houses of Pueblo Bonito contained few openings in the outside walls of the first floor, probably for reasons of defense. Most openings to this first floor were through the roof, while doors to the second and third floors entered off the roof terraces. The arrangement of functions was also similar to that of Acoma, with the large first floor providing food storage for this farming culture.

Judd reports that around A.D. 1050-1060, strangers to the old Bonitians, representing an unknown and quite different culture, moved into the region and were apparently welcomed into the Chaco Valley. Their influence upon the original inhabitants must have been extraordinary if modifications in shape and structure of the settlement are any indication (fig. 2.25).

These self-confident and remarkably skilled builders moved into the community with no apparent resistance from the old Bonitians and immediately launched a vast new program of expansion. During a twenty-year period, A.D. 1060-1080, they tripled the size of the original pueblo. Their techniques for construction were in advance of those employed by the old Bonitians and show a high degree of sophistication in the use of materials. The walls were no longer monolithic but were differentiated into rubble and adobe for the core of the wall with precisely shaped and fitted sandstone as the exterior facing. Roof timbers displayed fine craftsmanship, with pine and fir beams and poles supporting layers of dressed willows, pine boards, or cedar bark covered with adobe.

According to Judd, the two cultures of old and new Bonitians seem to have lived within the same building complex without intermingling to any great extent. They shared farming as a common activity but even here they operated as independent groups.

For unknown reasons, the entire complex was abandoned less than a century after its second phase of building was completed. A lowering of the water table in the region might have reduced their agriculture below support levels. The basis for this theory is that the Bonitians had cut down the forests that grew to the south of the settlement in order to use the wood, mainly for construction. Eliminating the groundcover produced runoff and erosion problems during flood seasons.

Because the water tended to run off rather than being absorbed into the ground, the water table was lowered below the reach of many plant roots, and the area's normally low annual rainfall of eight to ten inches was not sufficient to sustain crop growth.

The original pueblo was a simple building that satisfied the basic requirements of shelter and storage. Crescent-shaped, with its axis to the southeast at an azimuth of 150°, it measured 300 feet across the opening and 120 feet deep from the mouth of the opening to the outside of the curving walls on the north. The buildings were three tiers high and averaged 37 feet in depth. Like the units at Acoma, the first floor for storage of food was somewhat higher than the upper two. Its vertical height averaged 10.3 feet with a height of 9.4 feet for the upper two floors, totaling about 29.1 feet for the three floors.

Old Bonito displays the stepping terraces but not the distinct modular generation of Acoma. The common wall between individual housing units does not seem to be so clearly developed. By contrast, new Bonito demonstrates a clear modular generation, beginning from the walls of the old pueblo. As growth proceeded from the old crescent, there is evidence that it developed along a tangent extending to the east. This undertaking was abandoned, and the eastern arm of the semicircular plan was then completed by turning it to the south, as was the case with the western arm of the plan.

In a short twenty-year period, construction of the new pueblo engulfed the old crescent. A thin layer of spaces was added on the periphery of the crescent and its arms were extended to the south, spreading as they grew and finally terminating on an east-west line. The result was a semicircular plan 520 feet across its south face. The number of purely functional rooms for living and storage was vastly increased and in addition, many round kivas (special ceremonial structures) were built. The pueblo, at the height of its development, might have housed 1,200 inhabitants in some 800 rooms. At its highest development, Bonito's wealth brought traders from afar and regular attacks by covetous, nomadic tribes. Eventually, the pueblo succumbed, from the isolation and lack of food brought on by the lowered water table and drought. During its final years, the outer walls served as a fortress. All openings were sealed up and the once rich settlement suffered nearly constant harrassment. The end came about A.D. 1130 within a hundred years of its major building program.

The shape and orientation of the old crescent and the attempt to maintain the south-opening circular plan with the new construction suggest a special relationship to the sun. Observations made on the University of Southern California's heliodon using students' models based on the reconstructions of N. M. Judd bear this out to a remarkable degree. As the plan is oriented and positioned with reference to the cliffs a hundred feet to the north, the summer sun first strikes the western extremities of the old pueblo at 5:45 a.m., almost an hour after sunrise. At that instant, the sun's rays are parallel in plan to a line connecting the ends of the crescent. A sighting along that line from the west and across the two extremities of Old Bonito would reveal the sun at cliff's edge (fig. 2.26).

In the late afternoon a similar special relationship occurs. From 6:00 p.m. until summer sunset, a gap in the north face of the third floor allows the sunlight to penetrate to the upper terraces and to the eastern arm of the pueblo. Here the last rays of the sun simultaneously intersect two projected corners of a prominently placed section of the upper tier (fig. 2.27a). This special effect would have emphasized the limits of this part of the pueblo and would have insured its importance by sharp and detailed contrasts of dark and light.

Although summer sunrise cannot penetrate the pueblo at all because of the cliffs, and summer sunset penetrates in a controlled way through the gap in the northern wall, winter sunrise lights virtually the entire inside of the pueblo and, again, finds some corners of the eastern third tier in a special relation to each other. The projected south face of the upper tier is brightly lighted, and it stands out in sharp contrast because of the strategically shadowed surfaces on either side (fig. 2.27b).

The azimuth of winter sunset coincides precisely with a line drawn through the extreme limits of the crescent (fig. 2.27c). The result is a virtually complete reversal of the sunrise condition. Almost the entire inside of the crescent is in shadow. The significant exception to this is provided by a cutaway corner at the end of the western arm.

This removed section, which provided the special sighting of summer sun at cliff's edge, also allows winter sunset to finally strike the eastern extremity of the upper tier, thus reinforcing its apparent significance. Such special relationships seem remarkable and beyond the possibility of coincidence.

Old Pueblo Bonito

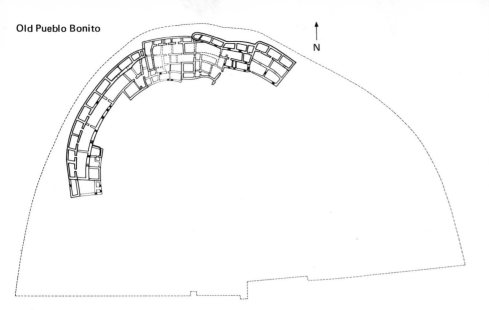

N

Fig. 2.24
Plan of Old Bonito. A tiered arrangement of two and three stories opening in a crescent to the southeast. The crude construction of monolithic sandstone walls with logs and mud used for floors and roofs has been dated at A.D. 919. Heavier lines represent higher tiers. *Source:* Neil M. Judd, *The Architecture of Pueblo Bonito,* figure 3.

Fig. 2.25
Plan of New Bonito. A vastly expanded, tiered arrangement containing 800 rooms built around Old Bonito during a remarkably short time of twenty years, A.D. 1060-1080. The construction showed a high degree of sophistication in the use of materials. The materials used in the walls were differentiated and roof timbers displayed fine craftsmanship. Heavier lines represent higher tiers. *Source:* Neil M. Judd, *The Architecture of Pueblo Bonito,* figure 2.

New Pueblo Bonito

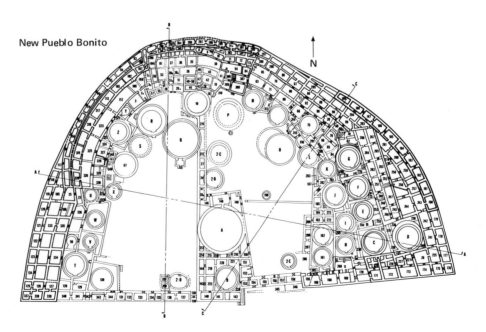

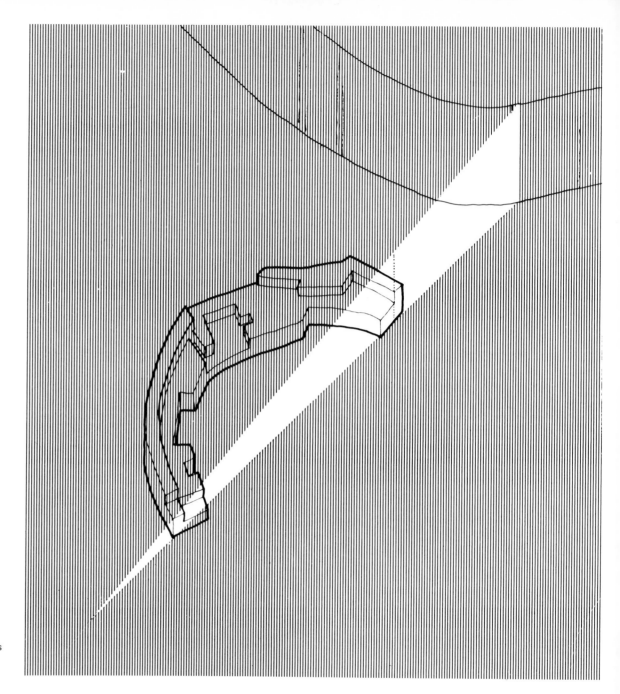

Fig. 2.26
Old Bonito. The hypotenuse of the right triangle represents the sun's rays at 5:45 a.m., summer solstice; when first light strikes the western extremity of the old Pueblo, a straight line sighting across the eastern extremity follows a ray to the sun at cliff's edge.

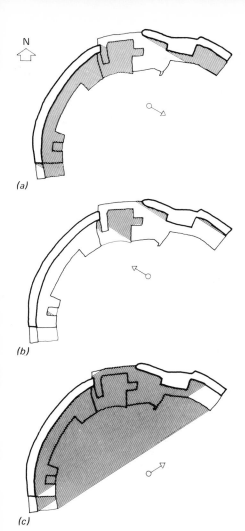

Fig. 2.27
Shadows of critical sun angles, Old Bonito. Sun azimuth is indicated by arrows (a) Sunset, summer solstice; (b) sunrise, winter solstice; (c) sunset, winter solstice. Such relationships show that the Bonitians used the dynamic interaction of sunlight and building to mark the passing seasons with great precision.

The aspects of the old pueblo that are distinctive and responsible for the special relationship to the sun are the open orientation to the southeast, the gap placed in the northern wall of the third tier, and the cutaway western corner. In comparison, the special feature of the new pueblo plan is its orientation directly to the south. The high walls around the outside of the semicircle tend to shut off the summer sunrise and sunset from the interior of the pueblo, while the low wall on the south tends to admit the winter sunrise and sunset directly into the central portion. Between sunrise and sunset at all seasons, the sun strikes the interior surfaces that make up the walls and terraces. The sun's sweeping motion, which alternately lights east faces and west faces, is made more evident by the circular shape of the plan.

As with the southern exposure of Longhouse at Mesa Verde and the tiered arrangement at Acoma, the forms of both Old and New Bonito suggest the possibility that the special relationship to the sun was more than visual; a closer examination of their shape and structure might reveal that, as with the other two examples studied, they tend to equalize seasonal energy profiles—i.e., they tend toward a steady state.

A calculation of direct incident energy per hour on both the old and new pueblos indicates higher summer profiles for both Old and New Bonito; the old pueblo shows a summer increase of 188 percent over winter while the new pueblo increases 233 percent in summer (fig. 2.28). New Bonito has generally higher energy profiles the entire year, but it also has a much larger surface area (130,000 square feet) compared to the old settlement (40,000 square feet). The result is that the two forms act somewhat alike with respect to incident energy per unit area;

their winter curves are nearly equal and only a somewhat higher summer profile appears for New Bonito (fig. 2.29).

This similarity of action based upon incident energy per unit area derives from the fact that all external surfaces on the two forms tend to act with nearly equal efficiency. The new form's efficiency is only 5 percent to 7 percent higher over the year than the old form; more important, its summer efficiency is not proportionately higher. In fact, the summer increase for New Bonito is 5 percent less than it is for the crescent of Old Bonito. The advantage of a reduced summer efficiency in receiving incident energy would begin to suggest possible attributes of the new pueblo beyond the more obvious improvement in construction techniques (fig. 2.30).

Both Old and New Bonito, like Acoma, show a considerably higher percentage of their total energy gain on the verticals during the winter and on the horizontals during the summer (fig. 2.31). Like Acoma, both use materials on each of the surfaces that would tend to balance the seasonal conditions regarding transmitted energy to the interior spaces. As would be expected, the difference in the size of the pueblos (340,000 cubic feet in Old Bonito; 1,350,000 cubic feet in New Bonito) produces a direct correlation in the magnitude of transmitted energy per hour, with the old pueblo showing much lower energy profiles (fig. 2.32).

Fig. 2.28
Incident energy. Summer increase of 188 percent over winter, Old Bonito. Summer increase of 233 percent over winter, New Bonito. Dotted lines indicate normal curve without effect of cliff.

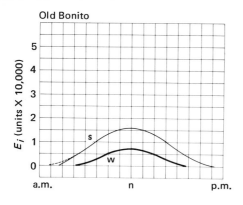

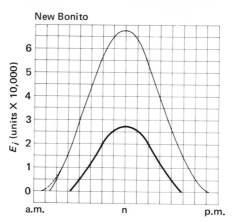

Fig. 2.29
Incident energy per unit area. When incident energy per unit area is graphed for the two pueblos, the curves tend to equalize.

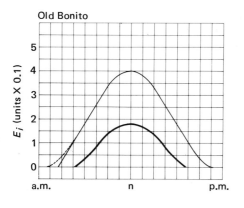

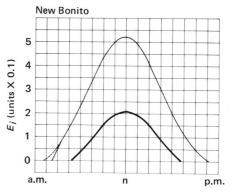

Fig. 2.30
Efficiency. Overall, there is only 5 to 7 percent difference in the efficiency of the way the surfaces of Old and New Bonito receive incident energy.

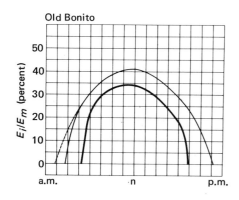

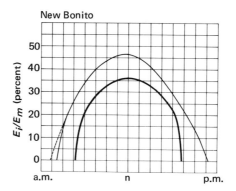

Fig. 2.31
Percentage of incident energy on vertical and horizontal. Old Bonito's curves are symmetrical with winter shown on left, summer on right. New Bonito's curves are asymmetrical; dark lines show winter, light lines show summer.

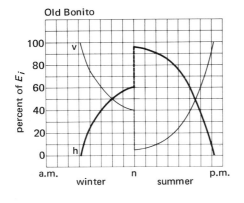

Old Bonito

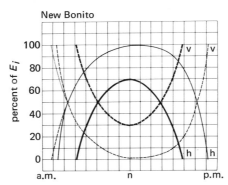

New Bonito

Fig. 2.32
Transmitted energy. Graphs reflect volumetric difference between Old and New Bonito.

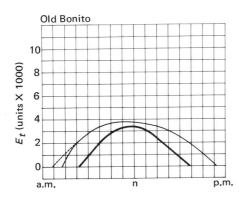

Old Bonito

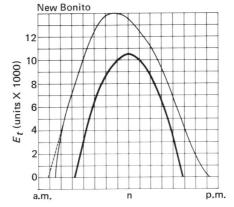

New Bonito

Fig. 2.33
Transmitted energy per unit volume. As with the graphs of incident energy per unit area (fig. 2.29) a plot of E_t/unit volume shows the two forms acting somewhat equally.

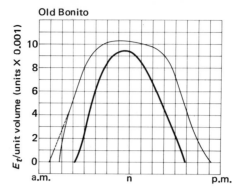

Old Bonito

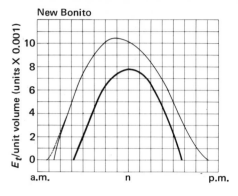

New Bonito

Fig. 2.34
Efficiency of Old Bonito in the way surfaces receive and transmit solar energy to interior spaces. Generally high stable winter efficiency (8 a.m. to 4 p.m.) in the way New Bonito receives and transmits energy.

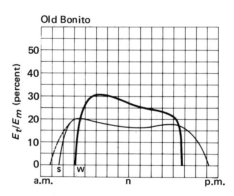

Old Bonito

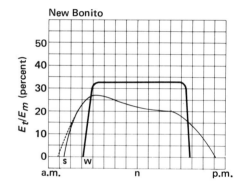

New Bonito

The graph curves show the symmetry of the old pueblo contrasted with the relative asymmetry of the new. The amount of energy transmitted to the interior of the new pueblo in the summer afternoon is lower than it is in the morning. This situation provides an advantage in a high desert region; the greater heat gain in the morning would more quickly overcome the chill of night, while the lower heat gain of the afternoon would help to overcome the effect of high ambient air temperatures.

Like the graphs of energy per unit area, a plot of transmitted energy per unit of volume shows the two forms operating somewhat equally, with a slight overall drop in the efficiency of the new pueblo (fig. 2.33). To some degree this can be accounted for by the lower surface-to-volume ratio of the new pueblo (if S/V is taken as unity for New Bonito, S/V = 1.44 for Old Bonito). Here again the graph indicates that the new pueblo is transmitting more energy per unit volume in the morning than in the afternoon. Added to the fact that New Bonito displays a proportionately lower summer efficiency than the old crescent, the subtle difference in the summer between morning and afternoon suggests the possibility that significantly different attributes were built into the new pueblo. Still, it is necessary to make some comparison of the efficiency of the forms as a whole.

A simple comparison of energy per unit of volume indicates that the old pueblo might have certain winter advantages;

but its real efficiency cannot be evaluated until all surfaces, including those through which winter heat losses may occur, are taken into account. When a comparison is made between the energy being transmitted to the interior of the pueblos (E_t) and the energy that might be transmitted if all available surfaces were receiving energy at 100 percent efficiency (E_{mt}; as if the sun were normal to them) some remarkable facts appear (fig. 2.34).

The old pueblo provides a 14 percent overall efficiency increase in winter, despite a shorter day (by four hours) and the greater attenuating effect of atmosphere because of the angle of the sun's lower winter altitude. Part of this difference is due to the effect of the cliff during the summer, but it is largely the result of a generally higher winter efficiency of the form during an eight-hour period from 8:00 a.m. to 4:00 p.m. Specifically, the summer curve shows an 18 percent efficiency from 7:00 a.m. to 5:00 p.m., while the winter curve declines gradually from a high efficiency of 30 percent at 9:00 a.m. to 21 percent at 4:00 p.m., averaging 26 percent from 8:00 a.m. to 4:00 p.m. While this situation would generally tend to provide an internally steady state over seasons, the curves do not suggest any special properties that might provide a subtler level of response to daily variation. By contrast, New Bonito not only develops a 15 percent increase in winter efficiency but the curves suggest that it would tend to provide a precise mitigation of daily variation.

An indication of the degree of precision that characterizes the functioning of New Bonito is provided by the winter efficiency curve for energy transfer. It is perfectly flat at 33 percent from 8:00 a.m. to 4:00 p.m. During this same eight-hour period the summer curve averages 22.6 percent. This amounts to a summer drop of 10.4 percent in average efficiency; but while this is a distinct advantage, the real significance occurs in the way this hourly difference is distributed. At 8:00 a.m. the seasonal difference in efficiency is 4 percent; by 4:00 p.m. that difference has increased to 15 percent. The reason is the steady and desirable drop in summer efficiency toward the late afternoon when ambient air temperatures are high and surfaces are warm from the day's accumulations of incident energy.

Both Old and New Bonito operate efficiently as energy systems that mitigate seasonal variation in insolation. Each has a higher efficiency curve in winter than summer. The truly remarkable fact about New Bonito is the precision of the curves. From sunrise to sunset during the winter solstice, the efficiency profile is absolutely flat, suggesting that the greatest advantage possible is being taken by the system to receive and store energy during the daylight hours to carry through the cold winter night. During the summer solstice, not only is the efficiency profile lower, as it should be to mitigate seasonal variation, but the curve is higher in the morning when ambient air temperatures are low and lower in the afternoon when ambient air temperatures are high. New Bonito mitigates daily as well as seasonal variations in insolation.

It is difficult to attribute such particular relationships to chance. The somewhat less regular efficiency curves for Old Bonito might conceivably allow such a question to be raised, but even here the precise visual phenomena resulting from the interaction of the sun, the crescent, and the site cannot be ignored. The quantification of such visual phenomena in energy terms strongly suggests that the Bonitians were aware of the relationships between the form of their constructions and the dynamics of earth and sun; in fact, they must have worked from a fairly distinct mental image or even from a two or three-dimensional physical model of form.

The evidence is convincing that they had a plan of action involving not only a generative increment (as at Acoma) but also the limits of generation, i.e., the form itself. First, there is the very strong visual recognition of the special times of day in the old pueblo. Sunrise and sunset of both extreme seasons are clearly emphasized in the way the sun strikes key surfaces. Second, there is the fact that the builders extended the original crescent arrangement, apparently making one false start, then correcting themselves to complete the semicircular plan of the new pueblo.[4] Third, there is the higher efficiency of both forms regarding transmitted energy to the interior volumes in the winter. Finally, there is the remarkable flatness of the winter efficiency curve for New Bonito accompanied by a summer efficiency that recognizes critical daily variation.

4. Judd, *The Architecture of Pueblo Bonito.*

These builders achieved, through the form of their constructions, a highly efficient energy system that tended toward a steady state. There can be little question that their actions were intentional and that the result was a purposeful system—a machine for equalizing seasonal and diurnal variations. What the Mesa Verde Indians accomplished with cave dwellings and the Acomas attained through the use of a highly developed generative increment, the Bonitians realized through the systematic generation of total form. In this sense they progressed beyond Longhouse and Acoma to a higher level of organization. They used the generative increment of the Acomas in a way that systematically transformed its simple, orderly repetition. The Bonitian increment was differentiated within a larger context so that an inevitable correlation existed between the internal differentiation or structuring of the system and its limits or shape. Like Longhouse, but unlike Acoma, the internal diversity of Bonito's form would have been reinforced over time by the movements of the sun. Its sweep of the great curving walls would have structured and enlivened the cycle of daily life. The plan indicates such a structuring; it is manifested as a specialization of the east, west, and central sections. These spatial differences of plan and the various activities they suggest must have been further delineated by the recurrences of light and heat.

Longhouse, Acoma, and Bonito can also be compared in the relation of their processes of building and their realization of purpose. Longhouse was a self-organizing system in which the limits were fixed by the site. Under these circumstances the process of construction became one of using up the cave's natural capacity to equalize the seasonal variations. The result was a highly differentiated internal arrangement that did not

realize its highest level of optimization until the spatial-temporal limits of the cave were reached. The end of the building process and the highest level of optimization occurred simultaneously with the using up of the cave's inherent capacity. By contrast, Acoma had no fixed limits upon its growth except the edge of the plateau; the relatively large size of the plateau would indicate, however, that this was not such a confining restriction. Beyond that, the shape of the repetitive increment, i.e., the tiered section, established the general attributes of the system as a whole. The terraced building section had been preorganized to act in a special way. The house, with its end walls covered on the east and west, comprised the essential increment and established the attributes of the system. Expansion did not provide higher levels of optimization in which seasonal variations were diminished toward a steady state.

Unlike Longhouse at Mesa Verde, Acoma did not have to build to use the capacity within predetermined and invariant limits. After the first increment was placed, the limits of the system remained variant and indeterminate; its growth was relatively undifferentiated. At the point when the first increment was placed, the highest level of organization was simultaneously reached as exemplified by the individual house in which there was greater internal differentiation than seems apparent in the plan as a whole.

Bonito combines attributes of both Longhouse and Acoma because it is pre-organized both at the level of a generative increment (the terraced unit) and at the level of total form. Like Acoma, some level of optimization was achieved by the old crescent with its essentially southern orientation of the terraced arrangement. Then came the industrious New Bonitians. It is evident from the special properties of the efficiency curves that these new builders were aiming at a specific purpose and did in fact achieve it with the completion of the form. The effect was to establish invariant limits upon the system. A second and higher level of optimization had been achieved than at Acoma, but like Longhouse with its site-determined and invariant limits, Bonito was fixed. The full realization of purpose had come with the completion of the form. They were powerless to reach beyond this level. Only a major change in technology could have allowed them to attain a third and still higher level of optimization in gaining a steady environmental state.

The comparison of these three early systems suggests the fundamental role of form in providing man with an essential degree of stability in his environment. By their shape and structure these settlements achieved a special and quantifiable relation to nature that is not unique in prehistory. Examples can be found that optimize other conditions. The extensive irrigation system of the Hohokoms on the present site of Phoenix, Arizona, represents an attempt to provide a steady environmental state by forming the land (fig. 2.35). Between A.D. 500-1400,

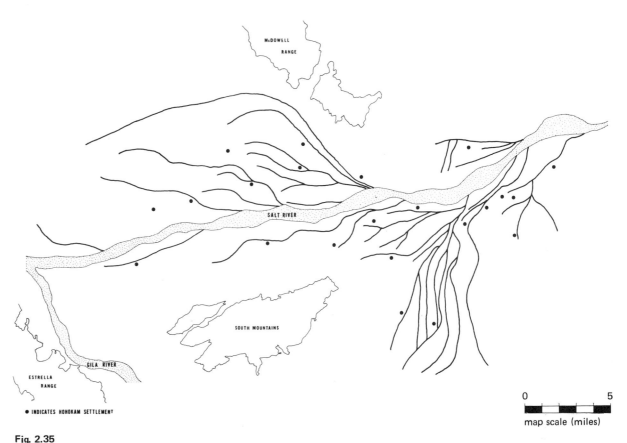

map scale (miles)

● INDICATES HOHOKAM SETTLEMENT

Fig. 2.35
The extensive irrigation system of the Hohokums on the present site of Phoenix, Arizona, represents an attempt to provide a steady environmental state by forming the land. Between A.D. 500-1400, these skilled engineers built several hundred miles of canals at gradients so accurate that some of the original beds are still used as part of a modern irrigation system.
Source: Annual Report of The Smithsonian Institution (Washington, D.C.: Smithsonian Institution Press, 1945), pp. 379-386.

these skilled engineers built several hundred miles of canals at gradients so accurate that some of the original beds are still used as part of a modern irrigation system.[5] As another example, for at least five hundred years, the uniformly directioned wind scoops atop the houses of Hyderabad Sind, West Pakistan, have caught the southwest wind. Their kite-like surfaces divert the air down and through the living spaces of each house, providing sufficient relief from the 98-120° F heat of summer. After cooling and refreshing the house, the air is pulled out the lee windows by the action of ambient breeze. Such a system not only keeps the houses well ventilated without the continuous expenditure of energy for mechanical devices, but it lends a special and identifiable form that distinguishes this city and its mode of living from another where environmental conditions are different.

The canal system of the Hohokoms and the wind scoops of Hyderabad Sind are but two additional examples of many in which men have employed form as the principle mode of adaptive response to the main recurring forces of nature. The comparative study of such responses suggests a general correlation between their level of organization and the attainment of purpose.

5. *Annual Report of the Smithsonian Institution* (Washington, D.C.: Smithsonian Institution Press, 1945), pp. 379-386.

The ultimate level of attainment of a steady state is increased by higher levels of organization. Both Longhouse and Bonito are clear examples of arrangements that must grow to predetermined limits before purpose can be fully attained. As expansion takes place, the system becomes increasingly differentiated; its parts take on special tasks. Beginning from a low level, optimization increases with the specialization of parts. With the placement of the last generative increment and the completion of the form, the fullest extent of purpose is achieved. The final degree of optimization is high and remains fixed.

In relation to the same purpose, Acoma maintains a fairly steady level of optimization after the placement of the first significant increment and throughout the entire building process. Specialization by parts of the settlement does not increase, so the level of organization tends to remain constant. These building arrangements, like natural systems in general, demonstrate an inverse relationship between the level of organization and the optimization of specific purpose. During growth, the lower level of differentiation produces an early but low level of optimization, as at Acoma; a higher level of differentiation during the growth process results in a later achievement of purpose but a higher level of optimization, as at Bonito and Longhouse.

While Acoma seems to suffer in this comparison, it has the advantage of flexible limits that may continue to expand. The level of optimization established by the simple, repetitive increment is not very high, but modification of the settlement's limits does not change that level. In fact,

since parts are not obviously specialized in their functional relation to each other and to the whole, they may be either added or subtracted without changing the particular attributes of the system as a whole regarding thermal variation.

It is evident that none of the three examples combines the advantages of indefinitely flexible limits and increasing levels of thermal optimization with growth. It is conceivable that Bonito might have achieved a higher level of optimization with an improved technology that allowed the construction of taller buildings or the use of materials with a greater range of thermal coefficients; but for the life and technology of its time, the Bonitian settlement must be recognized as one of the major achievements of pre-Columbian America. Beyond that, and more generally, the pueblos offer an intriguing architectural heritage and a promising legacy that has been generally ignored. The use of form to reduce the consumption of organic fuels and yet achieve a high degree of equilibrium can be studied with profit by any society, however technologically advanced.

Part Two

Owens Valley, California, as a Case
Study in Ecological Planning

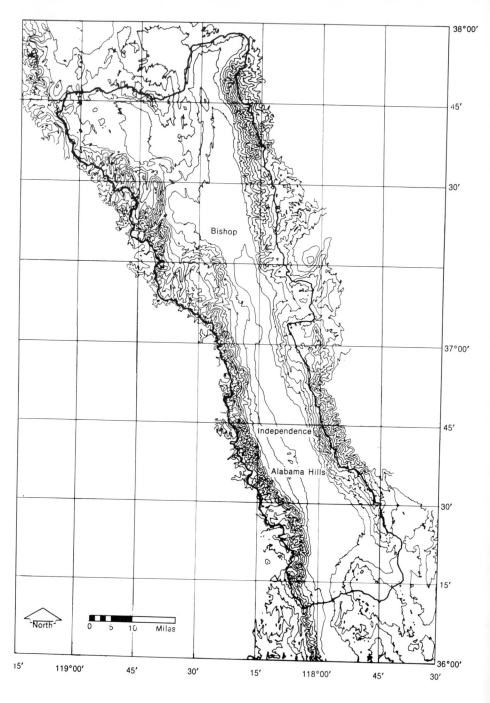

Fig. 3.1
Owens Valley, California,
stretches 100 miles long and
20 miles wide between the
peaks of the Sierra Nevada
Mountains on the west and
the Inyo-White Mountains
on the east. The dark out-
line shows the overall study
area.

In 1968, graduate students in urban design at the University of Southern California began a study of a large-scale application of principles correlating building form with natural variation. The specific purpose of this study was to investigate the use of building form to reduce energy expenditures in responding to natural variation at a regional scale. Earlier studies had shown the skillful use of form by the pueblo builders of the Southwest. Modern technology might allow an improved use of building form at a larger scale.

An exploration to find a modern correlation between form and natural variation requires a site that is rich with variety. A range of site conditions should result in characteristically varied form responses. Deep valley regions provide an example of such a site. Easy observations can be made on a great range of natural phenomena. In such places, the conditions of heat, light, water, and wind are likely to be different from one side of the valley to another. Large variations also occur from the valley floor to its rim, with lesser variations along the length of the valley.

Cyclical changes are superposed upon this rich spatial structure. There are day-night rhythms: surfaces become alternately light and dark, warm and cool; winds rise through the valley by day, descend at night, pausing regularly and reversing in direction twice each day. Such diurnal intervals lie within longer seasonal variations, which may be within still longer intervals. Owens Valley, California, a site with these strong spatial-temporal characteristics, was near enough to Los Angeles to allow frequent trips by the study team. The first step in the study was a careful ecological description.

The valley stretches a hundred miles long and twenty miles across at 37° north latitude, 13,000 feet below the peaks of the Sierra Nevada. Because of its strong ecological structuring, Owens Valley provides a remarkably useful study situation. The distance is relatively short from the Sierra crest east to the Inyo-White Mountains, but the valley provides a great range of ecological conditions, from subalpine and mixed coniferous forests in the mountains to high desert growth on the valley floor (fig. 3.1). The valley is oriented approximately north-south in the long direction but with a 20°-25° tilt to the northwest, with some interesting implications for the west-facing slopes of the Inyo-White mountain range. The mountains make the valley a closed water system, contained on the west by the Sierra Nevada (elevation 13,000-14,000 feet), on the east by the Inyo-White Mountains (about 10,000 feet), on the north by the higher elevation of the valley floor itself, and on the south by a small range of mountains that stop any major flow of water out to the Mojave Desert.

This unique and impressive valley was selected as an appropriate area for the study of land-sensitive planning techniques, not for potential settlement. As the study progressed, it became even more clear that for several convincing reasons intensive settlement should not take place there. The valley is a delicately balanced ecosystem, and urbanization would disturb this balance. Only a small portion of Owens Valley could be safely settled, and even this would require great care. Many of the regions of the valley are low-diversity ecological domains that would require a long time to heal the scars inevitably left by development. The rate as well as extent of any development would have to be highly controlled, and development techniques in use today do not responsibly direct growth in such areas.

In addition, settlement in Owens Valley is inadvisable because of its role as a major water resource for the city of Los Angeles. As part of the development of this water supply, the city had purchased about 300,000 acres of land in Owens Valley, situated mostly on the valley floor. The land is administered by the Los Angeles Department of Water and Power, whose primary responsibility is the operation of the Los Angeles aqueduct system, which presently furnishes close to 80 percent of the city's water supply. The department has adopted a management policy that accommodates a variety of uses, including various forms of recreation, compatible with its primary responsibility of safeguarding the water resources of the city. Significant development would threaten the quality and quantity of this supply, and would tend to disturb the watershed areas, which have stabilized since the construction of the aqueduct. Los Angeles is now dependent upon a water source that has been available to the city for sixty years.

The valley also provides a fine recreational resource, primarily for the people of the Los Angeles region, but also for other urbanized areas of the western states. Such a resource is much needed and provides in addition to hiking, camping, and sightseeing, a major protected habitat for several animal species, including the Tule elk.

Fig. 3.2
Topographic and geologic
features of Owens Valley,
California.

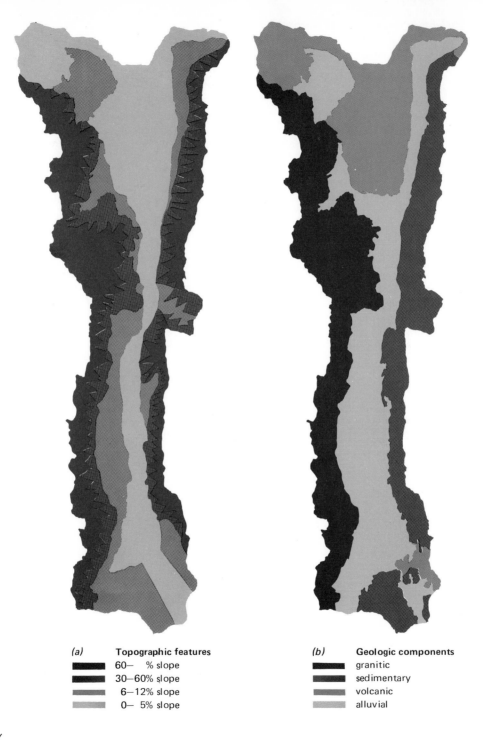

Topographically, the valley's shape ranges
from the very steep slopes of the Sierra
Nevada on the west to the gentle gradient
of the valley floor and on to the softer
contours of the Inyo-White Mountains on
the east. The most significant characteristic of the shape of the valley is the rapid
change of gradient in the east-west direction when compared to the north-south
(fig. 3.2a).

The second component of the form of
this reference system is its structure or
geological makeup. The Sierras are generally granitic formations, the Inyo-Whites
are sedimentary, and the valley floor itself is alluvial. The northern portion of
the valley is intruded upon by a lava flow
that has split the valley into two prongs
of a fork. The alluvial fill ranges in depth
from a few inches to 2,500 feet and is
contained by a watertight bedrock formation acting as a basin for water running
off the Sierra slopes (fig. 3.2b).

Only recurrent force actions allow adaptive responses. A single occurrence either
lies within the response capacity of a system or it destroys the system. Apparently,
there is no alternative, there cannot be an
adaptation unless the force recurs. The
main recurrent component of the environment is solar radiation.

(a) **Topographic features**
■ 60— % slope
■ 30—60% slope
■ 6—12% slope
■ 0— 5% slope

(b) **Geologic components**
■ granitic
■ sedimentary
■ volcanic
■ alluvial

Solar Radiation

In this relatively narrow valley with its long axis in the north-south direction, the sun rises on some portions before others. As the sun rises in the east it hits the Sierra crests first, and as the shadow from the Inyo-Whites recedes to the valley floor the entire western part of the valley is lighted and heated in the morning. From about midmorning until midafternoon the valley floor is in full light and receives its maximum direct insolation. As the afternoon approaches, the west-facing Inyo-White slopes receive their maximum direct insolation until the sun begins to disappear behind the Sierra crests, causing the shadow to rise up the Inyo-White slopes. The gentle crests of the Inyo-White Mountains are the last part of the valley lighted at night (fig. 3.3).

The Sierra side of Owens Valley receives its maximum insolation in the morning, when the ambient air temperatures of the valley are low, while the Inyo-White slopes, facing west and slightly south, receive their maximum insolation in the afternoon, when the ambient air temperatures of the valley are high (fig. 3.4). This fact has a pronounced impact on the life systems of the valley and would be a major factor in generating frameworks for settlement that take into consideration natural force action.

On the east side of the valley, heat is added to heat; the direct incident energy from the sun reinforces an ambient heat condition. On the west, nature performs a balancing act. The slopes receive their maximum insolation when ambient air temperatures are low, contributing to the great differences apparent from one side of the valley to another.

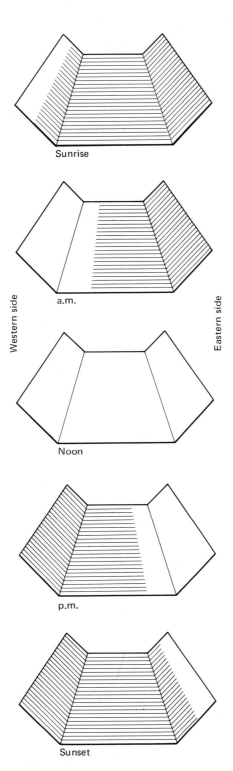

Western side

Eastern side

Sunrise

a.m.

Noon

p.m.

Sunset

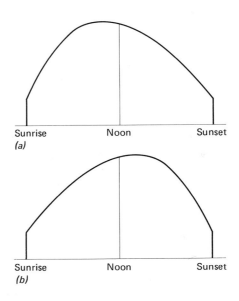

Sunrise Noon Sunset
(a)

Sunrise Noon Sunset
(b)

Fig. 3.3
Sun action on an idealized valley section. Shadows are cast from the east in the morning and from the west in the afternoon.

Fig. 3.4
Energy profiles of the Sierras: (a), western side of the valley and Inyo-Whites; (b), eastern side. East-facing slopes of the western, Sierra side of the valley receive maximum insolation in the morning when ambient air temperatures are low. West-facing slopes of the eastern, Inyo-White side receive maximum insolation in the afternoon when ambient air temperatures are high.

Fig. 3.5
Incident-energy domains.
The valley was subdivided
into 22 domains with dif-
ferent insolation properties
resulting from orientation.

Fig. 3.6
Ambient air temperature
domains. Air temperature
drops an average of 3.5° F
for each thousand feet of
vertical ascent. In Owens
Valley, the temperature
drop from valley floor to
Sierra crest is about 35° F.

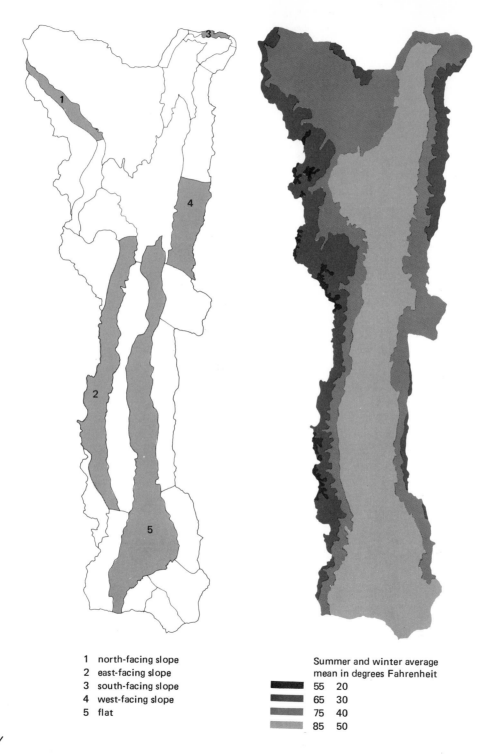

1 north-facing slope
2 east-facing slope
3 south-facing slope
4 west-facing slope
5 flat

Summer and winter average
mean in degrees Fahrenheit

	55	20
	65	30
	75	40
	85	50

To further refine the measurement of the
valley, areas were distinguished by the differences that resulted from sun energy
upon their form. The objective here was
to establish a structure in which insolation on one part could be distinguished
from that on another (fig. 3.5). Within a
part, the condition is relatively constant,
but from one part to another there is a
distinction across an edge. The fact that
an edge carries information that distinguishes adjacent parts is of critical importance in considering any framework for
settlement that attempts to respect the
land and its resources.

Ambient air temperature is a second
thermal phenomenon related to insolation but with somewhat different spatial
and temporal characteristics. It is primarily a function of elevation, with the temperature dropping an average of 3.5° F for
each thousand feet of vertical ascent. In
Owens Valley one of the results of the
temperature variations is displayed by
the extreme contrast between the alpine
conditions of the Sierra crests and the
high desert conditions of the valley floor.
From the crests to the floor the change
in elevation is about 10,000 feet, representing an average temperature drop of
about 35° F. The result is a dramatic
range of conditions within a relatively
short distance. A clear layering is evident
in the sharp demarcation of the snow line,
accompanied by similarly clear and strong
demarcations of plant and animal life from
one elevation to another. The result is a
second set of areas based on ambient air
temperature (fig. 3.6).

Wind

The wind in Owens Valley can be reduced to three component forces for analysis. The first, the westerly, blows fairly consistently off the Pacific Ocean and up the Sierra rise to the crest. It carries great amounts of moisture, which are deposited primarily as snow on the Sierra crests. In the spring the snow melts and runs off to fill the basin. When certain valley conditions exist, the westerly becomes extremely unstable, resulting in a spectacular phenomenon called the Sierra Wave. It rises off the crest of the mountains and fluctuates between very high elevations and the valley floor (fig. 3.7). Glider pilots have set world altitude records on this Sierra Wave, but the more normal condition is less dramatic, with the effect of the westerly diminishing when it reaches midvalley.

Wind tunnel tests, conducted at the University of Southern California, in which the westerly has been simulated on a typical cross-section through the valley (fig. 3.8), indicate a high concentration of isobars on the Sierra slopes, with a diminishing impact from the westerly on the valley floor, shown by increased spacing of the isobars (fig. 3.9).

The weakening of the westerly on the valley floor allows a second component of the wind structure to become dominant—the so-called mountain-valley winds. These winds result from the cyclical heating and cooling of the valley and the Mojave Desert to the south. During the day the hot air rises through the valley to the north and at night settles back through the valley to the south, producing a daily cycle of change in the wind direction from north to south on the valley floor.

Thermals, which rise through the lateral valleys up the slopes during the day and back down during the night, comprise the third component of wind structure in the valley. This daily cycle also produces winds in the east-west direction upon the mountain slopes.

From these three components of the wind, a composite structure allows one area to be distinguished from another while within a single area the conditions are generally consistent (figs. 3.10, 3.11). The results of wind action can be seen, for example, in the dune formations that lie on the top of the lava flow in the northern part of the valley. As the lava cooled, its surface became subject to wind action. Dunes finally stabilized and plant materials accumulated on their slopes (fig. 3.12). With a slope orientation of north-south, there is the additional phenomenon of sun action melting the snow from the south slopes while leaving it on the north, producing a clear differentiation from one orientation to another as a result of both sun and wind action. This north-south distinction appears on water-generated land forms as well (fig. 3.13).

The duning phenomenon is of considerable interest and has been the subject of several studies, including the important pioneering work of the physicist R. A. Bagnold. The studies conducted by the Department of Architecture at the University of Southern California were guided by an interest in phenomena related directly to wind-blown sand, and partly by a general interest in the responses of forms to environmental force action.

1. See Ralph A. Bagnold, *The Physics of Blown Sand and Desert Dunes* (New York: William Morrow and Co., 1941).

Fig. 3.7
The Sierra wave phenomenon.

Fig. 3.8
Topography of wind-test
section taken midway up
the valley's length between
the Sierra and Inyo-White
crests.

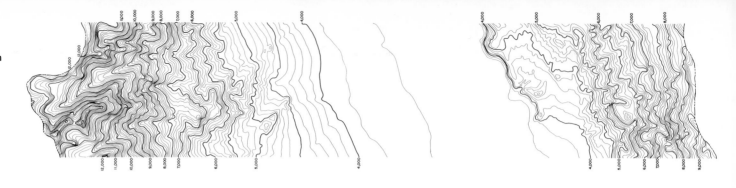

Fig. 3.9
Wind pressure isobars of
test section. Under normal
conditions, the impact of
the Westerlies diminishes
at the base of the Sierra
Nevada Mountains.

Fig. 3.10
Composite wind structure
of test section.

■ westerly
■ mountain-valley and
canyon thermals
■ bubble effect
■ mountain-valley thermals

Fig. 3.11
Wind domains. Winds in the
valley are generated both
from inside and outside
conditions.

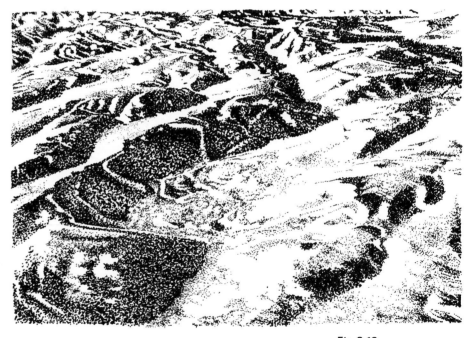

Fig. 3.12
Lava dune formations
(produced by wind action)
located in the northern part
of the Owens Valley.

■■ westerly
▨▨ mountain-valley and
canyon thermals
▧▧ bubble effect
▨▨ mountain-valley thermals

Fig. 3.13
When slopes are oriented to
the north and south, sun
action produces a clear differentiation from one orientation to another.

In a gravity environment, a sand cone with a natural slump angle is stable; its form is differentiated in the vertical direction so as to produce an equal stress throughout the pile of sand. At the top, where loads are small, the cross-section is small. At the bottom, where the loads are greater, the cross-section is larger, producing a more or less constant force per unit area throughout the pile.

This stable form can be unstabilized by changing its environment. What was stable under the action of gravity becomes unstable when another environmental force is added—in this case wind, simulated in the cross-section of a low-velocity wind tunnel. Under these new conditions, the form of the sandpile adapts, and certain conditions can be measured as this adaptation takes place (fig. 3.14).

One of the interesting things to measure on the pile of sand as it transforms and attains stability in its new environment is the relation between its contained volume and its exposed surface. The change in the surface-to-volume ratio (S/V) can be taken to represent an index or a coefficient of the susceptibility of any system to environmental force, which acts as a stress or a displacement upon that system. When the environment of the sand pile is changed from one of gravity to one of gravity and wind, a transformation to a more stable configuration occurs. In the early stages of this change, surface area increases rapidly and volume is quickly decreased through a loss of sand. As a more stable shape is attained, transformation slows and the rate of change in S/V diminishes, approaching a steady state (fig. 3.15).

Something else happens during the transformation of the pile of sand. The range of pressure on the original is very great— that is, the variation of force effect is at a maximum insofar as the action of wind is concerned. After the form has stabilized in response to the action of both wind and gravity, the range of pressure conditions upon the sandpile is minimized by comparison with the original range (fig. 3.16). A general principle can be drawn here that correlates certain conditions: *A minimum differentiation of form in relation to force action produces a maximum variation in the force effect; a maximum differentiation of form in relation to force action produces a minimum of variation in the effect of that force.* This generalization holds for phenomena in time as well as in space.

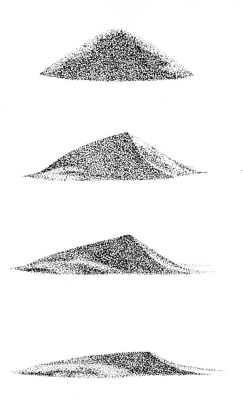

Fig. 3.14
The adaptation of a sand-pile to the action of wind. These tests were conducted in a low velocity tunnel where wind direction is from left to right. (Based on work done by Pierre Koenig at the University of Southern California, 1966.)

Fig. 3.15
Surface-to-volume ratio tends to increase at a decreasing rate, leveling off as a form achieves dimensional stability as a result of force action, i.e., wind. (Based on work done by Pierre Koenig at the University of Southern California, 1966.)

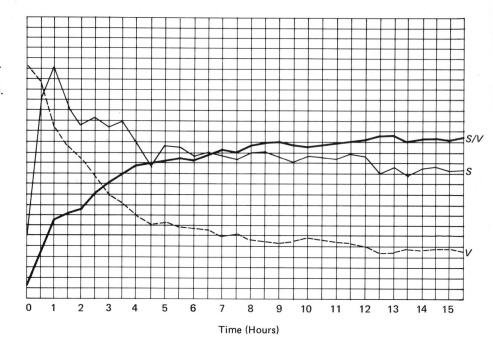

S/V

S

V

0   1   2   3   4   5   6   7   8   9   10   11   12   13   14   15

Time (Hours)

Fig. 3.16
Wind pressure isobar comparisons of a more stable sandpile and a less stable sandpile. (Based on work done by Pierre Koenig at the University of Southern California, 1966.)

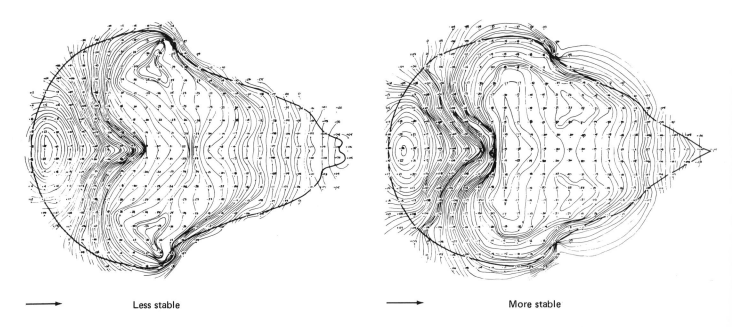

Less stable

More stable

Water

As the westerlies come off the Pacific Ocean and up the Sierra rise, they carry moisture that is deposited along the Sierra crest in average magnitudes of 50 inches a year. As these westerlies move on across the valley, they have very little moisture left to deposit, so that the valley floor itself receives not more than three inches of precipitation annually. In a distance of about ten miles there is a precipitation differential of approximately 47 inches. The result is a dramatic range of environmental conditions, with the variations occurring in the east-west direction across the valley (fig. 3.17).

As a result of the extreme amount of precipitation on the Sierra crest compared to the valley floor or the Inyo-White crest, virtually all the stream action runs from west to east on the Sierra slopes, with virtually no continuously running streams from east to west off the Inyo-White slopes (fig. 3.18). Because of this, the contrast in plant and animal life from west side to east side is also extreme: relatively lush vegetation occurs on the west side, especially in the north, with a barren and desert quality on the east.

While almost no precipitation hits the valley floor, especially on the eastern portion, some snow does fall along the northern Inyo-White crests during the winter. When this snow melts it produces a run-off that carries sediment to the base of the mountains, where it is deposited as alluvial fans on the basin floor. The result is a unique and remarkably pure formation, since no precipitation acts directly upon the fan to erode it and transform its pure shape. It remains a classic and stable form, sometimes visually reinforced by agricultural irrigation techniques that terminate at the base of the fan where the slope begins to rise (fig. 3.19).

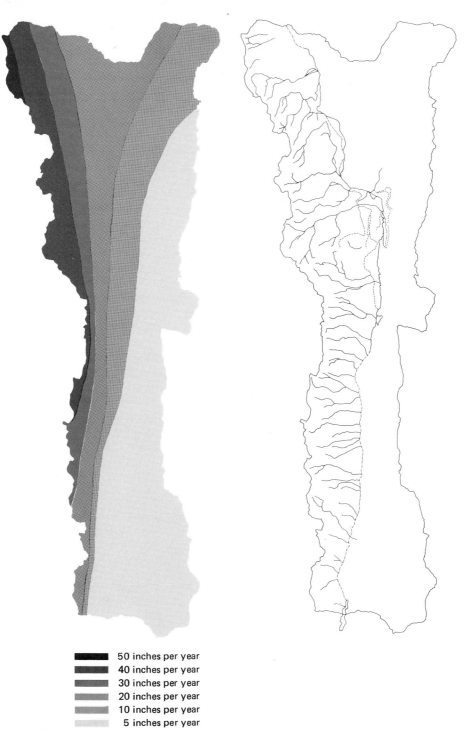

- ▇ 50 inches per year
- ▓ 40 inches per year
- ▒ 30 inches per year
- ▒ 20 inches per year
- ░ 10 inches per year
- ░ 5 inches per year

Fig. 3.17
Equal precipitation domains.

Fig. 3.18
Perennial creeks and Owens River.

Fig. 3.19
An alluvial fan formed by erosion.

Certain kinds of measurements can be made to establish the tendency of streams to transform themselves in the direction of stability. As part of the Owens Valley study at the University of Southern California, stream action was simulated on water tables, with the lateral movement of the stream recorded cinematically and measured. Beginning at the source and moving along the stream until it terminates in a fan on a flat surface, measurements of lateral movement were made at various points along the length of the simulated stream. Graphs of lateral movement plotted against time indicated much less lateral movement upstream than downstream during the process of stabilization of the stream system as a whole (fig. 3.20).

Stabilization involves lateral movement, or ambulation, and modification of the stream gradient through a process of erosion until some steady state is achieved. Lateral movement and the establishment of a steady gradient are related, so that to modify the gradient would result in an increased lateral movement while a modification in the lateral movement would result in an increased rate of erosion to bring the gradient into balance.

One of the tragedies in the southeastern part of the United States has been a consequence of the practice of channeling streams as they flow through agricultural land where they might be naturally inclined, through a process of lateral movement, to change their course. Channelization is aimed at retarding the lateral action of the stream by making the sides of the stream impervious to erosion. What is ignored in this procedure is the fact that

the only way a stream can stabilize itself along its entire course is through lateral action. Eliminating the possibility of that action at any point along the stream, especially on nearly flat land where it tends to exhibit the greatest amount of lateral movement, results in the instability of the entire stream system from one end to the other. Stream action is then directed to re-establish a steady state by changing its gradient with an intensive new stage of erosion. With increased erosion upstream come increased rates of deposit downstream; with increased cutting upstream comes increased debris, which deposits itself downstream on the very agricultural land meant to be saved by the channelizing process. Now farmers who originally supported the program in an effort to reduce flooding and changes of stream course have increased their resistance to channelizing as longer range implications have become clear. Perhaps their efforts will bring the whole program under more careful control.

In addition to stream action, Owens Valley is characterized by a high water table that forms a great natural reservoir (fig. 3.21). Since the valley is a closed water system, once the water has accumulated in the basin it can only get out naturally by means of evaporation and some underground leakage. The valley floor itself bears the marks of low-gradient stream action, in which the Owens River has been ambulating back and forth across the valley floor leaving erosion marks, salt deposits, and oxbows in its wake.

Fig. 3.20
Graphs of lateral movement plotted against time indicate that much less lateral movement occurs upstream than downstream during the stabilization of the stream system. (Based on work done by Emmet Wemple at the University of Southern California, 1966.)

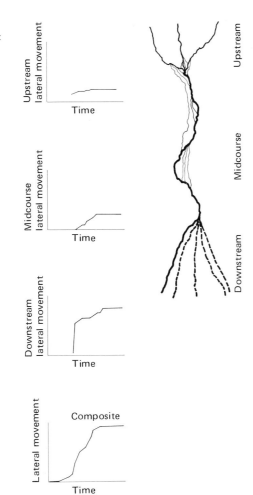

Fig. 3.21
Existing ground-water basin.

Composite Force Action

While the forces of sun, wind, and water
can be separately considered for measurement, their action in composition produces
the general conditions of Owens Valley.
Responses to such a composite structure
can be seen in the life systems of the valley. Plants, for example, arrange themselves according to that structure (fig.
3.22). Segments of the structure tend
to be narrow in the east-west direction
and very long in the north-south direction. The distribution of plant species
follows this arrangement. A much higher
degree of diversity in plant materials is
found across the valley than along its
length, and some species tend to arrange
themselves continuously from one end of
the valley to the other. Across the valley
in an east-west direction the variety is
very great; changes in plant material occur in quick succession reflecting the
great variety of states. The Piute Indians
of Owens Valley established their territories in an east-west direction to take
maximum advantage of that great diversity of plant life. By migrating across the
narrow dimension of the valley they en-
countered the greatest range of useful
states in the least distance.

Fig. 3.22
Plant-life communities.

■ barren

■ subalpine forest—white bark
pine, foxtail pine, lodgepole
pine, bristlecone pine.

■ mixed coniferous forest—lodgepole pine, jeffrey pine, pinyon-
juniper.

▒ inland sagebrush—rabbitbrush,
bitterbrush.

░ high desert—shadescale scrub,
creosote bush scrub.

□ grassland

The first step in the Owens Valley Study had been a careful site description of a large region comprised of a variety of subregions. The variety was great primarily because of the extreme range of topography. The purpose of the second step in the study was to convert these site descriptions into useful expressions of building form.

The direct conversion of information about environmental forces to a specification that will help in the design of buildings requires recognition of the basic fact that, in general, the desirable internal state of a building is steady while the outside environment goes through cyclic changes. For this reason, while a static description is required and is certainly employed by designers today, the cyclic or dynamic character of the environment must also be recognized if the building form itself is going to help support a steady state.

The static aspect of environmental force can be measured in terms of magnitude and direction. Insolation, for example, can be measured as the amount of energy received at an instant from a certain direction. Wind velocity can be measured and its direction established at a particular time. But such static descriptions tell only part of the story. The dynamic aspect of environmental force must be measured in terms of variation and interval. The sun rises and sets daily and its zenith changes with the seasons. In Owens Valley, the westerlies vary at seasonal intervals while the mountain-valley and lateral thermals vary their directions daily. Precipitation, surface runoff, and ground water all vary with the seasons, while the water table fluctuates at intervals of a day, a year, or thirty years. Streams cycle through course changes at even longer intervals.

Maintenance Costs for the Built Arrangement

The cost of maintaining a built arrangement is a function of the amount of energy required to sustain the desired steady internal state while the external environment goes through its cyclic variations. In other words, stress upon the built arrangement can be measured in terms of the amount of energy necessary to maintain it; and the amount of maintenance energy is a function of the variation in force effect upon the arrangement.

Stress, as the term has been defined in this study, is not exclusively, or even primarily, a function of the magnitude or direction of force action, which describes how hot or how cold it is, how wet or how dry it is at any given time. Instead, stress is a function of the variations in those conditions. If we assume a given condition, for example -70° F, then a simple machine can be designed to operate at a high level of efficiency, so long as the condition persists. But let that condition vary to -30° F, and the -70° F machine is no longer right for the job. What sounds like a warming trend is not very good for the machine. The least that can happen is that the full capacity of the machine is not being used. A control problem is introduced: the machine or its operator must decide which condition is critical.

Day in and day out, cities like New York and Los Angeles operate their power supply systems at one-third to one-half capacity during some portion of the day. They were designed to handle the worst conditions possible and, as with the -70° F machine that operates during part of the time at -30° F, inefficiency results. The systems are not being used to full capacity, and expensive control problems are introduced by the necessity to shift energies around and to shut equipment down. High maintenance costs result in order to avoid the dangers inherent in heating up and cooling down devices such as steam generators.

This suggests that environmental perturbation may be seen more as a function of variation than of the absolute magnitude of any condition. Since the environment is comprised of sets of variables, stress on the built arrangement has been defined in this study as a function of variation at different intervals of all environmental forces acting on a site.

The composite action of all cyclic forces provided information to structure Owens Valley into domains of maximum and minimum magnitude of variation. Such a generalization allowed the obvious differences in the forces of sun, wind, and water to be ignored. Instead, concentration was on the more useful notion that where the composite variation is greatest, stress is also greatest.

1. See R. L. Knowles, *Owens Valley Study* (Los Angeles: Department of Architecture, University of Southern California, 1969).

Fig. 4.1
A simplified verson of the
stress domains shows them
approximately limited to
the geometry of the valley
as established by the two
containing slopes and a
horizontal plane.

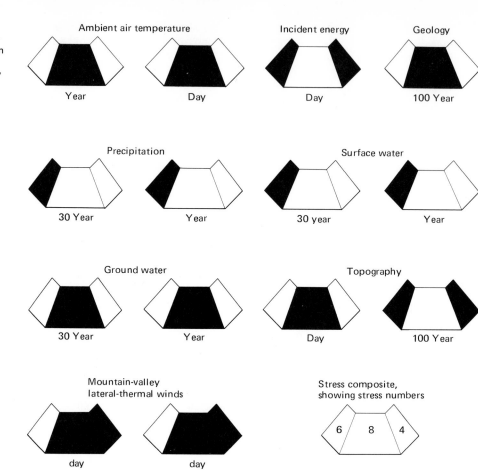

Ambient air temperature

Year

Day

Incident energy

Day

Geology

100 Year

Precipitation

30 Year

Year

Surface water

30 year

Year

Ground water

30 Year

Year

Topography

Day

100 Year

Mountain-valley
lateral-thermal winds

day

day

Stress composite,
showing stress numbers

6 8 4

■■■ maximum variation

Stress Domains

Owens Valley was subdivided into parts or domains characterized by the magnitude of force variation at an interval. (The study only recognized relatively large magnitudes of variation).

The interval of variation was carefully established, since different intervals tend to result in different classes of control problems. An example would be ground water that varies at intervals of a day, a year, and thirty years. There are three different control problems, although they are all caused by ground water.

The domains tend to reflect the shape of Owens Valley, with considerable overlapping where mountain slopes meet the basin floor. The largest useful stress domains would define the geometry of the valley as two containing slopes and a horizontal plane (fig. 4.1).

Variations of incident energy tend to be greater on the mountain slopes than in the basin over a daily interval. The result is maximum variation on the slopes and minimum variation on the valley floor. On a relative scale that applies only to the valley, maximum variation of incident energy over a single interval produces a stress value of *one*. In the example of incident energy, a stress value of *one* would be added to the mountain slopes. The composite stress value in that domain would increase with each additional force or force interval, thus distinguishing that domain from others in the Valley.

Variations of ambient air temperature occur at daily and yearly intervals on the valley floor. Since there are two intervals involved, producing two different sets of control problems, the result would be a stress value of *two* on the valley floor.

Variations in precipitation occur on the west slopes of the valley. There are two intervals involved, the obvious seasonal one and a longer interval of thirty years. For a truly responsive system, each interval would represent a different control problem. Consequently, insofar as the system is concerned, the domain represents a stress value of *two*.

One result of precipitation is surface run-off from the western slopes. Variations in this domain occur at the same two intervals as precipitation, that is, one year and thirty years, providing a stress value of *two*.

Another result of precipitation is ground water in the basin; this leads to cyclic variation in the height of the water table. Such variation occurs at the one-year and thirty-year intervals. In addition, the water table varies at a daily interval due primarily to evaporation. The result is a stress value of *three*.

The domains of maximum variation of wind occur on the valley floor and east slopes. The valley floor is affected primarily by the so-called mountain-valley wind; the slopes are affected primarily by lateral thermals. Both winds vary by day and by year. The effects of the westerlies tend to be constant and therefore do not count as a recurring variable. The stress in this domain is *two*.

There are two conditions that vary and produce stress in the valley at an interval arbitrarily referred to in the study as a "century," not because these conditions are known to recur precisely every hundred years, but because they recur at relatively long intervals with enough regularity to allow an adaptive response. The first of these is topography, or variations of topography, which results primarily from the ambulation of streams. Since ambulation tends to be cyclic it has been classed as a stress.

The second condition that varies at the "century" interval is geology. It might be argued that geologic variations are irreversible and therefore not cyclic or recurrent. The basin may be an exception since geologic conditions vary as a result of steam ambulation over a very broad flat area. The topography remains essentially unchanged in this area of high water table while the stream moves back and forth. As the stream moves, the composition of the soil changes in a cyclic way. Such a domain would pick up a stress of *one*. (Two related facts should be emphasized here. The first is that maximum and minimum magnitude of variation in recurrent force effect is a characterization of Owens Valley and recognizes only major distinctions in the magnitude of variation from one part of the valley to another. The second fact is that the study was only concerned with distinguishable sets of natural conditions in the valley because its purpose was to find separate form correlations for different sets of natural variation. Any stress condition that pervaded the entire valley was ignored on a scale of stress that only had relative validity. For example, variations of incident energy occur with nearly equal magnitude over the entire valley at a yearly interval. Such variations affect the entire valley and were not taken into account in making distinctions of form response.)

Fig. 4.2
Stress construct. Domains are distinguished one from another by the number of environmental forces acting at maximum variation. Darker areas represent higher stress.

Stress Construct and Stress Coefficient

After separate maps were made for each recurring force, the maps were overlaid and the number of forces acting at maximum magnitude of variation were summed within each domain of a composite construct (fig. 4.1). This summing of component forces produced a simple number, a *stress coefficient* to describe the perturbation of several forces acting with maximum variability in a domain. It also produced a ranking of domains within the valley on a stress scale that would allow identification of high and low stress domains. The result was a *stress construct* (fig. 4.2) that distinguished one domain from another as a function of the number of environmental forces acting at maximum magnitude of variation.

The summing of all possible stresses gives a theoretical maximum stress coefficient of *fourteen*. This theoretical maximum is never attained in the valley. The highest value is *twelve* and it occurs where basin floor meets mountain slope. In that transitional area between slope and flat, the highest stress coefficients can and do occur. Where the greatest variations occur in the environment of Owens Valley, there, too, occurs the greatest apparent variety of life forms. We might also expect the greatest variety of man-made forms to occur in this area.

Surface-to-Volume Ratio and the Measure of Susceptibility

Analysis of the Owens Valley produced a stress range from *zero* to *twelve*. Upon that simple scale, which generally describes the environmental stress in a domain as the number of forces acting with maximum variation, one domain can be distinguished from another on the basis of its stress coefficient.

If stress is defined in that way, susceptibility of the built arrangement can be described as a function of the ratio between exposed surface and contained volume. The more the exposed surface for the contained volume, the more susceptible the arrangement. This surface-to-volume ratio (S/V) or the coefficient of susceptibility can be correlated with the stress range on a site and the susceptibility of a building can be matched to the stress in a domain.

The specific values for the S/V range in this study were arbitrary. The intent was to establish a principle relating building susceptibility to environmental stress on a relative scale of differentiated sensitivity. While further study is needed to establish useful limits, the ones derived did provide a relational rather than absolute description of response to stress, just as the stress description itself is relational within the context of Owens Valley as an ecosystem. (Concern for a larger system would produce a different stress range and require different limits on the S/V range, but the description would still be in relation to some context.)

The general relation between S/V and stress in the Owens Valley study was based on the notion that higher stresses require lower coefficients of susceptibility expressed as S/V; lower stresses can be correlated with higher coefficients of susceptibility. Beyond this general relationship, it was necessary to establish a specific and optimum correlation between stress and S/V. A specific stress range had already been established. Specific values were required for S/V. They were derived by placing limits upon size and shape, two attributes of form that affect S/V.

The Effect of Size and Shape

The correlation between *size* and S/V can be explained by considering an expanding cube. A unit cube in contact with the ground upon one of its faces exposes five unit surfaces, while its volume is one; thus, $S/V = 5$. If the edge dimensions of that cube are doubled, its surfaces total 20, while its volume is 8; then $S/V = 2.5$ or half that of the smaller cube (fig. 4.3). We say that the smaller cube is more susceptible to environmental stress than the larger, simply because big things have smaller surface-to-volume ratios than small things.

S/V is, to a lesser extent, a function of shape and can be demonstrated by comparing the same volume in two different configurations.

Taking the larger of our two original cubes and rearranging it into eight unit volumes will produce a higher S/V in each case. First, arrange the eight unit volumes in a row so that eight faces are in contact with the ground plane; then $S/V = 3.25$ (fig. 4.4). Next, rearrange the eight units of volume into a tower shape; then $S/V = 4.12$, higher than the row and the cube of equal volume. (Orientation to the ground plane also becomes a factor in this case because surfaces in contact with the ground are not counted.)

A shape's complexity also affects S/V. Simple shapes generally have a lower S/V than complex shapes of the same volume (fig. 4.5), so size and shape together determine the coefficient of susceptibility by determining S/V. Large and simple shapes have a lower S/V and are less susceptible. Small and complex shapes are much more susceptible, with a higher S/V.

Fig. 4.4
The shape of the form has an effect on its surface-to-volume ratio.

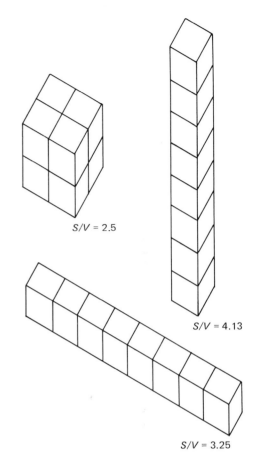

$S/V = 2.5$

$S/V = 4.13$

$S/V = 3.25$

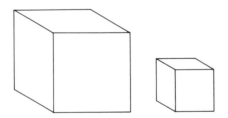

Fig. 4.3
Doubling the dimensions of a cube decreases its surface-to-volume ratio by one half.

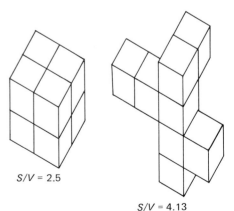

$S/V = 2.5$

$S/V = 4.13$

Fig. 4.5
Simple shapes generally have a lower surface-to-volume ratio than complex shapes of the same volume.

Surface-to-Volume Range in the Owens Valley

In developing a correlation between environmental stress and a coefficient of susceptibility, a logarithmic scale can be used to provide the most sensitive differentiation of S/V response where the stress is lowest. (In nature a logarithmic scale often pertains where the range of conditions to be met involves differences between numbers of quite different magnitudes. In this case, an increase of stress from 1 to 2 amounts to an increase of 100 percent, while an increase from 11 to 12 corresponds to a stress increase of only 9 percent. The increases are not proportional and require a logarithmic response.)

In order to establish a useful logarithmic curve of S/V response to stress, some finite values were developed in the Owens Valley study. For this purpose a tower with edges in ratio of $1:1:64$ units established the upper limit for S/V. A flat $8:8:1$ shape provided a lower limit.

A convenient unit cube dimension of 6.25 feet provided specific dimensions for the smallest volumetric building increment or module that might be useful in deriving flexible building arrangements. This dimension came from systematic subdivisions of the smallest land increment (100 feet) that appropriately described steep or complex topography of the Valley (fig. 4.6). The highest S/V attainable from a tower shape of $1 \times 1 \times 64$ units (fig. 4.7) at 6.25 feet to a unit, is calculated as follows:

$$S/V = \frac{257\ (6.25)^2\ (100)}{64\ (6.25)^3} = 64.0\ \text{ft}^{-1}$$

257 = number of exposed unit surfaces
 64 = number of unit volumes

A multiplier of 100 is used in all calculations of S/V to provide simpler numbers. (Units will henceforth be ignored.)

To establish the lower end of the scale, an arbitrary unit dimension of 400 feet provided specific dimensions for the largest building shapes. This dimension lay in the same proportion to the largest land increment describing flat land in the valley (3,200 feet) as 6.25 feet did to the smallest land increment (100 feet). The lowest S/V attainable from a flat shape of $8 \times 8 \times 1$ units (fig. 4.7), at 400 feet on a unit side, is:

$$S/V = \frac{96\ (400)^2\ (100)}{64\ (400)^3} = 0.375.$$

These two different shapes and sizes provided a range of S/V of 64.0 to 0.375. The specific values are arbitrary, as are the shapes, which are extreme if converted directly into building forms. However, it is possible to see that a correlation might be made between function and the size and shape of enclosure which, in turn, are matched to conditions at the site. In principle then, activities could be zoned onto the land partly as a function of the correlation between form and natural variation.

At this point, the extreme values in a stress range of 1 to 12 have been inversely related to the extreme values in a range of S/V of 64.0 to 0.375.

However, an optimal relationship between stress and S/V depends upon establishing a range of S/V responses for a specific stress coefficient as follows:

Step 1. Determine an increment of difference (X):

$$X = \frac{\text{range of } S/V}{\text{sum of log progression}}.$$

a. Range of S/V = Max S/V − Min S/V
   = 64.0 − 0.375
   = 63.625.
b. Sum of log progression = 4,095 (table 4.1), or

$$X = \frac{63.625}{4,095} = 0.0155.$$

Step 2. Determine S/V range for each stress coefficient:

Stress 12:
Min S/V = 0.3750
Max S/V = 0.3750 + (1 × 0.0155)
   = 0.3905
Range = 0.3750 to 0.3905

Stress 11:
Min S/V = 0.3906
Max S/V = 0.3905 + (2 × 0.0155)
   = 0.4215
Range = 0.3906 to 0.4215

Stress 10:
Min S/V = 0.4216
Max S/V = 0.4215 + (4 × 0.0155)
   = 0.4835
Range = 0.4216 to 0.4835

Stress 9:
etc. . . .

This process is continued throughout the entire stress range with the result that the S/V range for high stresses is small while the S/V range for low stresses is large (fig. 4.8).

Step 3. Determine optimum *S/V* for each stress coefficient.

The optimum *S/V* within a range (determined in Step 2) was arbitrarily set as that number which, when compared to the numerical extremes of the range, is proportionally the same (table 4.2). For example, the *S/V* range associated with a stress of three is 16.2315 to 8.2956. The optimum coefficient within this range is 11.6040. This number's proportional relationship to either 16.2315 or 8.2956 is 71.5 percent. (While the exact method for setting an optimum value is arbitrary, the need for such a value will be made clear in Chapter 5.) We have:

Opt *S/V* = *y*

$$\frac{y}{16.2315} = \frac{8.2956}{y}$$

$$y^2 = 134.6$$

$$y = 11.6$$

$$\frac{\text{Opt } S/V}{\text{Max } S/V} = \frac{11.6}{16.2} = 71.5\%,$$

$$\frac{\text{Min } S/V =}{\text{Opt } S/V} = \frac{8.3}{11.6} = 71.5\%.$$

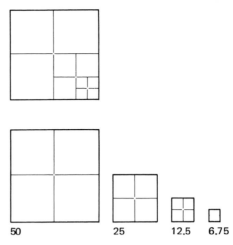

Fig. 4.6
The unit cube dimension of 6.25 feet was derived from subdivisions of the smallest land increment (50 feet) that appropriately described steep or complex topography of the valley.

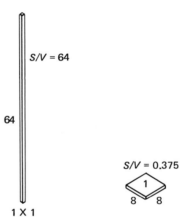

Fig. 4.7
The upper limit of a surface-to-volume range was established with a thin tower, the lower limit with a large flat shape.

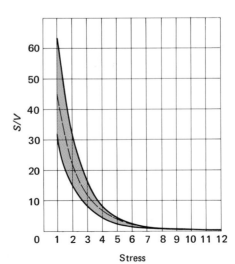

Fig. 4.8
Logarithmic graph correlating surface-to-volume ratio to stress. Gray area indicates surface-to-volume ratio range for each stress value.

Table 4.1 Stress and Log^2 Progression

Stress	Progression
1	2,048X
2	1,024X
3	512X
4	256X
5	128X
6	64X
7	32X
8	16X
9	8X
10	4X
11	2X
12	1X

Table 4.2 Surface-to-Volume Range: Optimization

Stress	Surface/Volume Range		
	Maximum	Optimum	Minimum
1	64.0000 70.8%	45.3235 100.0%	32.1036 70.8%
2	32.1035 71.1%	22.8250 100.0%	16.2316 71.1%
3	16.2315 71.5%	11.6040 100.0%	8.2956 71.5%
4	8.2955 72.0%	5.9744 100.0%	4.3276 72.0%
5	4.3275 73.6%	3.1831 100.0%	2.3436 73.6%
6	2.3435 75.8%	1.7773 100.0%	1.3516 75.8%
7	1.3515 79.6%	1.0753 100.0%	0.8556 79.6%
8	0.8555 84.6%	0.7243 100.0%	0.6076 84.6%
9	0.6075 89.1%	0.5411 100.0%	0.4836 89.1%
10	0.4835 92.8%	0.4490 100.0%	0.4216 92.8%
11	0.4215 96.0%	0.4047 100.0%	0.3906 96.0%
12	0.3905 97.9%	0.3823 100.0%	0.3750 97.9%

Stress Construct:
First Framework for Settlement

The stress construct, a map of diverse stress on a site, provides a framework for specifying S/V as an expression of susceptibility, a form coefficient for buildings. Such a specification is not subject to change. It persists over time as a useful guide in generating settlement. As a result, settlement would be differentiated in its susceptibility to environmental stress just as stress itself is differentiated over the site.

Location, Form, Metabolism

The stress construct takes into account two of the three response mechanisms used by nature. The three are *location, form,* and *metabolism.* The stress construct allows location and form to be considered as related response mechanisms for built systems. This is particularly significant because of our past inclination to depend almost exclusively on metabolism (mechanical systems) to maintain a steady state within building envelopes. This singular mode of response has been possible because of a seemingly unlimited capacity to generate energy. It has had the advantage of quick responsiveness and a high tolerance for uncertainty in providing for the energy needs of our growing cities; and so long as this dependence upon a single mode of response resulted in a healthy system, questions of location and form in the built arrangement could be ignored. In fact, the response range of mechanical systems is limited, as problems of peak loading now prove. The capacity of this response mode is now reaching natural limits; there must be diversification of response capacity to include alternatives which have not been considered heretofore.

Slope-Orientation Construct: Second
Framework for Settlement

A specification of S/V related to stress values is a general form descriptor. It is related to the fact that the main recurring environmental forces have predictable degrees of variation. A second form descriptor is concerned with the more static attributes of force action that have been mentioned before, magnitude and direction. A second useful construct can be based on these.

An analysis of the site based on the magnitude and direction of force action is essential to determine how buildings interact. Two factors influencing their interactions are slope and orientation of the land. One way to describe potential differences of interaction, from one degree of slope to another or from one orientation of slope to another, is to place a common reference upon various conditions of slope and orientation and to then measure the variations in magnitude and direction of force effect.

Slope-Orientation Domain

In the Owens Valley study, the common reference was taken to be a vertical line of unit height which cast a shadow upon the land as a result of the effect of sun acting upon the reference (fig. 4.9). Maintaining a constant height for the reference allowed slopes and orientations to be compared by comparing the areas influenced by the shadow (fig. 4.10). The result was a description of the interaction of site and environmental force that distinguished one place from another. Stress is a dynamic function of recurrence; *area of influence* is a static spatial function. Stress distinguishes among intervals of time to account for the same force causing a system to respond at different intervals; area of influence can only distinguish one force

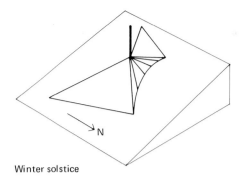

Winter solstice

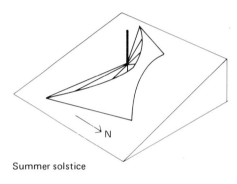

Summer solstice

Fig. 4.9
A hypothetical vertical line of unit height would cast a shadow that moves as the sun passes through daily and seasonal cycles. The total area affected by the moving shadow would vary with the steepness and orientation of the slope.

Fig. 4.10
The area affected by a
shadow cast from a vertical
line is matched as closely
as possible to a rectilinear
geometry. Within the rectilinear unit there is an upper
limit on the volume that
can be built without casting
shadows upon adjacent units
during critical periods of
insolation. The result is a
specification relating maximum building height (*H*)
to land area (*A*). (All *H/A*
values multiplied by 10^{-4}.)

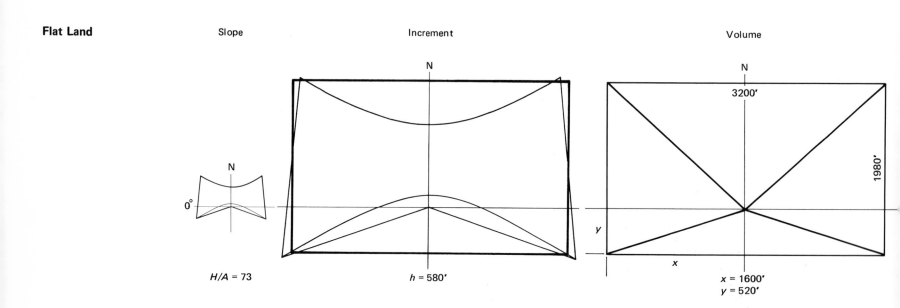

Flat Land

Slope

Increment

Volume

$H/A = 73$

$h = 580'$

$x = 1600'$
$y = 520'$

South Orientation

Slope	Increment	Volume

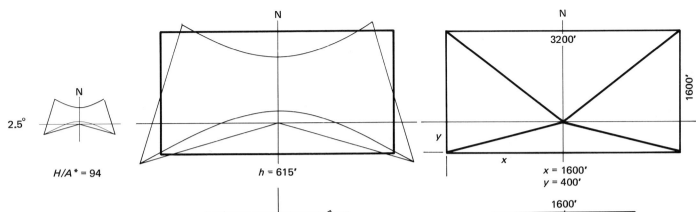

2.5°

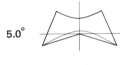

H/A* = 94

h = 615'

x = 1600'
y = 400'

5.0°

H/A = 101

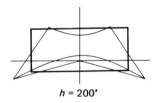

h = 320'

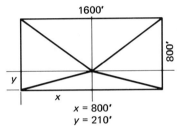

1600'

800'

x = 800'
y = 210'

10.0°

H/A = 124

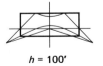

h = 200'

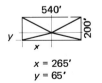

930'

400'

x = 460'
y = 100'

15.0°

H/A = 116

h = 100'

540'

200'

x = 265'
y = 65'

30.0°

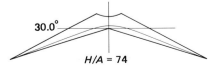

H/A = 74

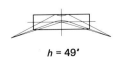

h = 49'

460'

100'

x = 230'
y = 49'

*Height constant

East Orientation
(reverse shadow for
West Orientation)

Slope

Increment

Volume

2.5°

*H/A = 77

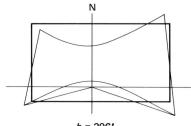

h = 296'

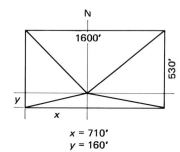

N

1600'

530'

y

x

x = 710'
y = 160'

5.0°

H/A = 75

h = 143'

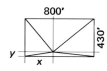

800'

430'

y

x

x = 325'
y = 51'

10.0°

H/A = 53

h = 65'

400'

338'

y

x

x = 112'
y = 112'

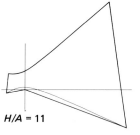

15.0°

H/A = 11

h = 21'

200'

200'

y

x

x = 32'
y = 62'

*Height constant

North Orientation

Slope	Increment	Volume

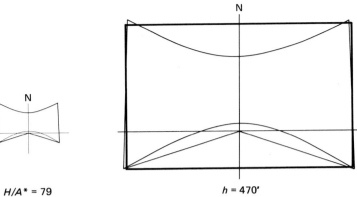

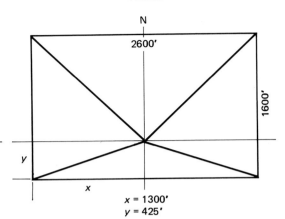

2600'

1600'

2.5°

H/A* = 79

h = 470'

x = 1300'
y = 425'

5.0°

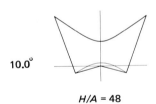

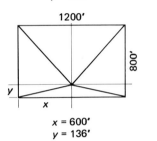

1200'

800'

H/A = 95

h = 210'

x = 600'
y = 136'

10.0°

610'

400'

H/A = 48

h = 94'

x = 305'
y = 37'

15.0°

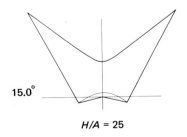

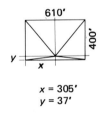

290'

200'

H/A = 25

h = 32'

x = 145'
y = 8'

*Height constant

Fig. 4.11
Slope-orientation construct.
A single stress domain (see
fig. 4.2) is structured into
parts that can be distin-
guished by their slope
and orientation.

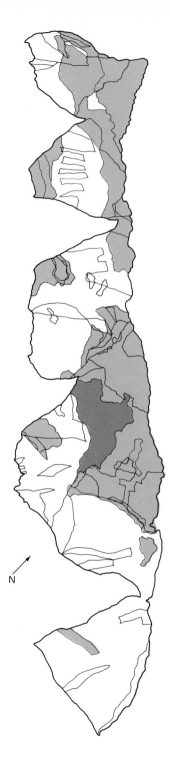

N

from another, not the intervals at which
they recur. Stress recognizes the differences between magnitudes of variation in
time; area of influence recognizes the
difference between magnitudes of influence in space.

Area of influence is characteristic of a
particular slope and orientation. Generally, as the slope increases, the area of
influence increases independent of orientation, while north, east, and west slopes
produce larger areas of influence than
south slopes. The area of influence is as
useful in describing differences in force
effect from one slope and orientation to
another as the stress coefficient is in describing differences in stress from one domain to another. In fact, it describes a
second kind of domain within which
slope and orientation are relatively constant. (Any directional force may be
handled in approximately the same way,
but this choice was made because of the
generally overriding importance of insolation in determining the energy necessary
to maintain an internal, thermal steady
state. In some circumstances, however,
other directional forces might become
critical and in such cases they would determine the area of influence. Examples
might be a situation in which strong winds
tend to blow with relative consistency
from a particular direction, or where the
direction of surface runoff due to precipitation would make certain orientations
of building more critical than others.)

Area of influence has been used to structure a single stress domain into parts
which can be distinguished from one
another as a function of slope and orientation. The result is a *slope-orientation
construct* comparable to the stress construct but at a different scale (fig. 4.11).

Surface-to-Volume and Height-to-Area: Form Specification

Both of the foregoing constructs lead to an initial and general limitation on form. The stress construct limits form as a function of the susceptibility of buildings to an environment comprised of many forces which share the common property of recurrence. The slope-orientation construct sets an initial and general limitation upon form as a function of interaction since any object placed upon the land within the area of influence of a building is obviously going to be affected in some way by shading. What is needed is a description of form response to the effects of slope and orientation comparable to the S/V response to stress. This new form limit should deal with a single force, insolation. To have specific dimensional properties, the area of influence, which is based on a unit height and is relational, must be converted into a dimensional relationship between height and the area influenced: This is done by means of the height-to-area ratio (H/A). The conversion required several descriptive steps leading to a building increment.

Incrementation of the Land

To develop the concept of incrementation we shall again consider the specific form of Owens Valley and apply to it a grid scaled to the important topographical features. Where the features are smaller, the grid is smaller. Where the form of the land is simple and flat, the descriptive increment is larger (fig. 4.12).

It would seem reasonable to match building sizes to descriptive land increments but mismatching often occurs in new growth. The results can be seen in the Los Angeles basin, for example, where the land is flat and where initial settlement took place with the generation of small building components proliferating across the basin floor. Now, as the city matures, larger elements replace small ones on the flat land. The initially small subdivisions of land have been collected into larger and larger packages. This is a natural consequence of the maturation of settlements, of the transformation to higher levels of organization. In this process land parcels are collected, streets are closed, blocks are connected by overpasses and underpasses, and smaller blocks merge to form larger ones. This process is generally unplanned and usually hectic. It produces the continuous disruption of present-day urban life.

Topography can tell us something about what can go on the land. For example, a land increment, as described before, can place some initial limitation on the plan dimensions of the building increment. But another requirement would be a height limitation if adverse modes of interaction are to be avoided during growth.

While the development of building height criteria may seem unnecessary if we built with regard for our neighbors, we are not evidently in control of the situation. What is sought here is a formalization of what seems only reasonable, namely that buildings should not shade each other unduly. The result is a height-to-area ratio (H/A) that limits building height and area of influence as a function of slope and orientation.

Within the height and area limits of a building increment, objects may be placed in some predictable relation to one another. This relationship is predictable in terms of the rate and direction of interaction among parts of a built arrangement. Since our ultimate purpose is to produce a system that represents some balanced response to nature, such a description of interaction is absolutely necessary.

Within the increment of interaction, the relative positions of parts of a built arrangement determine how they are going to interact. For instance, buildings placed to the north and south of each other interact at a different set of rates than those placed to the east and west of each other. The consequences, insofar as the supply of energy to each building is concerned, are different. As with the Acoma pueblos, there is a critical north-south spacing, below which the buildings to the south shade buildings to the north during the winter. Such a direction-dependent interaction has an effect upon the maintenance cost of those buildings over an entire year. Buildings placed to the east and west of each other interact in a direction which affects their maintenance cost over a daily interval.

Fig. 4.12
Size incrementation for
Oak Creek section. In a
typical cross-section of the
valley, gentle slopes are
described with larger increments; where the land
steepens and becomes more
complex in its configuration,
the increment becomes
smaller.

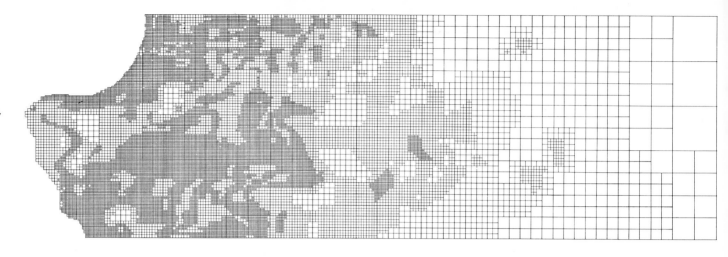

An attempt to match the land increment with the area of influence of a vertical reference introduces a problem pertaining to a difference in geometry between the two. Different sized squares were used as a convenient descriptor for the form of the land. The shape of the area of influence produced by the sun shadow from a vertical reference is quite different; but if an upper height limit on buildings is to be established, the geometries of the land increment and of the area of influence must be related. (It should be mentioned that the use of squares to describe the land is a convenience. Further investigation might suggest a more appropriate geometry.) While the squares shown on the site (fig. 4.13) are generally useful for describing the topography, the critical dimension on the grid lies in the direction of slope insofar as variations in the area of influence are concerned (fig. 4.14).

It is useful, therefore, to conventionalize the site into slopes on the cardinal points and eliminate those lines of the grid that lie in the direction of the slope, preserving only those that would be required in matching the up-and-down slope variations in the area of influence (fig. 4.15). This procedure frees one dimension of the square grid for a closer matching of the shadow (fig. 4.10). As figure 4.10 has shown, the matches between geometries are only approximate. The major portion of an area of influence is contained within the increment of interaction allowing relatively small magnitudes of shadowing outside.

What had been established up to this point in the Owens Valley study were two constructs or descriptions of land-force interaction and two building speci-fications or descriptions of building form based on the constructs. The first con-struct was derived from a dynamic de-scription of the natural environment. The variation in force action at a particular interval of recurrence was viewed as a stress upon a system: the greater the var-iation, the greater the stress; the more forces acting or the more intervals repre-sented, the greater the stress. The con-struct distinguished one area within the Valley from another as a function of the number of forces acting with maximum variability on a scale related to the valley.

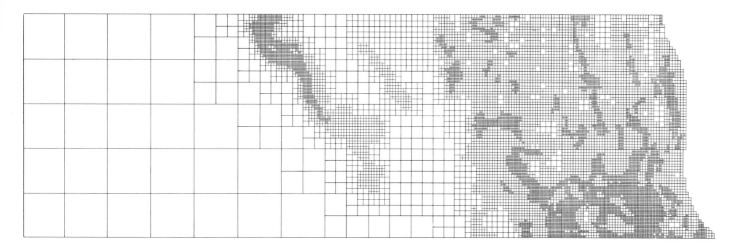

These areas were called stress domains. A scale of stress was related to a coefficient that described the susceptibility of a built arrangement. The degree of susceptibility was expressed as a ratio between the exposed surface and contained volume of a system. This ratio (S/V) provided a first general form descriptor when dimensional limits were applied. The object of applying the form descriptor was to match the susceptibility of buildings to environmental perturbation and thus to reduce the energy required to maintain their steady state.

The second construct was derived from a static description of the environment. The magnitude of force action was expressed as a fixed area of influence resulting from the interaction between a force (sun), a vertical reference, and the land. The area of influence varied with slope and orientation and thereby provided a basis for distinguishing one slope-orientation condition from another. Different conditions established domains with characteristic areas of influence. The application of dimensional limits related to the shape of the land converted the area of influence into a second and more specific form descriptor. This descriptor related building height to its area of influence (H/A) and thereby provided a basis for sizing and spacing buildings. The object of applying this second form descriptor was to enhance the possibility of using energy from the sun to reduce the demand upon energy supply systems. Table 4.3 gives H/A values; these will be of use in Chapter 5.

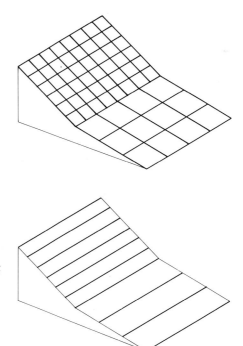

Fig. 4.13
While the squares are generally useful for describing the land, the critical dimension on the grid lies in the direction of slope insofar as variations in the area of influence are concerned.

Fig. 4.14
Grid lines that lie in the direction of the slope can be removed leaving only those that lie across the slope. The result is an approximation of a conventional topographic description.

Fig. 4.15
Slope-orientation construct.
The domain is convention-
alized into slopes on the
cardinal points and described
with only those lines of the
grid that lie across the slope.

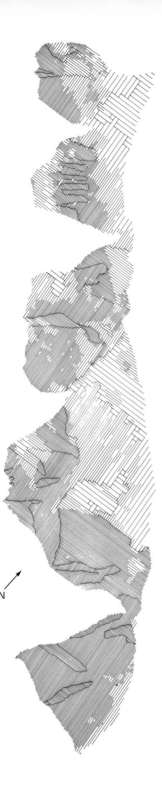

N

Table 4.3 *H/A* Ratios

Slope	Orientation				Increment
	North	East	South	West	
0°	0.92	0.92	0.92	0.92	3200'
2.5°	1.13	3.49	1.20	3.49	1600'
5°	2.19	4.07	4.70	4.07	800'
10°	3.85	4.80	5.38	4.07	400'
15°	5.50	5.00	9.26	5.00	200'
30°	0.00	0.00	10.70	0.00	100'

Note: All values $\times 10^{-4}$. *H/A:* 200' $\times$ 200'E = 20'/40,000 sq ft = .0005.

5
Natural Associations and Network Development

Up to this point in the Owens Valley study, a site description had been directly converted into an expression of building form. The procedure, if not its final expression, owed much to modern efforts by landscape architects and regional planners, and especially to Ian McHarg at the University of Pennsylvania, who has successfully applied the basic procedure of deriving useful descriptions of land-use from a rigorous description of site conditions.[1] The object of such prodecures is, of course, to build with respect for the diverse conditions of nature; in McHarg's own words, to design "with Nature."

The work in Owens Valley departs from that of McHarg and other large-scale planners in two respects. First, a direct expression of building-form rather than land-use was sought. This can be an additional help to planners and complementary to McHarg's work. Second, most planners derive an optimal expression of land-use from a site description and then depend on the uncertain arena of public and private regulation to determine how close the final plan approximates the optimal expression. In such an approach, the general application of an optimal description of land use is bound to be variously considered by developer and user as inadequate in some instances, repressive in others. While there will always be differences of opinion where planning control is concerned, the attitude taken by a group of planners at the University of Southern California was that some of the uncertainty resulting from "blanket" control could be reduced by differentiating the control. A more realistic planning framework for public and private regulation might anticipate circumstances where tolerances of building form specifications should be eased or strengthened.

In the Owens Valley study, the basis for this differentiated planning control was taken to be the preservation of the physical context of a building site. The context was described in terms of the diversities of adjacent site conditions. An attitude was taken that such diversity should be maintained and not greyed out by development.

In Chapter 4, expressions of building form were applied on a one-to-one basis. This application was considered to be general as when planners apply a rather precise description of land-use obtained from a rigorous site analysis. However, during the course of the study, there arose the questions that will be considered now. How rigorously should expressions of building form be applied to maintain site diversity while staying within reasonable tolerances of form specification for energy conservation? Should the response always be precise, or are there circumstances in which building specifications can be less than perfectly matched to a site condition? In other words, during the study there arose a question of the rigor of control in planning: How much control is enough?

The same question arises in the application of land-use proposals. McHarg describes such proposals as "an expression of physical, social and economic goals." They are generally applied with a degree of rigor finally determined by what McHarg calls "the combination of these goals and the public and private powers to realize them." The result is a plan reflecting the original proposals to a degree that cannot be known in advance.

Starting with the same values as McHarg regarding the preservation of diversity in nature, the urban design group at the University of Southern California set out to develop a control mechanism for predetermining rigor in applying building specifications.

The basic assumption in this undertaking was that optimum building specifications should not be determined in relation to discrete states without regard for adjacent conditions. Consequently, what was required was a context for each domain to provide a measure of an appropriate degree of control, neigher repressive nor inadequate to maintain site diversity.

The context was Owens Valley, where force-domains were viewed as associated parts of an overall ecosystem. Site inspection had already shown a close correlation between the variety of life systems and the variations of natural forces measured in the valley. The edges of force-domains could generally be drawn in the real space between plant domains (see fig. 4.2).

For two reasons a similarly close correlation with buildings was sought. The first was to conserve energy by matching development to site conditions: Buildings were not to be sited independent of natural variation, because a higher energy bill would be paid where the fit was poor. The second reason was based on a point of value for the character of the landscape itself: The visible distinctions resulting from the form of the landscape were to be reflected in the distinctions among built forms.

1. Ian McHarg, *Design with Nature* (Garden City, N.Y.: Natural History Press, 1969).

When energy conservation and site conservation are both valued objectives, the need for control becomes apparent by observing the boundary where adjacent force domains meet and where form specifications would be expected to change. This boundary is sometimes perceived as sharply drawn; sometimes it is more subtle. It is generally responding to some natural rhythm in which the interval may be short as the daily tides or long as the seasons of the year. (There may also be even shorter or longer intervals.)

A dramatic example of a sharply drawn boundary is the sea coast. The edge of the sea begins somewhere in the water and through a series of rich and complex transformations ends upon the land (fig. 5.1). In this transition, there is one condition recognized as *sea* and a second recognized as *land*; between, there is a *third condition* where change usually takes place in the most obvious way. A region that Rachel Carson in *The Edge of the Sea* has called the "marginal world" is comprised of those rather quick steps that are necessary to complete so total a transformation in such a small distance. From the land, through the intertidal zone, finally to the water itself, this meeting place has some attributes of both worlds. It is a realm of two languages, one of the sea and one of the land; and there all life is, in some degree, bilingual. A more detailed look reveals that any part of this "marginal world" seems to intimate a central theme. There can be found, in miniature, the same kinds of transition occurring as comprise the surround, so that at the edge of a tide pool there are tiny variations reminiscent of the larger scale of the shoreline as a whole.

When viewed at an instant in time, this scene reveals to the casual observer an incredibly rich picture; but it is only with observations made over time that events are perceived to have continuity and states appear to exhibit significant differences. As the days and seasons pass, impressions of the whole scene swing to and fro—at one time strident and unsettling, at another gentle and soothing.

More subtle is the edge of a forest where the tempo may not be so quick but where the cyclic forces of nature nonetheless produce a boundary where plant variety can be correlated with environmental variations. For example, the edge of a yellow pine forest may shift with variations in annual rainfall. If yellow pine, requiring relatively moist conditions, grows adjacent to chaparral, requiring less water, the pine will advance during wet years while the chaparral will advance during dry years. The result is a mixing of the two communities in a boundary zone where conditions are in constant flux at a relatively long interval (close to thirty years in Owens Valley). Considerable variation in plant morphology would be evident among samples taken near such a boundary and might even contain species not present toward the center of adjacent domains. (Big-cone pine can occur within the boundary between yellow pine and chaparral.) Away from such boundaries, variation in plant morphology may be less among samples and predictability of plant form would increase as the state of the domain becomes pervasive.

If the forms that envelop man's activities are to reflect the domainal variations of place and time so apparent at such boundaries, then it seemed that there must be a close correlation sought between the organization of natural and man-made systems. This is not to say that any attempt has been made here to directly model the complex interactions among parts of a community of people upon the complex interactions among life systems in the valley. But a building arrangement that is responsive to the same recurring forces that generate adaptive behavior in nature should exhibit some of the same organizational characteristics. Certainly the relation among force-domains that establishes the basic valley structure should be evident in the forms of development.

Domains can be distinguished in the valley by observing variations in the whole set of conditions that comprise the landscape. Such distinctions are a long time in the making and, in point of historical fact, provide the ultimate framework for settlement. This is obvious in the case of the Piutes of Owens Valley (see figs. 1.11-1.13).

Although it is clear that throughout the world natural conditions tend to persist long after the constructions of men have crumbled, over the short term men have been able to build over and grey out such distinctions and thereby, at least temporarily, to destroy the association among parts of the landscape that provide its character. No matter how carefully it is planned, development will obviously change the landscape, but it need not destroy the basic physical structure. Parts can be modified but the distinctions among those parts can be preserved.

Fig. 5.1
The edge of the sea begins
somewhere in the water and
through a series of transformations ends upon the
land.

At a large scale, the stress construct of Owens Valley reflects the physical structure of the valley as an ecosystem. Within this structure all of the life systems result from adaptation and the complex natural changes of biological succession defined by Eugene P. Odum as "an orderly process of community development that is reasonably directional and therefore, predictable. It results from modification of the physical environment by the community; that is, succession is community controlled even though the physical environment determines the pattern, the rate of change, and often sets limits as to how far development can go. It culminates in a stabilized ecosystem in which maximum biomass (or high information content) and symbiotic function between organisms are maintained per unit of available energy flow." [2] What were viewed earlier as discrete force domains could now, in Odum's terms, be viewed as interrelated ecological domains within a natural environment.

It seems possible to take one more step and to see in the association among ecological domains a framework for development within a man-made community. The framework would not dictate the precise locations of specific community activities, but it would provide a basic organizational reference for growth and change. Over time there would develop, as in the natural system, interactions among the parts involving energy exchanges. In such exchanges the "flow" tendency would be in the direction of higher levels of organization. This flow tendency has been described by Odum and others in both natural and man-made systems.

2. E. P. Odum, "The Strategy of Eco-System Development," *Science,* 164 (1969), 262-270.

Cities attract human and material resources and are an example that seems to support the biologist Margalef when he states, "There is always some regulation; one sub-system is more controlling, the other more controlled, and one of the parts pays a higher energy bill than the other." [3]

In the Owens Valley study, the assumption was made that a diversity of site conditions would generate a diversity of urban community functions with interrelations likely to develop over time. Therefore, the number and variety of adjacent domains would determine the potential for symbiotic energy exchanges in a community context.

The point may certainly be argued that symbiotic associations in today's city are often between distant places and are not a function of physical adjacency. However, such associations are costly to maintain and usually depend on the mobility of people and material. Energy required for mobility could be reduced by developing symbiotic associations among adjacent parts of an arrangement. If that were the case, the number and variety of a domain's associations could be taken as a measure of its "controlling" ability. This was taken to be the case in Owens Valley. In the study, a domain with many and varied adjacent domains was held to be in a "controlling" position and energies were considered likely to flow toward it,

3. Ramon Margalef, *Perspectives in Ecological Theory* (Chicago: University of Chicago Press, 1968), p. 13.

thus increasing its potential for organization and its importance as an interrelated community function. Conversely, a domain with few and similar adjacent domains would not control nor would it have a high potential for organization. It would not be critical to community development and would comprise a peripheral community function.

Whether a domain was in a "controlling" position or not became the basis for tolerance in applying form specifications. A controlling domain was allowed somewhat greater tolerances in applying form specifications for two reasons. First, its greater potential for organization is likely to generate a self-regulating tendency that makes planning control difficult and costly. If control tolerances are not eased in a situation like this, they will have to be applied repressively. Second, the identity of a force domain is taken to be a function of its contact diversity with adjacent domains. The more identifiable domain is taken to be the one with a greater number and variety of surrounding domains. In other words, a strongly identifiable domain is a "controlling" domain. But the identity of domains depends primarily on their boundaries. To insure that a domain will continue to function as an interrelated part of a community requires that the boundary be considered.

Unfortunately, modern development does not often respect natural boundaries and Odum's statement that communities modify their physical environment has a painfully familiar ring. He speaks of natural communities which must necessarily respect natural boundaries. Today's technology and the rate of urban growth make natural boundaries highly vulnerable.

Boundaries have been carefully considered in the Owens Valley study for two reasons: First, because the richness and character of the land depend on them; and second, because they represent potential diversity of community interrelations in the built environment.

Regarding the first point, preservation of the land's character would depend in some measure on the rigor of form specifications in regard to the state of a domain. As sympathetic development occurs within adjacent domains, an edge naturally occurs where the conditions for development change. Development based on the governing criterion of energy conservation will tend to enhance domainal boundaries. On the other hand, if development appropriate to one domain intrudes into adjacent domains, the results are a misfit for purposes of energy conservation and diminishment of the land's character because the natural edge is not supported by a constructed one.

Regarding the second point, the potential diversity of community interrelations would also depend in some measure on the rigor of form specifications. But here the number and variety of adjacent domains would seem to become a factor.

If each different state requires a different form specification, a domain surrounded by a greater number and variety of adjacent domains will eventually be surrounded by a greater diversity of potential interrelations as development progresses. Such a domain would have its community identity, and most likely its physical identity, insured by the diversity of contacts across its boundary. In Margalef's sense, it would be a "controlling" domain and would be in little danger of losing its identity as development takes place. Even if some of the edge segments comprising its boundary were greyed out by development, such a controlling domain could still maintain its identity. The identity of a "controlled" domain would be maintained by tightening its building specifications.

At the largest scale, the valley floor is an example of a controlling domain. It has a set of fairly consistent conditions different from a whole range of adjacent conditions on the adjoining mountain slopes (fig. 4.1). This fact is obvious on first inspection of the valley and was established in terms of the action of sun, wind, and water during the study. If the valley floor is considered to be a single domain, the range of conditions in the adjoining slopes may be viewed as many adjacent domains. In the case of this overview, the floor is clearly distinguishable from what surrounds it. The diversity of surrounding domains, whether measured as recurring forces or as natural life systems or ultimately as diversified community development, is great enough to insure the identity of the valley floor.

The situation of valley floor and mountain slopes provides a simplified view of the Owens Valley but one worth describing because it comprises the strongest first impression for the observer. Beyond that, successive observations reveal that, at a smaller scale, the identity of "controlling" domains may be measured in the same way.

From these observations, and where planning control is a function of the desire to preserve distinctions and to maintain the separate identities of force domains, a general principle can be drawn: There is an inverse relation between the identity of a domain (its ability to control measured as diversity of adjacent domains) and the rigor of planning control (measured as tolerances of form specifications).

Where a domain is "controlling" because of a high contact diversity with adjacent states and consequently a high potential for community interrelations, planning control will be eased and specification tolerances will be broadened. Where a domain is "controlled" because of a low contact diversity and low potential community interrelations, planning control will be increased and specification tolerances will be narrowed.

Fig. 5.2
Stress construct (*a*) and
adjacency network super-
posed on the stress con-
struct (*b*).

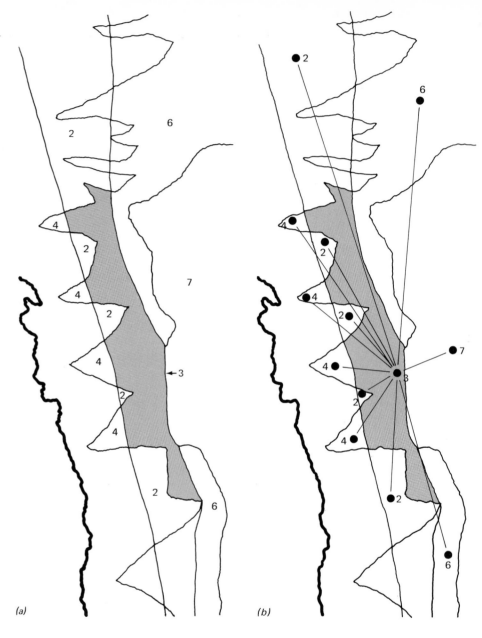

(a)

(b)

Network Development: Stress

In order to more precisely quantify the phenomenon of domainal identity and to relate it to planning tolerances, the domainal construct of Owens Valley can be translated into a simple network of points and lines upon which associations among domains may be more easily measured. In the network, a point represents a domain of force action and a line represents an edge between two adjacent domains. A controlling domain appears in the network as a point with many lines radiating from it indicating a variety of adjacent domains. The network describes the degree of tolerance allowed in applying building specifications by quantifying the diversity of potential community interrelations that can develop across the domainal boundary.

A controlling domain is less susceptible to a building misfit. By means of the network, differences of susceptibility from one domain to another can be recognized and can therefore provide a basis for optimization throughout the valley. The result would be a distinction between "controlling" domains in which a broad tolerance may be allowed in meeting building specifications and "controlled" domains in which little or no tolerance may be allowed. In order to explain the procedure, a sample force-domain can be selected from the Owens Valley network (fig. 5.2). The domain lies on the west side, near the intersection of slope and basin. It has a varied topography and orientation of slope and is surrounded by twelve adjacent domains, some steep and uphill toward the Sierra Nevada crest, others flatter and toward the basin floor. The domain has a recurring force condition defined by a stress value of three.

If the domain were considered without regard for its context within Owens Valley, the form specification appropriate to that stress value would be an *S/V* of 11.6 (table 4.2). But if the domain has a high contact diversity across its boundary, increased tolerances will be allowed in the ratio.

Any attempt to correlate building form with natural variations must take into account the intervals at which variation occurs. This seems particularly appropriate when the basis for correlation is taken to be the phenomenon of domainal identity, defined in terms of boundary conditions. As we have seen in the examples of sea coast and forest edge, such boundaries exhibit variety related to the interval of recurring sets of environmental conditions.

Therefore, the network used to describe the stress construct was developed with two components that were separately derived and then combined. This three-step process was necessary to account for the dynamics of recurrence in force action. Recurrence has been described earlier as being compounded of both variation and interval. The two component networks were based on these twin phenomena. Taking the steps in order, first the variation network will be developed. (Each step is accompanied by a simplified network of four points and four lines to make sample calculations as a model for the larger network being discussed.)

1. Variation Network (table 5.1)

1a. Diversity Coefficient (fig. 5.3).
The notion has already been stated that for planning, the identity of a domain was based on the diversity of its associations with adjacent domains. A coefficient of this diversity expresses variety and is determined by counting the different stress values in domains adjacent to the sample. The *diversity coefficient* appears on each point of the network (fig. 5.4). The sample domain (shaded) is associated with twelve domains; but there are only four different stress conditions represented among the twelve, resulting in a diversity coefficient of 4 on the point.

1b. Potential Coefficient (fig. 5.5).
The second step quantifies the potential for change in associations comprising the network by describing the likely energy flow between two adjacent domains. In the example drawn from the valley, the *potential coefficients* which appear on the line range from 1 to 3 (fig. 5.6).

1c. Control Coefficient (fig. 5.7).
The sum of potential on lines attending the point is called a *control coefficient*. It suggests the tendency of the point to dominate by virtue of the number of its associations, each association with a potential energy flow. This expression of control appears on the point, as 28 (fig. 5.8).

Table 5.1 Development of a Network for the Stress Construct

Step	Descriptor	Derivation	Figure number
1. Variation Network			
a.	Diversity coefficient (on point)	No. of different stress conditions	5.4
b.	Potential coefficient (on line)	Difference between diversity coefficients	5.6
c.	Control coefficient (on point)	Sum of potential coefficients	5.8
d.	Control vector (on line)	Difference between control coefficients	5.10
2. Interval Network			
a.	Diversity coefficient (on line)	No. of different interval conditions	5.13 - 5.15
b.	Potential coefficient (on line)	Difference between diversity coefficients	5.17 - 5.19
c.	Control coefficient (on point)	Sum of potential coefficients	5.21 - 5.24
d.	Control vectors (on line)	Difference between control coefficients	5.26, 5.27
3. Variation and Interval Network			
a.	Composite control vectors (variation plus interval)	Algebraic sum of compound control vectors	5.10 + 5.27 = 5.29
b.	Composite control coefficient	Algebraic sum of compound control vectors	5.30
c.	Final control vectors	Difference between compound control coefficients	5.31

1d. Control Vectors (fig. 5.9).
The final step in developing the variation network places a value and direction on the line which describes the probable direction of energy flow across an edge segment between the sample domain (Stress 3) and any adjacent domain (fig. 5.10). The number is derived from the difference between control coefficients on the points. In the example, when a control coefficient of 28 is compared to one of 14, the difference is a control vector of 14 on the line, in the direction of 28. This procedure is followed for each adjacent domain.

Control vectors indicate directional associations, the structure that interrelates domains; but the description is not complete since it is essentially a spatial description. What is required is a complementary description that recognizes the tendency of domainal boundaries to regularly shift their position or to cycle in and out of existence at recurring intervals. At a large and quite visible scale, the valley floor again provides a good example. Conditions of sun, wind, and water cycle at different intervals on the valley floor than on adjoining slopes. As a consequence, even though the intersection of mountain slope and basin is spatially fixed, the boundary cycles through time at different intervals depending on the particular force being considered (fig. 4.1). As the day passes or as seasons come and go, the edge that establishes the limit of a domainal state can also appear, then disappear only to reappear as conditions essential to its existence cycle through their regular changes. This temporal event can also be used to develop structural links among domains.

2. Interval Network (table 5.1)
In undertaking the development of an interval network it must be recognized that all edges do not exist at all intervals. An edge is considered to exist at an interval if one or both adjacent domains contain maximum-varying forces recurring at that interval. (The intervals of concern to us have already been described as day, year, thirty-year, and century.) The intervals at which a particular edge cycles or recurs are indicated on the line rather than on the point of the network since the line signifies an edge segment of a boundary. (The study of a particular stress domain established the intervals of recurrence of its edge segments, fig. 5.11.) If separate networks are drawn for each interval, some edges disappear since they only exist in time and may, in fact, not exist at a particular interval (figs. 5.13-5.15). (Separate networks can only be drawn for the example at intervals of day, year, and century, since no edge exists there at a thirty-year interval.)

The four steps required to develop the *interval network* are essentially the same as those taken for the network based on variation except that the diversity coefficient is derived from a temporal description of a boundary rather than a static description of the pervasive stress state of the domain (table 5.1).

2a. Diversity Coefficient (fig. 5.12).
A diversity coefficient is calculated for each point based on the number of interval combinations at the domainal boundary. This requires that a diversity value first be established in relation to each interval. For example, to determine diversity coefficients for the interval day, it was necessary to consider all edge combinations involving daily variations (fig. 5.13). There are two edges at a day-year combination and one at a day-year-century combination. Consequently, there are two different kinds of edge reflected in the daily network; the resulting diversity coefficient is 2. This procedure is followed for every point at all three intervals. (figs. 5.13-5.15.)

2b. Potential Coefficient (fig. 5.16).
The step for determining a potential coefficient is also taken separately at every interval but the diagram will only consider one interval. The procedure involves taking the difference between the diversity coefficients on adjacent points. Potential coefficients are shown on the line for each interval network (figs. 5.17-5.19).

2c. Control Coefficient (fig. 5.20).
As with steps *2a* and *2b,* this step for determining the control coefficient is taken at each interval. The diagram considers only one interval. The procedure involves summing the potential coefficients on the lines. Control coefficients are shown on the points for valley networks (figs. 5.21-5.23). Before moving to the final step in developing the interval network, it is necessary to develop a composite of the control coefficients at separate intervals. The result is a set of associated numbers listing control coefficients at intervals from the longest (century) to the shortest (day) as in the example: 5—century, 0—thirty-year, 10—year, and 2—day (fig. 5.24).

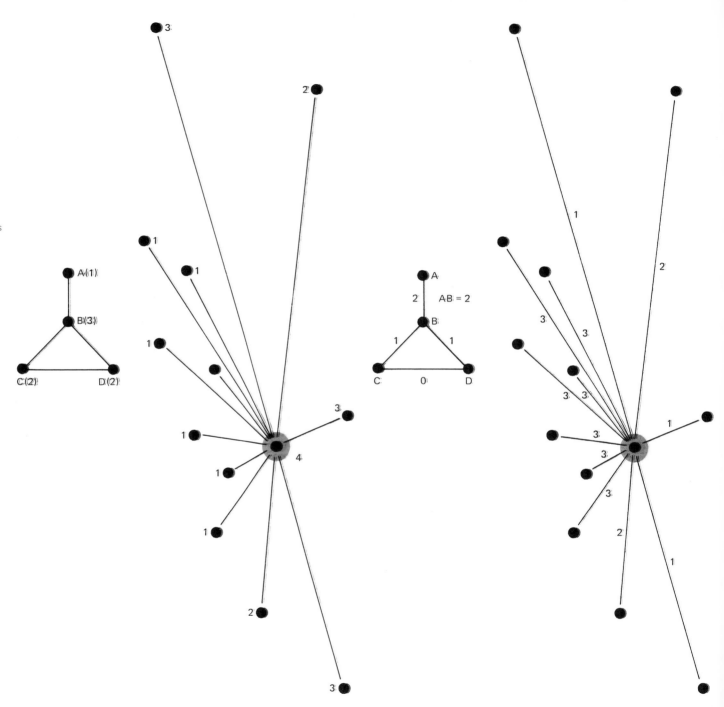

Fig. 5.3
Diversity coefficient (step *1a*). Diversity is measured by counting the variety of conditions adjacent to a point. In the diagram, conditions are shown as *A*, *B*, *C*, and *D*. The variety of conditions adjacent to a point is shown in parentheses.

Fig. 5.4
Variation network with diversity coefficients. In the Owens Valley network, diversity was measured by counting the variety of stress conditions in adjacent domains. The diversity coefficient (4) on the central point results from adjacent stress values of two, four, six and seven (see fig. 5.2*b* for stress values). Diversity coefficients on adjacent points result from their own adjacencies that are not shown.

Fig. 5.5
Potential coefficient (step *1b*). Potential for change in associations is measured by subtracting diversity coefficients and placing the difference on the connecting line.

Fig. 5.6
Variation network with potential coefficients. The potential for change in the structure of Owens Valley is described by numbers that express the likely energy flow between adjacent domains. (See fig. 5.4 for diversity coefficients that are subtracted to get potential coefficients.)

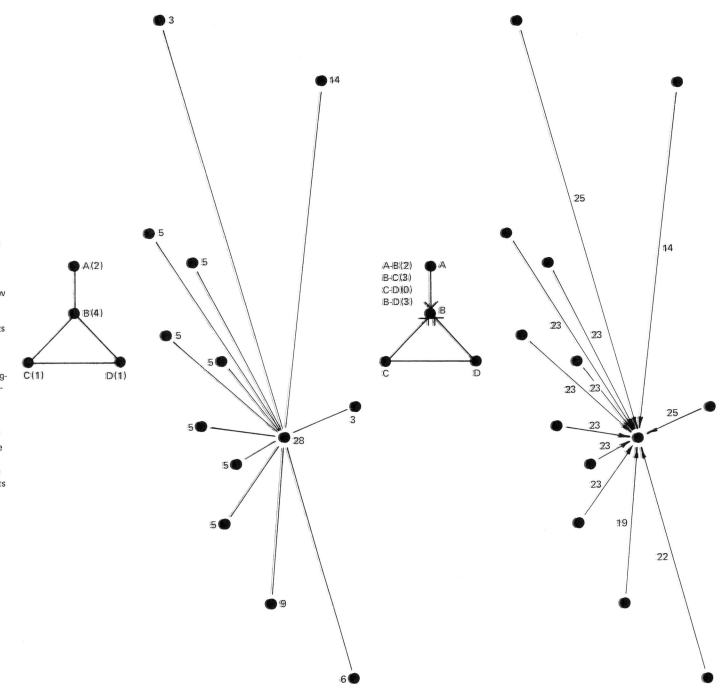

Fig. 5.7
Control Coefficient (step *1c*). Control is measured at a point by summing all potential values on lines meeting at that point.

Fig. 5.8
Variation network with control coefficients. The tendency of a domain to control transactions with adjacent domains in Owens Valley is measured by adding the number of associations and their potential for energy flow. (See fig. 5.6 for the potential coefficients that are summed to get the control coefficient.)

Fig. 5.9
Control vector (step *1d*). The direction of energy flow between adjacent points is measured as the difference between control coefficients on those points.

Fig. 5.10
Variation network with magnitude and direction of control vectors. Energy flow across an edge separating adjacent domains in Owens Valley is in the direction of the controlling domain. The probability of this flow is derived from the difference between control coefficients of the adjacent domains. (See fig. 5.8 for control coefficients that are subtracted to get the control vector.)

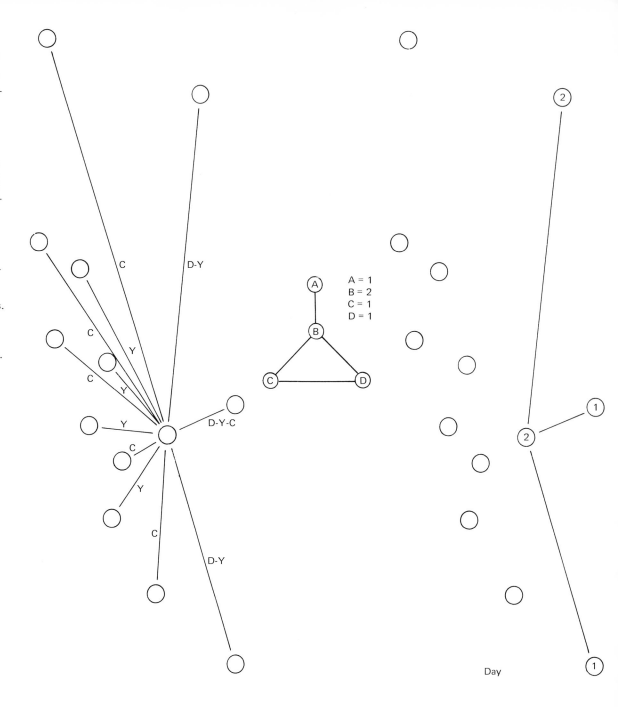

Fig. 5.11
Interval network. Stress construct is redefined as a network of adjacent domains with the interval of recurrence of the edge segments indicated on the line as *D* (day), *Y* (year) and *C* (century).

Fig. 5.12
Diversity coefficient (step *2a*). Diversity is measured by counting the variety of edge combinations that include a particular interval (fig. 5.11). Consequently, a different network must be made for each interval (figs. 5.13, 5.14, 5.15). Figure 5.12 shows a hypothetical set of diversity coefficients as a starting point for subsequent steps.

Fig. 5.13
Interval network (day) with diversity coefficients.

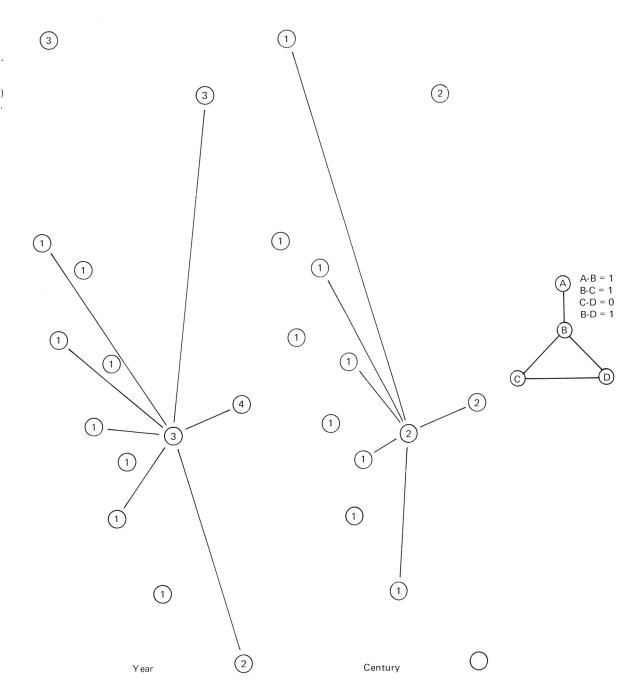

Fig. 5.14
Interval network (year)
with diversity coefficients.

Fig. 5.15
Interval network (century)
with diversity coefficients.

Fig. 5.16
Potential coefficient (step
2b). The potential for
change in associations is
measured by subtracting
diversity coefficients at a
particular interval and
placing the difference on
the connecting line.

Year

Century

A-B = 1
B-C = 1
C-D = 0
B-D = 1

Fig. 5.17
Interval network (day)
with potential coefficients.

Fig. 5.18
Interval network (year)
with potential coefficients.

Fig. 5.19
Interval network (century)
with potential coefficients.

Day

Year

Century

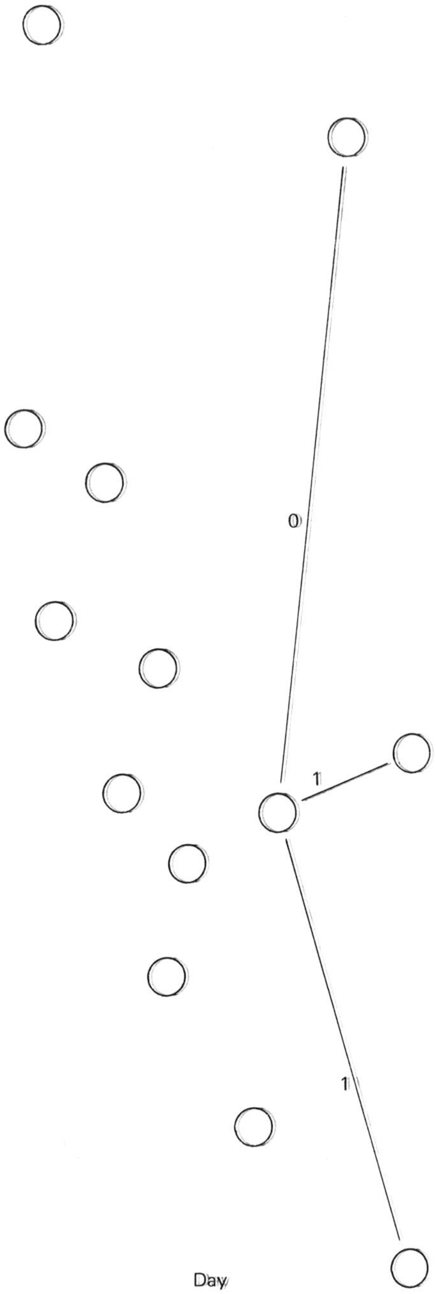

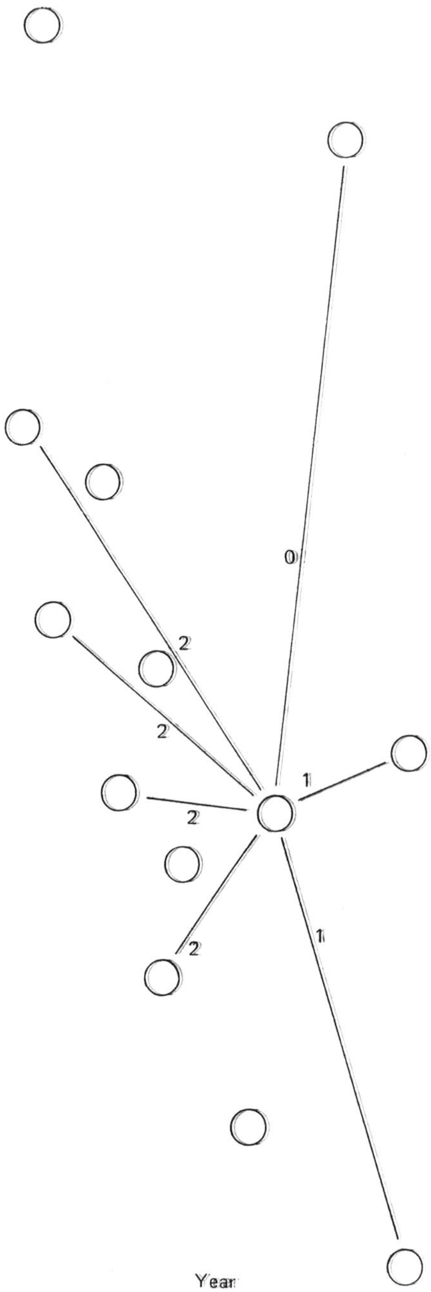

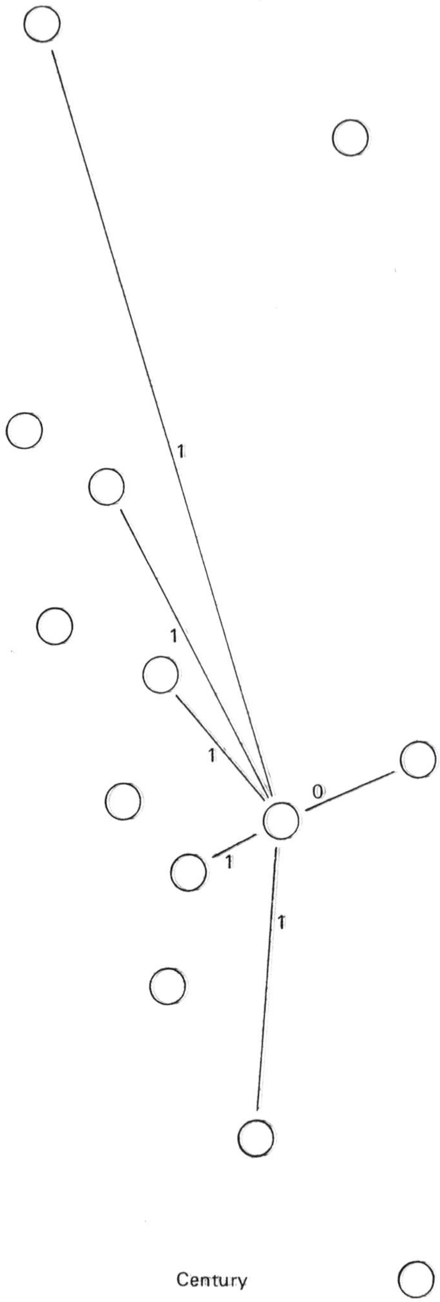

Fig. 5.20
Control coefficient (step *2c*). Control is measured at a point by summing all potential values separately for each interval.

Fig. 5.21
Interval network (day) with control coefficients.

Fig. 5.22
Interval network (year) with control coefficients.

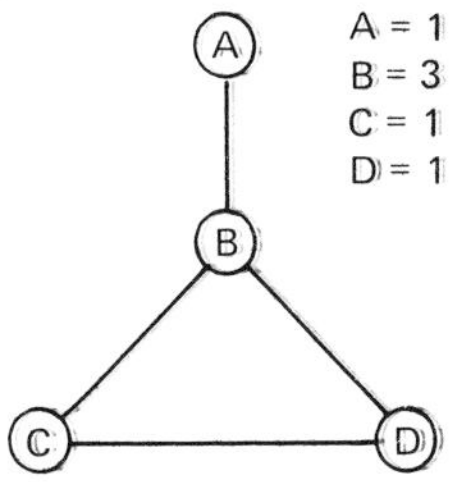
A
B
C
D
A = 1
B = 3
C = 1
D = 1

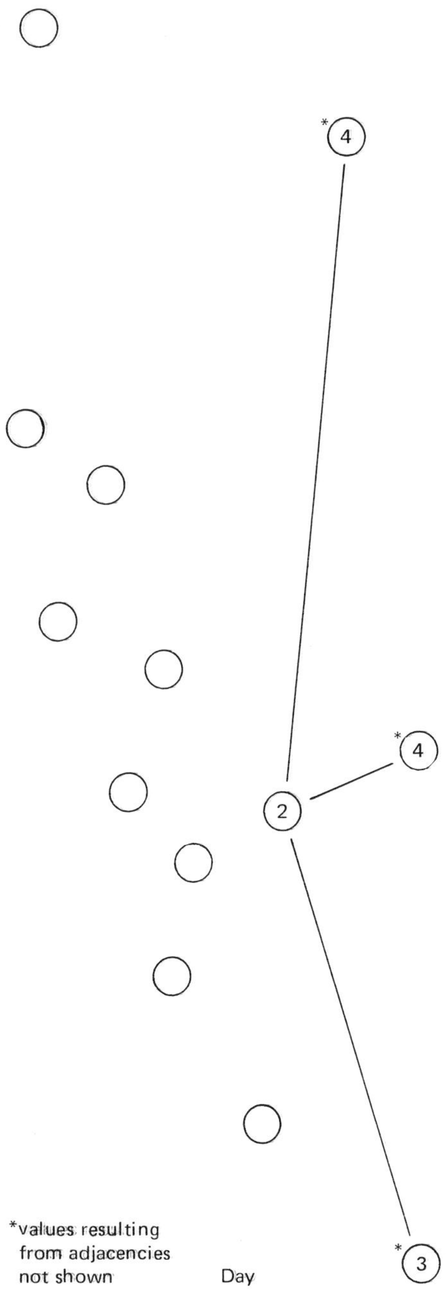
*4
*4
2
*3
*values resulting from adjacencies not shown
Day

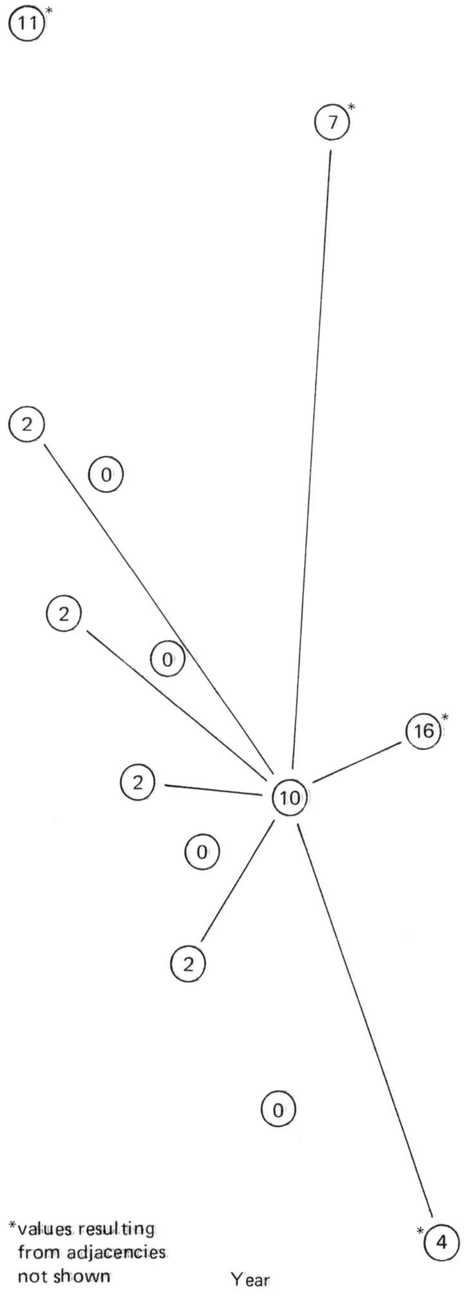
11*
7*
2
0
2
0
16*
2
10
0
2
0
*4
*values resulting from adjacencies not shown
Year

Fig. 5.23
Interval network (century) with control coefficients.

Fig. 5.24
Composite control coefficient. Before developing control vectors, all intervals must be recognized by listing control coefficients at intervals from the longest (century) to the shortest (day).

Fig. 5.25
Control vector. The intervals that establish an edge between two adjacent domains determine which control coefficients will be used to establish the vector. The sums of control coefficients at those particular intervals are then subtracted to get the magnitude and direction of the control vector.

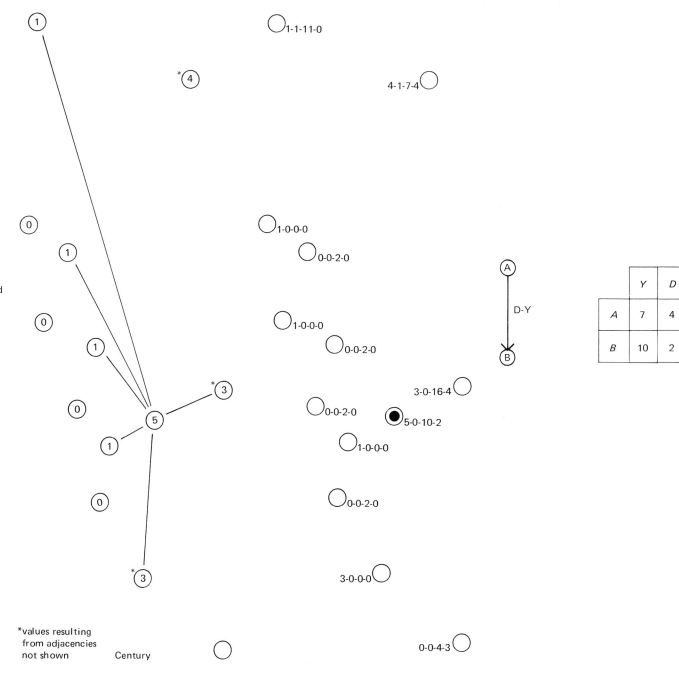

2d. Control Vectors (fig. 5.25).
Regardless of how many intervals have established control coefficients on the points control vectors can only be determined at those intervals that establish the edge immediately under consideration. The example involves two hypothetical points separated by an edge that recurs at only the daily and yearly intervals; therefore, even though Points *A* and *B* may have had control coefficients at intervals other than day and year, the only control coefficients considered for Point *A* are 7 and 4; only 10 and 2 are considered for Point *B*. The composite control coefficient for Point *A* is 7 + 4 = 11; for Point *B* it is 10 + 2 = 12. The control vector is the difference between those coefficients, 12 − 11 = 1, directed toward Point *B*. Vector values and probable direction of energy flow are shown on the line (fig. 5.27).

3. Variation and Interval Network (table 5.1)
The last step to develop a final network relating stress to a form response (*S/V*) requires combining the two separately developed networks for variation and interval (table 5.1).

3a. Variation-Interval (fig. 5.28).
Final control vectors are derived by combining the sub-networks for variation and interval that were required because of the twofold nature of natural recurrence. This procedure involves algebraically summing the vectors derived from the separate variation and interval networks. For example, if the variation network showed a vector of 6 directed to point *B,* and the interval network showed a vector of 3 in the same direction, the resulting composite vector value would be 9 to Point *B* (fig. 5.28, *top*). If the situation were 6 to Point *A* and 3 to Point *B* the algebraic sum would show a vector of 3 to Point *A* (fig. 5.28, *bottom*). For the valley network, *variation vectors* (fig. 5.10) are combined with *interval vectors* (fig. 5.27) and algebraically summed on the line (fig. 5.29).

3b. Composite Control Coefficients.
The composite vector values representing a combination of the two component networks are once again summed on the point, producing a composite control coefficient. This number for our sample domain is 316 (fig. 5.30). Similar numbers are shown on each adjacent domain; because vector values have been summed algebraically, some of the control coefficients have negative values.

3c. Final Control Vectors.
The final step involves taking the difference between adjacent domains to produce another and final set of control vector values. These values range from 244 to 493 with some numbers repeating (fig. 5.31). They will now be employed to establish a specification for the allowable *S/V* range.

Stress and Surface-to-Volume
The development of an allowable *S/V* range is based on a control principle, stated before, that relates the identity of a force domain to the rigor of planning control in such a way as to preserve the physical structure of an ecosystem (Owens Valley). Modern development often changes the basic structure of the natural environment.

One extremely useful expression of that change is the *S/V* of what is built because it places change into an energy context by describing building susceptibility to environmental stress. Up to now we have developed the point of view that susceptibility may be somewhat larger or smaller than the value corresponding to its designated stress coefficient. For example, a perfect building match or analogous coefficient of susceptibility for the Stress 3 domain previously discussed would be *S/V* = 11.6 (table 4.2). If a higher *S/V* were used, the building result would be relatively insufficient to handle the stress on the scale devised. The energy cost would be higher per unit volume to maintain that built arrangement than its relative position in the ecosystem warranted. On the other hand, a lower *S/V* would produce a redundant building solution, one that used less energy per unit volume than its relative position in the ecosystem would have predicted. In either case, the building does not precisely meet the site conditions.

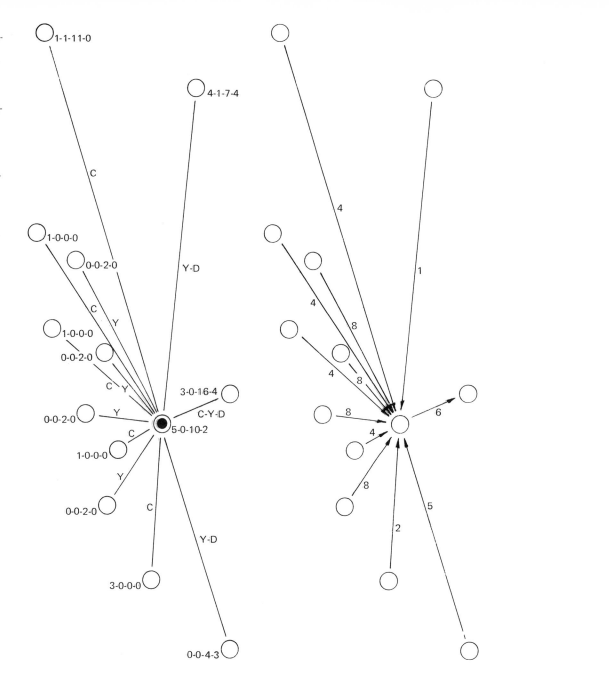

Fig. 5.26
Interval network with composite control coefficients (on points) and edge intervals (on lines).

Fig. 5.27
Interval network with magnitude and direction of control vectors.

Fig. 5.28
Composite control vectors. Variation and interval vectors are algebraically summed to get the magnitude and direction of composite control vectors.

$6 - 3 = 3$

$6 + 3 = 9$

Fig. 5.29
Variation-interval network with magnitude and direction of composite vectors. Variation vectors (fig. 5.10) are combined with interval vectors (fig. 5.27) and algebraically summed on the line.

Fig. 5.30
Variation-interval network with composite control coefficients. Composite vectors are summed for the sample domain and for adjacent domains. (Control coefficients shown for adjacent domains derive from their own various adjacencies that were developed but are not shown.)

Fig. 5.31
Variation-interval network with magnitude and direction of final control vectors. The difference between composite control coefficients (fig. 5.30) establishes final control vectors for the valley network.

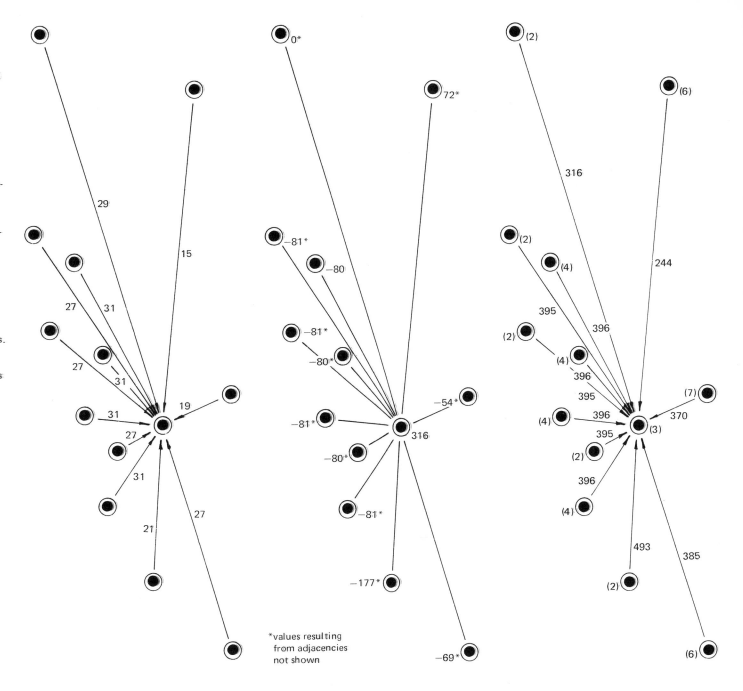

*values resulting from adjacencies not shown

Fig. 5.32
Variation-interval network
for Owens Valley. Each
point represents a stress
domain, each line an adjacency between domains.
The network shows a clear
separation between the
eastern (right) and western
(left) sides of the valley.

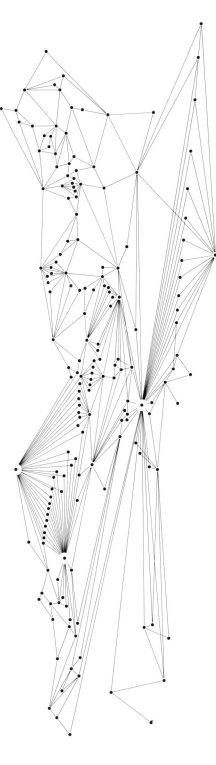

Tolerance of the Surface-to-Volume Ratio

Building specifications are derived from
an individual consideration of each edge
condition comprising the boundary of a
domain. Specification tolerances for S/V
are derived from the final control vectors
in the Owens Valley network. The vector
range for the whole network is 0 to 8,130
(fig. 5.32). This range represents the diversity of edge conditions within the Valley.
The largest vector (8,130) requires a minimum optimization while the smallest
vector (0) requires maximum. From this,
a scale is established in which the smallest
vector requires 100 percent optimization
and the largest one requires 0 percent
optimization.

The spread of vector values is not evenly
distributed, which suggests the convenience
of a nonlinear scale. The greatest number
of control vectors falls among the lower
values (1 to 100) rather than among the
higher values (1,000 to 10,000). The
actual vector distribution is as follows:
In the range from 0 to 100 there are 110
vectors; in the range from 100 to 1,000
there are 131 vectors; in the range from
1,000 to 10,000 there are only 87 vectors
(table 5.2). This uneven spread suggested
a need for increased sensitivity at the
lower end of the scale, where there is the
greater number of vectors but where the
difference from one to another is smallest.
To develop a scale of differentiated sensitivity segments of the range were divided
into the number of vectors in that segment
to produce a point in the distribution
curve (fig. 5.33): $110/(100-0) = 1.10$;
$131/(1,000-100) = 0.14$; $87/(10,000-1,000) = 0.01$. When plotted on a graph
these values generally describe a logarith-
mic curve, in which the lower end has a
greater sensitivity than the higher end.

The vector range (0 to 8,130) was then plotted on a log scale (0 to 10,000). Laid over this is a linear scale of required optimization that matches 0 percent optimization to the high end of the vector scale and 100 percent optimization to the low end (fig. 5.34).

Optimization across an edge can be determined by locating the vector value of the edge, and then matching to the optimization scale. For example, if the vector value were 10, almost 90 percent optimization would be required. If the edge were stronger, with a vector value of 3,000, only about 10 percent optimization would be required.

In the vector range from 1,000 to 8,130 (with an absolute vector value change of 7,130) there is only a 15 percent optimization range. This results from the fact that there are very few vectors of great strength. By contrast, where the vector value range is smallest and where there is the greatest number of vectors requiring the greatest degree of distinction, the graph shows more sensitivity. With this graph we are now able to establish a range of S/V (above and below the value of 11.6 derived from table 4.2) for the sample domain of Stress 3 with its associated vectors (fig. 5.31).

The maximum and minimum control vector values associated with the point establish an optimization range from 28 percent to 35 percent (table 5.3). This suggests that the Stress 3 domain is rather strongly defined requiring a relatively low degree of optimization. The S/V range is then determined by matching the percent optimization required to the range of S/V optimizations (table 4.2). For a Stress 3, 100 percent optimization has been taken as S/V = 11.6; for each adjacent domain, the value of S/V = 11.6 automatically becomes 0 percent optimization regardless of the magnitude of stress differential. For example, if a Stress 3 domain is adjacent to a Stress 4, the S/V that represents 100 percent optimization for one becomes 0 percent for the other. For Stress 3, 100 percent optimization is S/V = 11.6. For Stress 4, 100 optimization is S/V = 5.97; but each 100 percent optimization of S/V becomes 0 percent for the stress value in the adjacent domain. In this way we can establish a range, based on the distinctions across edges comprising a boundary.

Figure 5.35 plots the S/V value for the sample domain on a vertical scale on the left side. The right-hand vertical scale plots the extreme S/V values for the full range of all adjacent domains. The horizontal scale plots optimization required. The S/V required to match optimization for all edge segments of the domain results in values of 4.0, 4.5, 5.0, 8.0, 19, 19.5, and 20, providing us with a range of S/V. The low value is 4.0, the optimum is 11.6, and the high is 20.0 (table 5.4). The total range is from 4.0 to 20.0. Anything built within the sample domain must fall within that range both to match the prevalent stress condition and to distinguish responses in that domain from associated responses in adjacent domains.

Finally it should be noted that the range of S/V could not be simply identified by looking at the largest vector value because the range is not linear. For example, a Stress 3 compared to a Stress 2 provides a range of optimum S/V values from 11.6 to 22.8. The same Stress 3 compared to a Stress 4 represents a much smaller range from 5.97 to 11.6 (table 4.2).

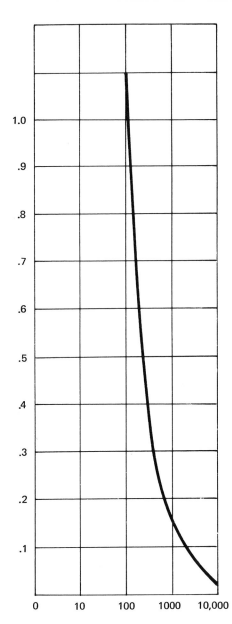

Fig. 5.33
Vector distribution curve. The spread of vector values is not evenly distributed, suggesting the convenience of a non-linear scale that allows greater sensitivity in recognizing distinctions where there is the greater number of vectors over the smallest value range.

Fig. 5.34
Vector value versus percent optimization. Optimization across an edge can be determined by locating the vector value of the edge and matching it to the optimization scale.

Fig. 5.35
Stress and optimization. The range of stress (converted to *S/V*) in adjacent domains determines the range of optimization for surface-to-volume ratio in the sample domain.

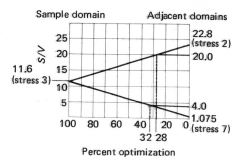

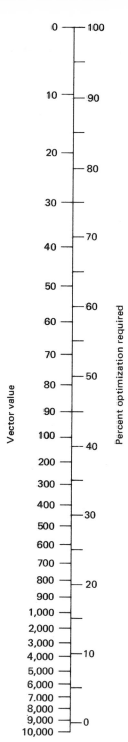

Table 5.2 Vector Distribution

Vector range	Vector quotient
0 - 100 = 110	110/100 = 1.10
100 - 1,000 = 131	131/900 = 0.14
1,000 - 10,000 = 87	87/9,000 = 0.01

Table 5.3 Control Vector Values and Percent Optimization

Vector	Optimization required %
257	35
328	33
409	30
408	30
505	28
379	31
382	32

Table 5.4 Control Vector Values for the *S/V* Range 4.0 - 20.0

Vector	Adjacency	Optimization required %	S/V range
257	stress 3 - stress 6	35	4.5 - 11.6
328	stress 3 - stress 2	33	11.6 - 19.0
409	stress 3 - stress 4	30	8.0 - 11.6
408	stress 3 - stress 2	30	11.6 - 19.5
505	stress 3 - stress 2	28	11.6 - 20.0
379	stress 3 - stress 6	31	5.0 - 11.6
382	stress 3 - stress 7	32	4.0 - 11.6

Network Development: Slope-Orientation

The discussion of control thus far has been concerned with the Owens Valley as a whole. The stress construct has been derived from an overview of recurring forces; the resulting control network has quantified relationships among large-scale land segments as a basis for developing tolerances in applying a general specification (S/V) of building form.

A closer view of the stress domains shows them to be comprised of smaller-scale slopes with different orientations. While these more refined earth forms may not be significant when determining the major configuration of natural forces in the valley, they are of significance in the siting of buildings with relation to one another. (See the discussion of slope-orientation, chap. 4.)

The need to consider how adjacent buildings interact with relation to cyclic natural forces requires a second construct which subdivides each large stress domain into smaller segments based on slope and orientation (fig. 4.10).

A control network can be developed for each construct contained within a stress domain. These new networks can be used to quantify relationships among smaller-scale land segments as a basis for developing tolerances in applying more particular specifications (H/A) of building form.

To demonstrate this, a single stress domain (the Stress 3 domain with previously determined tolerances for S/V) can be isolated and sub-structured by slope and orientation (fig. 5.36). Each of these smaller segments becomes a domain of consistent slope, oriented on one of the cardinal points. (Further refinement of slope angles and orientations other than the four cardinal points is possible and may usually be desirable, but this degree of refinement serves to describe the processes in this case.)

The slope-orientation construct, limited by the boundary of a single stress domain, is then provided with a network in which points represent a domain of consistent slope-orientation and lines represent edges separating domainal states (fig. 5.37).

The major difference between development of the variation-interval network and the slope-orientation network derives from the fact that the first required two sub-networks to define the state in time as well as space. Only one network is used for slope and orientation.

One domain, and its associations, has been selected for this discussion and is shown on both the construct (fig. 5.36) and the network (fig. 5.37). That portion of the network directly involved has been isolated for discussion (fig. 5.38). Its particular control-vector range is distributed near the high end of the total range (0 to 2,295) for the entire network. As with the stress network, the vector distribution for this total range is nonlinear. There are approximately as many vectors in the value range from 0 to 100 as there are from 100 to 1,000 (table 5.5), and in this case as well, a logarithmic curve better describes the range of distinctions involved from more subtle, at the low value

end of the scale, to less subtle at the upper value end (figs. 5.39, 5.40). The required optimization of the building height in relation to its area of influence (H/A) on the case-study domain is very low; it is approximately 2 percent for most edge segments comprising the boundary (table 5.6).

While the sample domain (15° east-facing slope) is adjacent to twenty-one domains (fig. 5.38), there are only five different H/A values represented (table 5.7). (The H/A values shown in table 5.7 were previously derived and shown in table 4.3) When these five values are shown in association with the H/A for the case-study domain and compared in terms of a scale for optimization, the result is an allowable H/A range for the domain of 0.1 to 5.4 (fig. 5.41). Because of the low optimization required (2 percent), the allowable range is nearly as great as the actual range of H/A (0.0 to 5.5) in adjacent domains.

The significance of this range of H/A is, as it was for the tolerance range of S/V, that the building specification need not be applied so rigorously; that the "description" of site conditions may be less than completely accurate. This lack of accuracy is allowed by the strength of identity of a domain that derives from contact diversity with adjacent domains.

This less-than-accurate site description allows modifications in the H/A ratio of 5.0 previously derived for a 15° E slope (table 4.3). Such modifications are produced by changing the ratio between building reference height and area of influence under the action of the sun. One major advantage to be gained by a tolerant range of H/A is the merger of building increments into more complex and more highly organized increments with greater potential diversity of building height, plan dimension, and interaction for purposes of energy conservation. (The procedures for this will be explained more fully in chap. 6.)

The S/V and H/A ranges provide two specifications for built form derived from the interaction between recurring natural forces and the form of the land. S/V is a general function of environmental perturbation, the composite of cyclic forces acting at a large scale. H/A is a particular function of insolation at the smaller scale of building interaction.

Up to this point, building specifications have been correlated with the interaction between natural forces and land form. The degree of rigor exercised in that correlation has been inversely related to the diversity of associations among force-domains. This attitude about control has been applied at the large scale of the whole valley and at a smaller scale of site distinctions. But the smallest segment yet defined is, in many cases, still large enough to require a framework for internal control over the size, complexity and sequence of community development. This requires some description of growth modes and the consequent types of control.

Fig. 5.36
Slope-orientation construct. Each segment of the construct is a domain of consistent slope, oriented on one of the four cardinal points. The entire construct is a single domain (stress 3) isolated from the stress construct (fig. 4.2).

Fig. 5.37
Slope-orientation network. Each point represents a slope-orientation domain; each line, an adjacency between domains.

Fig. 5.38
Slope-orientation network (sample section).

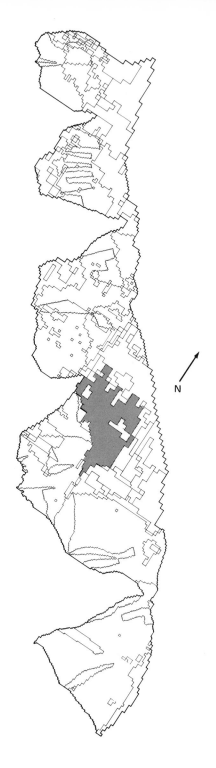

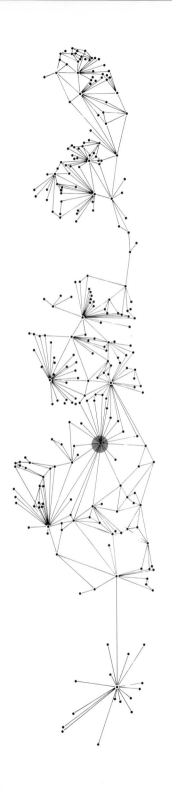

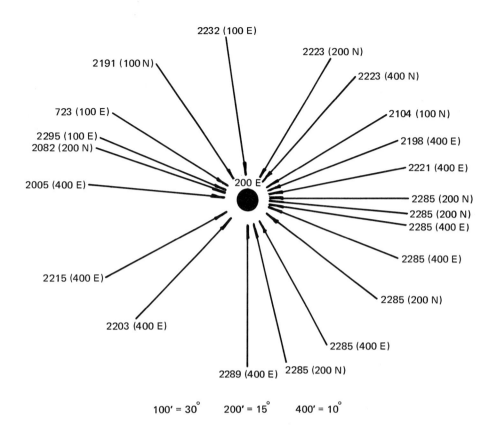

2232 (100 E)

2223 (200 N)

2191 (100 N)

2223 (400 N)

723 (100 E)

2104 (100 N)

2295 (100 E)

2082 (200 N)

2198 (400 E)

2005 (400 E)

2221 (400 E)

200 E

2285 (200 N)

2285 (200 N)

2285 (400 E)

2285 (400 E)

2215 (400 E)

2285 (200 N)

2203 (400 E)

2285 (400 E)

2289 (400 E)   2285 (200 N)

100' = 30°   200' = 15°   400' = 10°

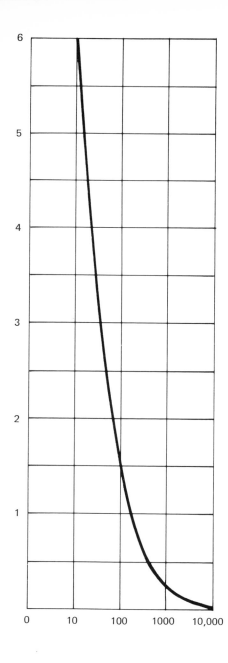

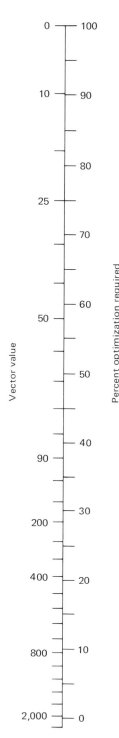

Fig. 5.39
Vector distribution curve
(see fig. 5.33).

Fig. 5.40
Vector value versus percent
optimization (see fig. 5.34).

Fig. 5.41
H/A versus optimization.
The range of slope orientation in adjacent domains
(converted to *H/A*) determines the range of optimization for *H/A* in the sample domain.

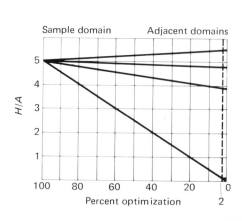

Table 5.5 Vector Distribution

Vector range	Vector quotient
0 - 10 = 60	60/10 = 6.00
10 - 100 = 140	140/90 = 1.60
100 - 1000 = 163	163/900 = 0.18
1000 - 10,000 = 61	61/9,000 = 0.01

Table 5.6 H/A Range ± 0.0 - ± 5.5

Vector	Adjacency	Optimization required %	H/A Range
2,232	200 E - 100 E	2	0.0 - 5.0
2,223	200 E - 200 N	2	5.0 - 5.5
2,223	200 E - 400 N	2	3.85 - 5.0
2.104	200 E - 400 N	2	3.85 - 5.0
2,198	200 E - 400 E	2	4.8 - 5.0
2,221	200 E - 400 E	2	4.8 - 5.0
2,285	200 E - 200 N	2	5.0 - 5.5
2,285	200 E - 400 E	2	4.8 - 5.0
2,285	200 E - 100 E	2	0.0 - 5.0
2,203	200 E - 400 E	2	4.8 - 5.0
2,215	200 E - 400 E	2	4.8 - 5.0
2,005	200 E - 400 E	2	4.8 - 5.0
2,082	200 E - 200 N	2	5.0 - 5.5
2,295	200 E - 100 N	2	0.0 - 5.0
723	200 E - 100 E	10	0.25 - 5.5
2,191	200 E - 100 N	2	0.0 - 5.0

Table 5.7 H/A

Domain	H/A	
200' X 200' E (15°)	5.0	case study domain
100' X 100' E (30°)	0.0	adjacent domains
400' X 400' E (10°)	4.8	
200' X 200' N (15°)	5.5	
400' X 400' N (10°)	3.85	
100' X 100' N (30°)	0.0	

Part Three   Diversifying Urban Arrangements

Part Three of this book is concerned with the relation between diversity and energy conservation in built arrangements. The notion that there is such a relation was introduced in Part One by describing the pueblos of the Southwest. There, diversity was observed at a small scale, in the forms of interacting buildings. The notion was further explored in Part Two where diversity became the basis for energy-conserving development of Owens Valley. There, diversity was measured at a larger scale. Specifications for development were matched to the ecosystem framework of Owens Valley and varied from one segment of the system to another in response to changing conditions of recurring natural force. Throughout Parts One and Two the governing criterion was based on the need to reduce the energy demands per unit volume of the built environment. This same criterion will now be used to apply the principles of interacting building-form within the context of the ecosystem of the Owens Valley. Overall site conditions will be met but, at this scale, the major distinctions of environmental stress and slope-orientation that were measured in Owens Valley cannot be used as a basis for diversity. What the planner needs at this intermediate scale is a framework for his own design that fits within the larger ecosystem framework. He needs a framework that controls the changing interactions between the forms of land and building and the recurring forces of nature as development takes place.

When the criterion for development is conservation of the energy required to maintain equilibrium, the perturbation resulting from the composite of all cyclic forces must be considered. But the main recurrence is insolation, and it must be taken into particular account. For this reason, the principles of growth and interacting form observed in the pueblos will be used in the design of a framework for development; and as with the pueblos, the governing criterion for seasonal insolation will be based on the mitigation of variation.

The daily and seasonal variations that result from sun action are common to most habitable regions of the earth. Before the industrial revolution and a plentiful supply of inanimate energy, building form and location were more likely to be responsive to nature, providing, as well, rich symbolic meaning. The south-oriented courts of the Greek houses of Olynthus, built around 500 B.C. became the center of family life. The court, surrounded by a gallery, allowed the warming winter sun to penetrate deeply into the interior of the house while shielding spaces from the intense summer sun (figs. 6.1, 6.2). The religion of the Acoma pueblo dwellers required three steps to get to heaven. The three-tiered houses of the Acomas were also an efficient way of relieving the impact of seasonal variations (fig. 2.15).

It is evident that expressive form is based upon the rhythms of nature; indeed the expression is dependent upon those rhythms for its completion time. The sun must pass through its cycles of seasonal variation before the complete set of interactions can be reviewed and appreciated.

Buildings in modern cities have tremendous dimensions when compared to the Greek house and the Acoma pueblo. They also interact; and because of their size and proximity the interaction occurs over long periods of time. But neither form nor location are planned for their considerable potential as responses to the natural environment. Building forms and their interactions may be simple or complex but the purpose for their forms and their interactions is generally set from the developer's point of view. The form of a modern building is most often limited by the commercial value of the land, by the limits of the site, and by any code restrictions having to do with how much of the site may be covered or possible restrictions governing setback. The way buildings interact with each other is usually not planned and remains a matter of circumstance that results from a rapid rate of change based on short-term profit. But form and the interactions resulting from location, seen in the pueblo studies, can be used to mitigate the effects of daily and seasonal insolation. In modern building, they could replace some of the need for mechanical support systems.

If we are willing to organize the increments, rates, and directions of that change around a clear purpose, cities like Los Angeles and New York could, within a decade, be transformed into energy-conserving systems. Our cities are being transformed anyway. Can we get more benefit from that transformation than higher land values and more office space?

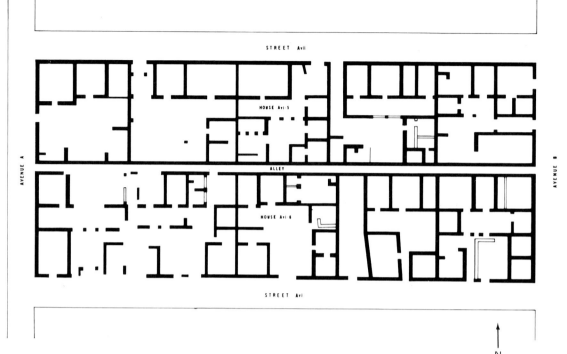

STREET A vii

HOUSE A vii 5

AVENUE A

ALLEY

AVENUE B

HOUSE A vii 6

STREET A vi

N

Fig. 6.1
Block at Olynthus. The plan of a typical block demstrates a great variety of house arrangements while adhering to certain constraints: the blocks were consistent in size and orientation; there were always ten houses per block; and each house was built around an open court on the south side regardless of

the location of the entrance from the street. Based on a drawing by J. Walter Graham from plans by Donald N. Wilber in *Excavations at Olynthus: The Hellenic House* by David M. Robinson and J. Walter Graham (Baltimore: The Johns Hopkins Press, 1938).

A planning framework that is based on natural rhythms and that respects constraints imposed by the shape and scale of the land will generate a richly diversified growth. The pueblos demonstrate this fact. The Owens Valley study reinforces it. In addition, such a framework can provide clues to the kinds of problems that will arise, and where and when they will arise. Such information allows the possibility of anticipating problems. Such a framework substructures the land into domains with unique sets of conditions. If each set of conditions requires a different growth mode, a different size, complexity, and sequence of construction then the problems associated with that set of conditions can be clearly distinguished from another set. The growth mode will determine a control mode. Size, complexity, and sequence of development determine the economic, social, and political institutions necessary for sufficient growth

Growth can be defined in a number of ways. For this study two growth processes have been distinguished and classified in terms of their different characteristics and the modes of control that seem appropriate to each. The first can be called *expansion*— a simple multiplication of like parts, an accumulation that exhibits low diversity, minimal complexity, and independence of functioning parts. Such development exhibits minimum differentiation. It generally appears as new or pioneer growth in urban development and is associated with a low degree of maturation; it is unstable and tends to change rapidly. While initial control over such growth is generally low, its tendency to change rapidly toward maturation and higher degrees of complexity require that control be maintained or even increased for a certain period.

The second mode of growth can be called *transformation.* Unlike expansion, the number of parts tends not to increase—it may even decrease—but the form changes. Each part becomes larger, more diverse and complex. Such development exhibits maximum differentiation. It generally appears with successive land uses in older cities and is associated with higher degrees of maturation. It is more stable and tends to change less rapidly. As something like a mature state is achieved, control can be relaxed.

Expansion and transformation can also be used to describe the phases of growth. Simple expansion occurs first, followed by transformation through increasing levels of complexity that leads to a predictable and functioning system. When towns and cities grow slowly, with ample time for adjustment, or when increments, rates, and directions of growth are prescribed by a built-in set of instructions combined with an environmental limit on resources to which the system is adapted, growth is predictable; expansion, transformation, and their attendant degrees of differentiation occur in a predictable sequence. However, when the instructive mechanism is malfunctioning or nonexistent and when the resources necessary for growth are unregulated, maturation is adversely affected, as it is in the modern city. The modern city is an expanding but perpetually immature and unstable arrangement. If its growth is to be differentiated to increase stability and to help limit its indiscriminate expansion, the attendant control must also be differentiated. This fact was recognized in the study of Owens Valley through the use of a framework that made a general distinction among domains defined in terms of natural cyclic forces. Now a more refined and specific distinction will be made between development at the boundary and the interior of a single force domain.

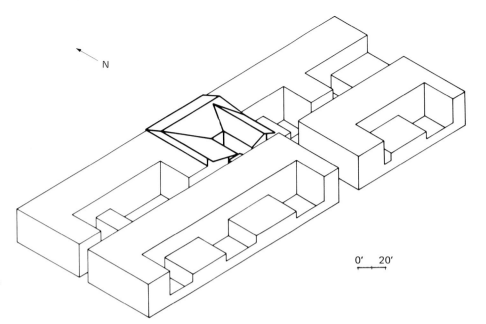

N

0' 20'

Fig. 6.2
Isometric of Olynthus block. Building volumes at Olynthus take advantage of the south orientation of the court. One house has been shown in greater detail to indicate the extent of overhang that acted to exclude summer sun and admit winter sun. (Reconstruction of building height, roof slopes and overhang of one house within an Olynthus block based on sun studies made at the University of Southern California in 1967 by G. Anderson, M. Dubin, J. Parkin, and D. Williamson.)

Such a distinction must be made in recognition of the different levels of variability and, therefore, predictability from one part of a domain to another. In its analysis of recurring natural forces in Owens Valley, the University of Southern California group had recognized the boundary of a domain by the greater variety of force conditions there. Sample measurements made while approaching the edge displayed greater variation while toward the center of the domain a general state was pervasive. Measurements over time supported the spatial observations. Conditions tended to change more at the domainal edge than toward the center in response to the cyclic forces of sun, wind, and water. The result was a higher degree of predictability of composite force action in the center of a domain than toward its edges.

The USC group also observed what appeared to be a correlation between predictability of force action and predictability in the distribution of plant species. In moving toward the boundary of a force domain, a change of location often produces a change of plant species and changes of conditions over time reduce the stability of plant life. Toward the center of the force domain, samples are more consistent.

Such observations suggest the need for a planning framework that recognizes the special problems of domainal boundaries. The edges that comprise boundaries are an interface between two different sets of force conditions. They are the "third condition" referred to in Chapter 5. A framework that recognizes the uncertainty of this "third condition" must, in addition to any initial specification, constrain the transformation of edge development over time. There can be accumulation and simple expansion to prescribed limits, but no transformation to greater levels of complexity and diversity. Since transformation is primarily a function of interaction among parts of an arrangement, it can be avoided by reducing the possibility of interaction, that is, by establishing a condition characterized by a relatively low level of organization. Small and independently acting parts that have little possibility of merging and transforming themselves into larger and more highly organized parts would be more likely to respect the domainal edge. The initial control over such an arrangement of independently acting parts can be relatively low but must be maintained over time. Further away from the edge, parts of the built arrangement can be gathered together into larger interacting groups.

Such groups require a higher degree of initial control over their growth; but that control can be reduced as the arrangement matures. While these larger increments could not be so responsive to edge conditions, they can be tolerated at the interior of the domain so long as they respond to the pervasive state of cyclic forces. Here, diversity in the built arrangement may increase through a process of transformation. Maturation over time and functional considerations other than those of preserving natural diversity may properly take dominance.

From these requirements a general principle can be taken that governs the location within a domain, the mode of growth, and the control attending that location.

At the boundary of a force domain where conditions are less predictable, the mode of growth must be maintained at a low level of organization by means of a control system that does not allow transformation over time. Here, the physical environment rigorously limits development. Toward the more stable center, where there is a pervasive physical state and greater predictability, a more complex mode of growth can be established by means of a control system that allows maturation through a process of transformation. Here, development becomes more controlled by diverse community needs.

Following this principle, settlement can take place within a domain in such a way that the land and its development becomes an arrangement of interdependent parts. The purpose of that system can be described in terms of the interrelationships among parts.

Settlement on these terms can anticipate where the greatest change will occur over time and can provide for that change by properly designing the institutions necessary to regulate it. Such information is vital if society is to avoid the traumatic consequences of unanticipated change.

Organizational Levels of Growth

In order to deal specifically with modes of growth and control, a site has been abstracted from Owens Valley as a case study. The site faces east on a 15° slope at the foot of the Sierra Nevada mountains. It is located in a slope-orientation construct that substructures a Stress 3 domain (figs. 5.37, 6.3). It carries three specifications for building form: The first is a range (S/V = 4.0 to 20.0) derived from the large-scale stress construct of the whole valley and determines building susceptibility to general perturbations; the second is also a range (H/A = 0.1 to 5.4), from the smaller-scale slope-orientation construct, and established the ratio between building height and its area of yearly sun shadow; the third is not a range but is an absolute ratio between insolation on the winter solstice and the summer solstice. This third specification is aimed at overcoming the peak loading effects of seasonal variation. Within a planning framework, each independent increment of development (which may be comprised of one or several buildings) must meet a ratio, E_W/E_S = 1.0. Failure to meet that criterion for seasonal insolation in combination with the S/V and H/A specification-ranges derived from the study of Owens Valley will be considered grounds for not building. The ranges for S/V and H/A apply to the whole site and come from the control mechanisms that relate contact diversity at a domainal boundary to specification tolerances; the greater contact diversity develops a broader specification range. But every built increment must lie somewhere within those specification ranges.

In devising a framework for the development of such a site, the attitude has been taken that growth should be a structured and understandable process that will not continue beyond certain limits. Furthermore, a series of trade-offs may be allowed based on maintenance costs. For example, when the decision is made to grow cheaply and expand through a simple, repetitive process, the criteria affecting development are the most rigid; few options are allowed. When development is more diversified and more comprehensive in its organization, restrictions are eased; the number of options goes up. This suggests that growth may be organized at more than one level. Depending on which level is used, there is more or less freedom to specify building with respect to the land. For this case study, growth has been considered at three organizational levels starting with the lowest and moving to the highest. The levels have been classified under three descriptive terms: *order, structure,* and *system.*

Order

The lowest level at which growth may be organized can be demonstrated with an applied framework that is undifferentiated and that derives the size and shape of its basic unit (200' × 200') from a 15° slope and east orientation (fig. 4.10). The increments comprising it are arranged in an orderly way, but the orderliness does not suggest the direction nor limits of growth (fig. 6.4). If development were planned at this level, the framework would provide a basic increment size but not a basis for varying the size or complexity of parts from one place to another. The information provided by such a framework is minimal.

Like the undifferentiated grid that has provided a framework for much urban growth in the nineteenth and twentieth centuries, the *order* level framework tends to be a good device for measuring or describing change as it occurs but a poor one for directing it. This is true in the sense that when a city grows, some parts change faster and press harder against the grid. Consequently, the grid is more restrictive in some places and gives less trouble in others. It thus acts as a reference against which to measure change.

Each square on the grid is considered to be a potential building site in this study, and the attitude has been taken that buildings located with no other control over their interactions shall not shade adjacent sites during the critical periods of insolation.

The result is a simple pyramidal shape on each square describing the maximum allowable volume without extending the influence of that volume significantly past the limits of the square (fig. 6.5). As might be expected, the high point of the volume shifts its position relative to slope and orientation. (The height of the volume as well as the increment shape also change with slope and orientation, fig. 4.10.) Within these volumetric limits, parts of a built arrangement can be organized to interact in some predictable way. Any extension of form beyond those limits, however, produces unpredictable interaction with adjacent increments. The resulting uncertainty of such interaction across boundaries has forced today's almost exclusive reliance upon power-consuming mechanical devices. Uncertainty could only be reduced by containing and organizing interaction within manageable limits. At this level of planning, critical shadows must be contained within the single increment.

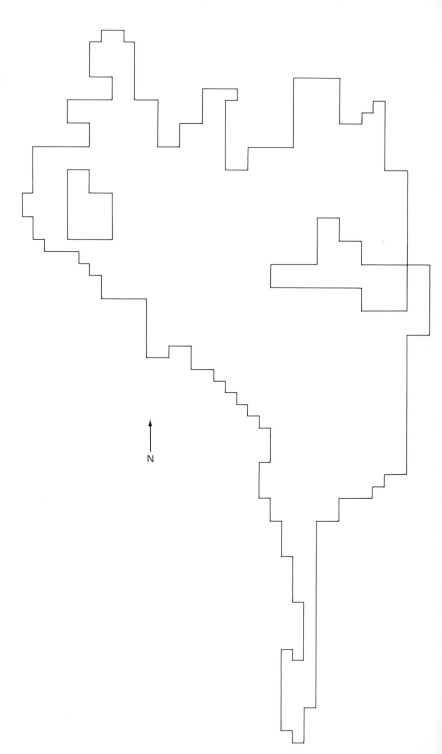

Fig. 6.3
Slope-orientation domain.
(See fig. 5.36.) A site abstracted from Owens Val-
ley faces east on a 15° slope
at the foot of the Sierra
Nevada Mountains.

N

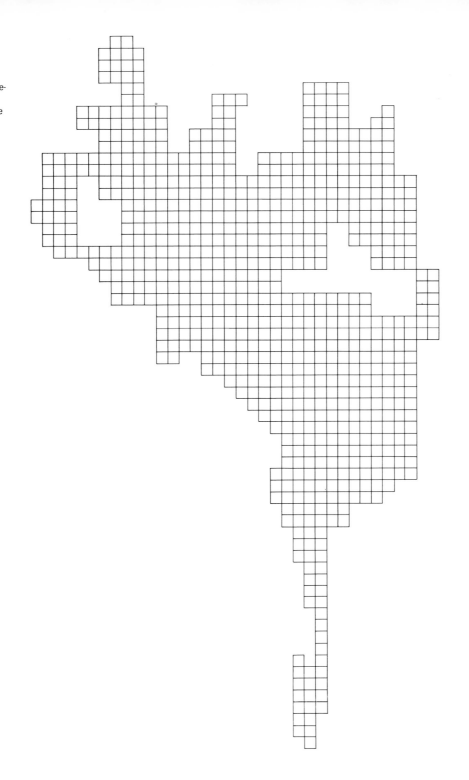

Fig. 6.4
Order level growth. The
first and lowest level at
which growth may be or-
ganized is *order*. The framework at this level is undifferentiated. The size of the
grid squares is 200 X 200
feet. (See fig. 4.10.)

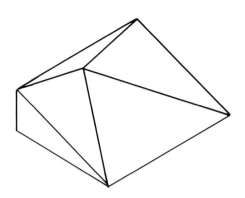

Fig. 6.5
Pyramidal shape. Each square in the grid contains a maximum allowable volume that could be built without extending shadows beyond the square during the critical insolation period of each day.

To demonstrate this, a kind of "clocklike" arrangement of planes can be placed on the heliodon. The planes can be moved to study different building configurations and so long as they stay within the volumetric limits, their shadows will remain within the site. Their interactions can be studied as the sun moves and casts shadows (fig. 6.6). The shading influence of planes can be seen to change in magnitude and direction while the influence is contained within the arrangement during the critical periods of energy reception from the sun. These periods are from 6:00 a.m. to 6:00 p.m. in the summer and from 8:00 a.m. to 4:00 p.m. in the winter. (These times would vary with latitude.) Before these hours in the morning and following them in the afternoon, insolation is significantly reduced by the effects of the atmosphere, and the direct energy influence of the sun can be ignored. (Re-radiation might become a factor to consider in determining the form of a building. However, its importance has not been generally determined and it is not considered here.)

If each such increment were to represent the upper limits of a single building that did not shade and thereby modify the energy being received by adjacent buildings, the result would be a very simple and repetitive growth mode. The results of its multiplication would exhibit a low degree of variety among parts with one part functioning essentially like another and all parts functioning independently of one another. Whatever can be done to employ building form as an adaptation mechanism must be done within the confines of the single increment.

At this level of planning, the size of building increments can be distinguished from one force domain to another (derived from Owens Valley), but size within a domain is consistent and, in this particular case, relatively small. There is no systematic attempt to increase complexity or to interconnect basic increments. The study found that under conditions where each building increment was independently expected to meet the three specifications (S/V, H/A, and E_W/E_S) no building could take place.

Structure
The applied framework that demonstrates the second level at which growth may be organized exhibits directionality (fig. 6.7). If our intention is to instruct the complexity of growth, rather than merely providing a framework that must modify with increasing diversity as maturation tends to take place and for which a constant and reactive control would otherwise be required, some information must be introduced. To do this we can structure the force domain to recognize the difference between edge and center. This second framework provides, in addition to the orderliness supplied by the grid, a directionality in growth.

Aside from the need to change building specifications from one force domain to another across an edge for purposes of energy conservation, directionality in the structure framework also derives from the notion that domainal identity should be valued for its own sake and is most clearly perceived at boundary conditions. But in the center of a domain, associations (intradomainal and community controlled) can be developed without loss of identity.

Throughout the entire domain, the *structure* level framework respects the principle stated earlier relating location to the modes of growth and control. In this framework, if each square is considered to be a potential building site, an increase of size toward the center of the domain allows for the possibility of greater built diversity. This is true simply because there are more potential building options on a large site than on a small one.

If there is an advantage in larger land-increment size, there may also be a disadvantage depending upon relative position in the domain. As Gulliver reflected, "Nothing is great or little otherwise than by comparison," and comparison in this case depends upon proximity to the domainal edge. If the increment is too large at the edge, the result may be a change in the character of the domain over time and a modification of domainal associations. Increments should not be too large nor too small in this directional description of a domainal state.

Even though care is required when growth is more highly controlled in this way, there are some advantages. One is the greater design freedom possible regarding interaction among buildings. For example, because land increments have been made larger toward the middle of the applied framework, the small building increments of the previous grid might be systematically gathered together into larger and potentially more complex and diverse arrangements (fig. 6.8). Our simple "clocklike" arrangement of planes, which could only be manipulated within a single reference height, now becomes an increasingly complex arrangement toward the center of the domain. The levels of organization achieved by gathering units together are referred to by the number of original

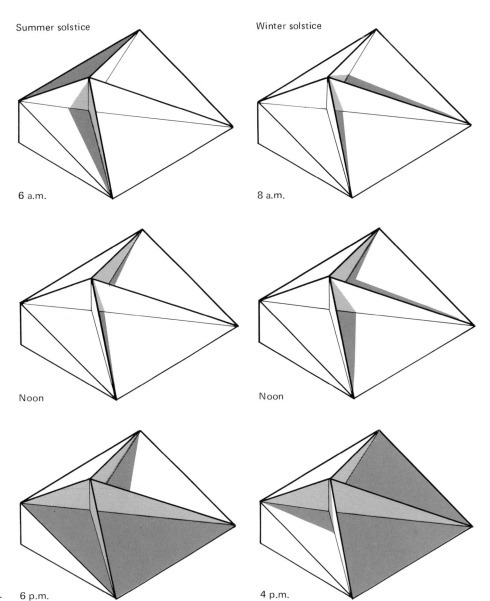

Summer solstice

6 a.m.

Noon

6 p.m.

Winter solstice

8 a.m.

Noon

4 p.m.

Fig. 6.6
Clocklike arrangement of planes. Planes can be used to study different building configurations within the pyramid of volume allowed on each square of the grid.

Fig. 6.7
Structure level growth. The
second level at which growth
may be organized is *structure*. The framework exhibits directionality in relation to the domainal boundary.

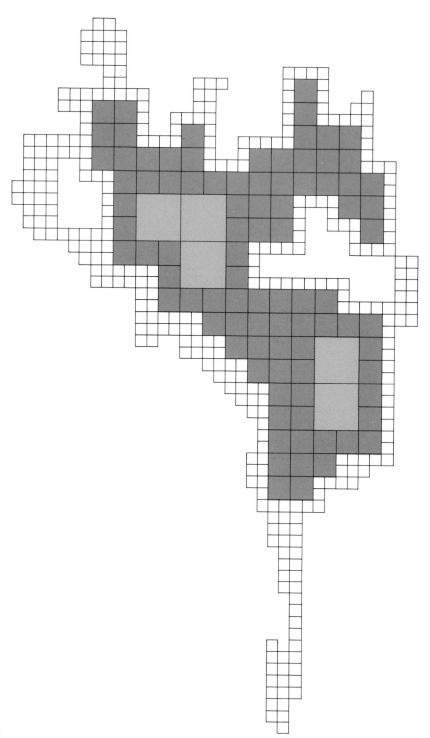

increments in a group, i. e., *One, Four, Sixteen,* and so on. In this study, group-ing occurs by doubling both edge dimen-sions beginning with 200', 400', 800', etc. The highest level of complexity in the study domain is *Sixteen* (fig. 6.9). The slope-orientation network does allow an *H/A* range that will tolerate *Sixteens* (fig. 5.42).

While the interactions within such a highly organized unit are complex when com-pared to the first example, the attitude taken about its limits is the same. Inter-actions within the increment may be or-ganized to take place in a predictable and systematic way relative to some purpose; but one increment, whether it is simple or complex, will still avoid shading an-other (fig. 6.6). If the sun is to be the energy source, then the condition to be met is that no increment may deprive an adjacent one of its resource. However, within an increment, parts may shade each other by design. They may interact to modify their individual energy recep-tion; but all parts must be considered to comprise a single purposeful arrangement, which must be totally considered as a function of energy utilization. (To reduce adverse interaction, the sub-structure of smaller planes has been removed from the near vicinity of the largest planes in the *Sixteen,* fig. 6.9).

From this viewpoint, the increasing com-plexity demonstrated by the planar ab-stractions of buildings suggest greater de-sign options in the range of building sizes, shapes, and modes of interaction. All are important factors in developing form-response capability to mitigate the effects of environmental perturbation. Equally important, all are factors in developing a richly diversified community.

The case-study demonstrated that sufficient capacity to achieve the three specifications (*S/V, H/A,* and E_W/E_S) accumulates as the level of complexity increases. Near the edge individually acting basic increments still do not allow building. As *Ones* are accumulated into groupings of four with proportionally higher levels of complexity and interaction, the larger planar references of the *Four* can be converted into buildings, leaving the smallest references still unbuilt. As *Fours* are gathered together to produce *Sixteens* with still higher levels of complexity and interaction, all planar references representing a range of three building sizes within the *Sixteen* can be built (fig. 6.7). The advantage gained by controlling complexity and size in this way is evidently not just in meeting the specifications but is also in the potential to build diversity into a growing community.

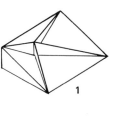

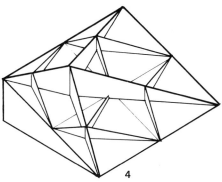

Fig. 6.8
Organizational levels (1 and 4). Basic increments can be systematically collected into groups of increments that allow potentially more complex and diverse building arrangements.

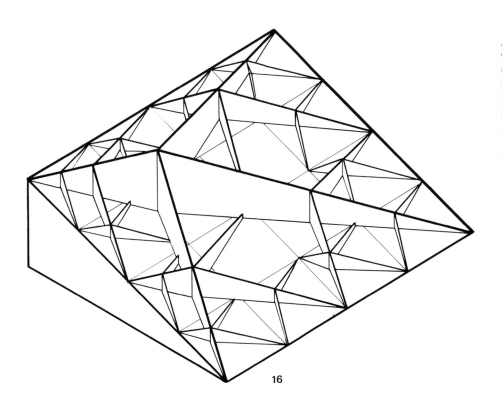

Fig. 6.9
Organizational level (16). Within a complex and diversified arrangement, parts may shade each other by design. To reduce adverse interactions, the substructure of smaller planes has been removed from the near vicinity of the largest planes.

Fig. 6.10
System level growth. The
third and highest level at
which growth may be organized is *system*. The framework at this level exhibits
orderliness, directionality,
and variety in the shapes
as well as sizes of the increments comprising it.

System

The third and highest level at which
growth may be organized can be demonstrated with an applied framework that
is completely differentiated (fig. 6.10).
Not only is the edge of the framework
different from the center, but large and
small squares in the previous grid have
been grouped into an array of distinguishable shapes. The intention at this
level of organization is to plan the sequence of growth as well as the complexity and size of its increments. Each of
the parts comprising the *system* framework can be viewed as a unique component of a constructed arrangement.

What could only be viewed in the *order*
framework as isolated building events,
and in the *structure* framework as events
organized with regard for a natural boundary, can now be viewed as events potentially integrated into the spatial and temporal development of a community.
Each of these parts of the *system* framework derives a potential community
function from associations just as the
domains of Owens Valley derived their
functions from associations within an
ecosystem.

Now, if each component of the framework
is considered to be a building site, the
possibilities for built diversity are potentially the highest yet. Not only can the
basic unit be clustered to generate higher
levels of organization as described at the
second planning level, but those clusters
can be interconnected in a variety of ways
to form other than square arrangements.

Each component of this last framework was viewed as potentially the most highly organized unit of development containing the maximum built volume in equilibrium with the physical environment. A vital strategy for such development was modeled on natural succession: control over the sequence of constructive events leading to a maximization of built volume and symbiotic function per unit of available energy flow.[1]

From this viewpoint, the successive interconnection of building references adds an important capability to mitigate the effects of seasonal insolation. Planar references, suggesting the limits and orientations of buildings, can be connected in directions which effect seasonal variation (fig. 6.11). When broad surfaces can be generated to face south, the effect is to equalize seasonal insolation as with the south-facing pueblos (chap. 2). If interconnection becomes a part of the successional process in which the direction of that interconnection and the direction of building growth is controlled, still more of the potentially buildable arrangement can be constructed (fig. 6.10). For example, because of interconnection, many *Fours* can be completely developed thus adding to the built diversity of the arrangement as a whole. This, of course, depends upon the maximum level of initial planning and the greatest differentiation of control and even then, the *Ones* near the end cannot be built; but otherwise, the overall result is an increase in the amount of building that can take place on the particular slope-orientation domain while meeting the three specifications set down as a basis for a decision to build.

1. E. P. Odum, "The Strategy of Eco-System Development," *Science,* 164 (1969), 262-270.

This study demonstrates that control of the sequence of development as well as size and complexity results in equilibrium for a greater and more diversified built volume. Implied in this is the increased possibility for choice. This choice is available for both the developer and the user. The developer benefits from an increased number of alternative ways in which he can put parts together if he is willing to accept an increased level of initial planning over what is built. The result is that, over time, the system increases its own capacity to maintain equilibrium by alternative means. This diversified ability to achieve equilibrium through a successionally constructive process relieves the necessity to depend exclusively upon the use of "manufactured" energy to maintain a steady state. A benefit is the reduced problem of peak loading.

Increased alternatives during the constructive process and reduced maintenance control over time have a parallel for the individual user. Increased initial control in the built arrangement is manifested as increased diversity, the enrichment of the built environment. The enrichment occurs at a building scale comprehensible to the individual. It lies within his ability to understand and to make decisions that depend upon perceived distinctions. Secondly, the anticipation of a successional process by controlling size, complexity, and sequence during the constructive process insures a higher degree of predictability. The unpredicted, and therefore painful, changes that now accompany the tendency of any unplanned arrangement to diversify for its proper function are avoided. At the same time, the environment is protected and the uncertainty involved in relying exclusively upon increasing rates of energy input to maintain an unplanned development is reduced.

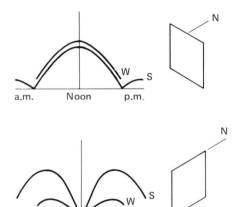

Fig. 6.11
Orientation. Seasonal insolation on a vertical plane with its broad faces north-south (*top*) tends to equalize. Broad faces east-west (*bottom*) receive much more insolation in summer than in winter.

Network Development and Optimization

Previous discussions of networks (based on stress and slope-orientation constructs) were aimed at developing a control tool for preserving natural domainal associations. At a scale below our interest or capacity to further structure the land as a function of recurring force action lies the intradomainal scale of community development. It is here that focus narrows to the associations that derive from interacting building forms. This is the point at which our interest in preserving natural associations gives way to developing constructed ones; and with this shift, a new use for the network emerges. The original use was aimed at maintaining existing, natural associations on the land. These will be maintained within the applied building-framework by holding to the ranges for S/V and H/A derived from the Owens Valley study; but a range suggests the possibility that some building increments may be near the upper limits, some near the lower, some may use up more of the range, some less, depending on their size, complexity, and interconnection; and conceivably some building groups may not be able to meet the specifications at all. Tolerances for each building group depend on location within the planning framework and this suggests a new use for the network: To develop associations within a framework where none existed and to transform small parts into larger, more diversified groupings which can be sustained in their associations at minimum energy cost. It is, in short, to distinguish between associations which can attain equilibrium through a growth process and those that cannot.

As was discussed earlier in this chapter, insolation is an important factor in maintaining equilibrium. This has been recognized by applying, without tolerances, an absolute specification that equalizes summer and winter insolation ($E_W/E_S = 1.0$); the network deals only with tolerances for S/V and H/A. Each increment of development must meet the absolute requirement for E_W/E_S within the tolerances for S/V and H/A determined by the planning network.

The essential ability of the network to determine such tolerances is based on a measure of diversity that distinguishes the parts of an arrangement. In the Owens Valley networks (chap. 5), diversity was a function of the different states of adjacent force domains. The purpose of the network was to preserve domainal identities, thus conserving the existing natural associations between domains that share common edges. In the growth networks now being discussed, diversity is a function of the number and variety of related parts comprising planned units. The purpose of the network is to develop new, artificial associations by transforming simple and independently acting units into larger and more complex constructed arrangements for which there can be a viable, developmental strategy other than the familiar one of repeating like units. Because the purposes of the valley and the growth networks are different, the method of calculating diversity is different. For this study, the diversity coefficient is calculated to be the product of the number of original increments combined (1, 4, 16) and the number of reference heights (1, 2, 3). The diversity coefficient for a *One* is $1 \times 1 = 1$; for a *Four* is $4 \times 2 = 8$; and for a *Sixteen* is $16 \times 3 = 48$. When interconnection is involved, the above coefficients are multiplied by the number of increments being interconnected. These calculations will be discussed for each organizational level of control.

Order Level Network: Maximum Optimization

The *order* level network contains the maximum number of points and the minimum diversity (fig. 6.12).

Beginning with a Diversity Coefficient of 1 on each point of the network (1 increment $\times$ 1 reference ht. = 1), then following the four steps previously outlined (table 5.1) produces a Control Vector of zero on each line.

Development carried on at this level of organization does not distinguish one part of the domain from another (fig. 6.4). Since control is relative, not absolute, there is no basis for differentiating the level of optimization required to maintain the separate identities of parts. It would be arbitrary to drop optimization of building specifications of any part below that of any other; they must all be optimized to 100 percent ($S/V = 11.6$; $H/A = 5.0$), and the control necessary to maintain the distinctions among parts over time would be maximum.

Growth would occur in such an arrangement by the simple process of multiplying like parts, i.e., by a constructive process that depends upon the mode of growth called expansion. If such a uniform arrangement were considered desirable, it could be maintained only by the exertion of maximum, perhaps repressive, control to prevent symbiotic tendencies from developing within the domain.

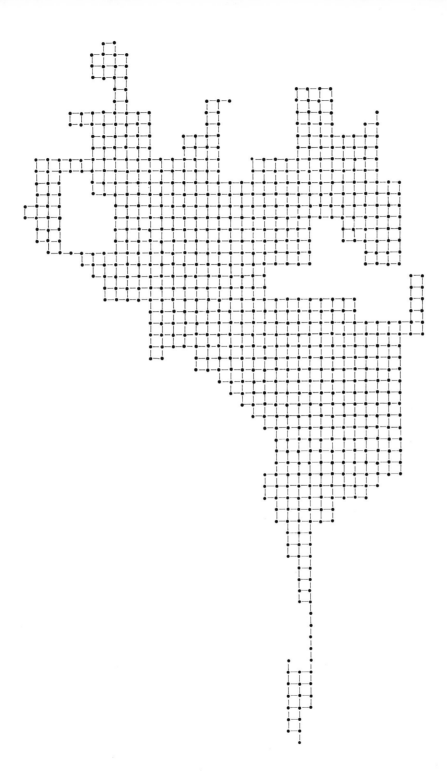

Fig. 6.12
The order level network contains the maximum number of points and the minimum diversity.

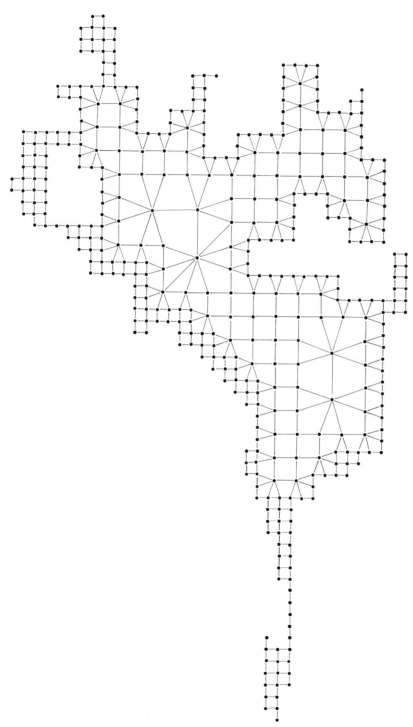

Fig. 6.13
The structure level network contains fewer points and greater diversity. It recognizes maturational tendencies characterized by accumulating diversity.

If such internal tendencies were restrained, symbiotic function would occur only between the domain as a whole and adjacent domains. Intradomainal associations would be minimized. All parts would tend to merge into an undifferentiated whole.

An example of such a growth mode can be seen in low-diversity suburbs and many slum clearance projects that are internally lacking in the diversity essential to a functionally complete or spiritually rich life; associations are with distant places. The transportation price is high to maintain those associations; but, in some cases, there is no other choice for the people involved.

Structure Level Network: Moderate Optimization

For many reasons, large developments of uniform building size and shape (which generally determine uniform function) are difficult to maintain in their original state. There are diversifying influences at work. As such developments get older, communities begin to emerge through a process that involves the gathering together of some land parcels to allow for larger buildings and the subdivision of other parcels to allow for an increasing variety of functions. This need for diversity in communities is recognized at the second level of organization where the regular grid from the first level is intentionally structured.

The resulting network describes fewer points and greater diversity (fig. 6.13). It recognizes maturation tendencies characterized by accumulating diversity. It also recognizes the edge by maintaining there the most appropriate land descriptor for this domain, that is, an increment 200 feet on a side and where $H/A = 5.0$. This increment is allowed to systematically merge by a process that doubles its edge dimension and quadruples its area as development occurs further from the edge (fig. 6.14). The transformation of small increments into larger ones would occur as follows using the number of original increments that are combined to identify the new increment: a *One* contains one original increment and measures 200 feet on a side ($H/A = 5.0$); a *Four* contains four original increments and measures 400 feet on a side ($H/A = 2.5$); a *Sixteen* contains sixteen original increments and measures 800 feet on a side ($H/A = 1.25$). This number progression (1, 4, 16) provides only half of the diversity coefficient. The other half is provided by the increasing variety of building height references as increments are merged (1, 2, 3, and so on).

Insofar as the action of the sun is concerned, an increased land area would allow an increased building height without influencing adjacent increments by shading. At the same time, the allowance of increments to merge transforms independently acting *Ones* into interacting *Fours*; *Fours* can be transformed into *Sixteens* with still higher levels of interaction. If building height references are allowed to accumulate in this transformation, the *Four* contains not only the original reference height derived from the H/A ratio that characterizes this particular domain ($H/A = 5.0$), but a second height reference related to the new area. The *Sixteen* picks up a third reference height.

This progression of reference heights (1, 2, 3) provides the second half of a diversity coefficient at the *structural* level. The two parts are then multiplied. Following the four steps previously outlined (table 5.1), beginning with a diversity coefficient that varies with the increment size, produces control vector values that will also vary. They will be generally low at the edge (where the diversity coefficients and adjacencies are low) and high toward the center. While a good many vectors still carry a control value of zero, there is a range that did not occur at the *order* level where all vector values were zero. As a result, some variance from 100 percent optimization is possible. The range of S/V and H/A can be broadened, especially toward the center of the domain where the volume of building as well as the variety of its components is potentially greater. Of course, the realization of all potential building is a function of control vector values. If construction were to take place at the *structure* level, tolerances for a broader range of S/V and H/A are increased as is the possibility for achieving $E_W/E_S = 1.0$. Whether the *Fours* and *Sixteens* shown in the plan (fig. 6.7) could actually be built depends upon how much variance the network will tolerate (fig. 6.13).

Fig. 6.14
(a) Three increments of interaction are shown. One, Four, and Sixteen represent three different organizational levels of development. Building height, area of interaction, and the complexity of the arrangement increase with the level of organization. (b) The ratio between maximum building height and the area of interaction resulting from that height (H/A) decreases at a decreasing rate as the level of organization increases.

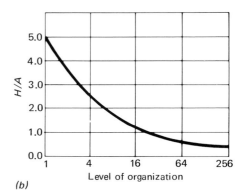

Sixteen	Four	One	
800'	400'	200'	Plan view
84'	42'	21'	H
640,000 sq. ft.	160,000 sq. ft.	40,000 sq. ft.	A
1.31×10^{-4}	2.63×10^{-4}	5.25×10^{-4}	H/A

(a)

(b)

Differentiated Control

The directional nature of the framework at this second level of planning suggests the necessity for differentiated control. Such control would have two components: One deals with initial and long-term control over the interaction between building form and natural force; the second deals with the stringency of state description required to maintain the associations among natural domains based on the interaction between land form and natural force. To satisfy both requirements, *the control system must be differentiated.*

Consider first the control question involving the interaction between built forms and natural forces. The biologist J. T. Bonner has pointed out the correlation between size and generation time in organisms and has drawn a parallel with man-made constructions. He states, "Since each generation is mainly a period of growth, a period of construction, it simply takes longer to build something large than something small, just as it takes longer to build a skycraper than a one-room shack."[2] The benefit derived from larger size (and potentially greater complexity) in construction is greater protective capacity against environmental stress. The cost is either a longer period for construction or greater initial control, or both. As longer periods of time are allowed for adjustment during construction, the initial control can be reduced. Since such extended time periods are not often allowed today, initial control over larger and more complex built arrangements is essential; but as equilibrium of greater amounts of volume is achieved, control

2. J. T. Bonner, "The Size of Life," *Natural History,* 78 (January 1969), 40-45.

can be relaxed. This situation would be reversed for small constructions. They have less capacity to achieve equilibrium because of their high surface-to-volume ratio, but there is an immediate control benefit. The *order* level framework is repetitive and, in this case, the small size and lower complexity require less initial control over construction; on the other hand, their inherent instability requires that control be maintained over time (hence the problem of peak loading in power supply). There are spatial as well as temporal implications involved in the interaction between buildings and the natural environment. Both can be outlined as follows:

Inside of Domain. Larger, more complex constructions have a greater ability to achieve equilibrium; require maximum initial control (or a long period of adaptive growth); as development progresses, control can be relaxed.

Edge of Domain. Smaller, simpler constructions have less ability to achieve equilibrium; require minimum initial control (or a short period of adaptive growth); because there is minimum interaction and development is fast, control cannot be reduced. (Control must not be reduced if the edge is to be respected.)

The second question raised by the intentional prestructuring of protective ability in the *structure* framework deals with the stringency of state description required to maintain the domainal associations that result from the interaction between land forms and natural forces. Any transformation of a domainal edge is bound to have some effect upon the internal state; but the edge of one domain is also the edge of an adjacent domain. The edge

is a transition between two states; it must "speak two languages." Its displacement or modification through man-made development therefore affects the identities of associated domains. If an edge is entirely ignored, the resulting loss of perceived diversity in the built environment might be important to those who will live in what is built.

Kevin Lynch has written about the correlation between the readability of edges and man's ability to act in his environment.[3] According to this view, the recognition of natural edges not only conserves the perceived associations of the land, it increases the likelihood that man can better understand and use what is built.

The technique described here for respecting the domainal edge, and therefore the associations among domains, involves an intentional restriction upon the relative abilities of edge and center to mature and to transform as development takes place. There are spatial as well as temporal implications involved in this restriction upon building that would respect the interaction between natural forces and the land. They can be outlined as follows:

Inside the Domain. Greater community-controlled transformation is allowed where the domainal state is pervasive and where there is less danger of losing natural distinctions at the edge; inside, where natural associations are not critical, constructed associations become maximized.

Edge of Domain. Less transformation is allowed where the edge is respected; where natural associations are critical the physical environment controls development and constructed associations are minimized.

3. Kevin Lynch, *The Image of the City* (Cambridge, Mass: MIT Press, 1960).

Growth in such an arrangement would
not occur by a simple process of multiplying like parts as at the *order* level. It
would occur through transformation as
well as expansion. The result would no
longer be uniform throughout. The natural tendency to mature is recognized.
The potential for community function is
structured into the arrangement by providing for a variety of building sizes and
complex interactions. The control of increment size and complexity produces
intradomainal associations that recognize,
in a directional way, the relationship between domainal edge and center.

System Level Network:
Minimum Optimization

The arrangement at the *structure* level is
easier to maintain than that at the *order*
level because it recognizes maturation
tendencies; but some zero vectors still
occur. The assumption in this study is
that such edges, if built, would probably
disappear with maturation. Based on that
assumption, all edges attended by a zero
value in the network are eliminated and
increments are allowed to merge. The result is the *system* level framework. It represents the highest level of planned organization. The network contains the
smallest number of points, the highest
diversity, and it graphs associations within the domain that most closely approximate a mature state for the framework
(fig. 6.15).

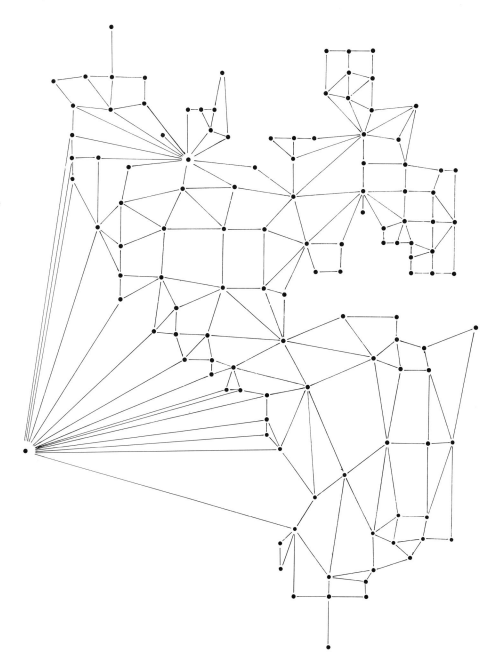

Fig. 6.15
The system level network
contains the smallest number of points, the highest
diversity, and no zero values on the vectors. It graphs
a distribution of information within the domain
that most closely approximates a mature state for
the framework.

Fig. 6.16
System level network
(sample section).

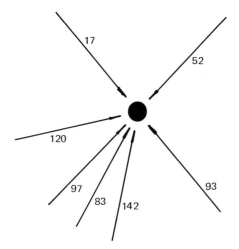

The diversity coefficient on points of the network is, as it was for the previous networks, a function of the number and variety of parts comprising a building increment of the domain. The coefficient for such a building increment is a product of the number of original squares comprising an increment of interaction (4), the number of reference heights (2), and the number of increments of interaction comprising the unit (7). The diversity coefficient for this particular successful unit (shaded in fig. 6.10) becomes $4 \times 2 \times 7 = 56$.

A diversity coefficient is determined for each point of the network followed by the steps previously outlined (table 5.1). The result is a larger range of control vector values for a smaller number of points than occurred in the previous two networks. These values are shown for the example (fig. 6.16).

The step to determine optimization from the vector value range necessarily differs from that used for the stress and slope-orientation networks. They were concerned with describing the associations that result from the interactions between land forms and natural forces. This network is intradomainal, concerned with describing building-scale associations that result from the interaction between built forms and natural forces.

The land-force networks contained control vectors individually related to an edge segment of the domainal boundary. Each vector carried instructions based upon an association between two states, each with its own S/V or H/A descriptor. The allowable range of each specification was derived from the relative value on the vector.

The building-force network is intradomainal and therefore intrastate. The specification ranges for the domain as a whole have already been established. The task now is to determine what portion of that land-related range can be handled by the varying capacities of planned increments within the domain and what will be their individual roles in satisfying the general state, while maintaining their own interdomainal association. Where the potential of a unit (to achieve $E_W/E_S = 1.0$) is high and the identity of the domain is not endangered, optimization of S/V and H/A may be lowered and the specification range can be broadened up to the limits for the domain as a whole; where the protective capacity of a unit is low and the character of the domain is susceptible, optimization must be kept high, up to the limit of 100 percent optimization for the natural domain.

The role of a building increment in maintaining the general state of a domain has been determined by describing its unique context in the domain, its condition with relation to the successional units surrounding it. This was taken to be its average condition and from it was developed an average vector value to describe it. In the case of the sample domain, there are eight vectors with a total value of 604. The average vector value representing the relative condition of the unit is $604/8 = 75.5$ which was then used to determine what portion of the S/V and H/A ranges for the domain could be used by that unit in fulfilling its role.

Following this departure from earlier techniques, a vector distribution was developed as was done for previous networks (table 6.1) and, as before, a logarithmic curve most closely matched that distribution (fig. 6.17). Vector values ranging

from 0 to 1,000 were then plotted log-
arithmically against a linear scale of percent optimization. An average vector
value of 75.5 for the sample unit produced a value of 23 percent for the required optimization (fig. 6.18). This optimization applies to both building specifications attending the domain. Converting it into a range for *S/V* and *H/A* requires a plot of the relationship between
associated values within the domain rather
than among domains as was done before.
The *S/V* values for a Stress 3 domain
that were to be shown in association were
11.6 (representing 100 percent optimization) and the two values 4.0 and 20.0
(representing the entire *S/V* range for the
domain). These associated values were
plotted against a linear scale of optimization (fig. 6.19). An optimization of
23 percent produces a range of *S/V* from
5.5 to 18.2 for the sample unit. Using
the same procedure produces an *H/A*
range from 1.2 to 5.4, a range that in-
cludes the *H/A* value of *Fours* that comprise the successional unit (fig. 6.20).
This completed the establishment of
building specifications that were aimed
at conserving two sets of associations: The
first, among domains, resulted from the
interaction between environmental forces
and land forms; the second, among building increments designed after a strategy
of sequential development, resulted from
the interaction between built forms and
environmental forces. The object of conserving land-force associations and generating building-force associations was the
same: to provide the diversity essential
to stable systems. The level at which development is organized for this purpose
determines how much freedom can be
taken with the size, complexity, and sequence of construction.

Table 6.1 Vector Distribution

Vector range	Vector quotient
0 - 10 = 41	41/10 = 4.1
10 - 100 = 131	131/90 = 1.5
100 - 1,000 = 61	61/900 = 0.061

Fig. 6.17
Vector distribution curve.

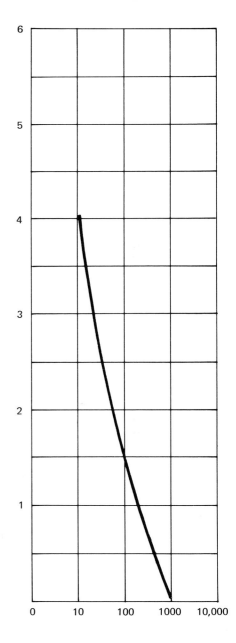

Beyond that, the level at which development is organized determines how many tools can be effectively used to achieve equilibrium with the environment. Nature evidently uses three: location, form, and metabolism. In the modern world of building, we tend to rely almost exclusively upon metabolism by providing sufficient energy for the vital processes to maintain equilibrium. But what about location and form?

The first framework recognized the importance of location. At the *order* level a regular grid determined only the size of a basic building increment. The size of the increment was based on topography and orientation of the slope with regard to insolation. Both conditions vary from one place to another, making grid size a function of location.

The second framework recognized the importance of form and changes of form over time. At the *structure* level, the size of building increments was differentiated thereby allowing the potential for greater levels of complexity in some areas of the framework. The basic increment was maintained on the periphery of the framework. Toward its center, basic increments were gathered into larger building sites where a number of buildings might be developed with a variety of sizes and relationships. In such a framework, the achieved level of complexity is a function of built form and transformations over time.

Finally, the third framework recognized the importance of metabolism as one of three related modes of response to environment. At the *system* level, building increments of different size and complexity were joined thereby allowing the potential for interconnecting built forms. The sequence of such interconnections is critical to the maintenance of equilibrium at every stage of development. If our objective is to reduce the energy required to maintain equilibrium, the sequence of development becomes a continuous and dynamic function of building metabolism.

What we have here in this final framework is control over the critical adaptive mechanisms; size of building as a function of location, complexity as a function of form, and sequence as a function of metabolism. We achieve a built extension of all three natural adaptive mechanisms—location, form, and metabolism—by specifying size, complexity, and sequence of constructive events for the purpose of energy conservation.

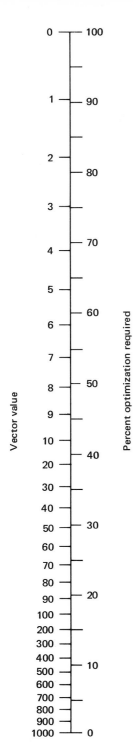

Fig. 6.18
Vector value versus percent optimization.

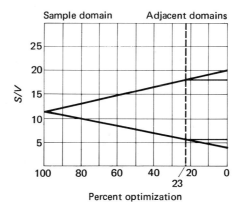

Fig. 6.19
Allowable *S/V* range (5.5-18.2).

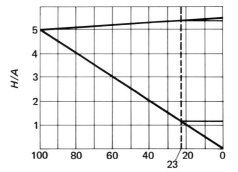

Fig. 6.20
Allowable *H/A* range (1.2-5.4).

7
The Shape and Structure of Buildings

Within the constraints of the frameworks developed in the last chapter, individual buildings can be shaped and structured to reduce the effects of environmental variation. Over the past nine years, the study of form as a building response has been in process at the University of Southern California's Department of Architecture. The work has focused on the control of daily and seasonal insolation, which has been achieved by generating forms with relation to daily and seasonal movements of the sun. To show how this can be done in the context of a large-scale planning reference, previously developed constraints will be simultaneously applied in a case study of development (chap. 8). First, however, some of the techniques of form generation will be described in this chapter.

The pueblos of the Southwest provided some principles of interacting building form. These principles, if applied at a faster rate with today's technological ability to buildings of larger scale, ought to provide the means for relieving some of the pressing energy problems.

The basis for equilibrium in the pueblos was the mitigation of daily and seasonal variation. This was partially accomplished by the overall shape of the buildings and partly by the structure, i.e., the selection and use of materials to enclose space.

Shape

One technique for developing responses to insolation is to generate shapes by using the rays of the sun as a generator. A line, representing the sun's rays, can be moved in space as the sun rises and sets. The moving line generates a surface. Since the sun takes a different path from one season to another, the surfaces generated by its daily sweep will not be the same. Their insolation characteristics will vary. Some of the surfaces generated in this way have desirable insolation properties, and they can be used to enclose single buildings or to define the limits of frameworks to accommodate development over time. This is basically what is involved in shaping. But to gain specific control over daily and seasonal insolation (the energy profile of a shape) requires more particular control over the generation process. While there are many techniques for shaping, they all use variations on a three-part procedure, and only one technique based on this procedure will be discussed here. For this we will use the case of a 15° east slope for which a pyramidal volume has already been developed as the basic building increment in a planning framework (fig. 7.1).

Orientation

The first part of the procedure pertains to orientation or changes in orientation in the plan view of a generated surface.

Orientation is a function of the particular season chosen for the generation of a surface by casting shadows from the vertex of an imaginary pyramid to the sloping surface of the ground (fig. 7.2). Such generated surfaces vary with slope and orientation but they provide a planar reference to which volume can be added.

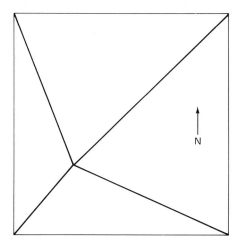

Fig. 7.1
Intersecting lines within the square indicate the vertex of a hypothetical pyramidal volume that can be built on the site, and the location of the highest shadow-casting reference.

Fig. 7.2
Orientation. Three different
seasons are chosen to cast
shadows from the vertex of
an imaginary pyramid to
the sloping surface of the
ground. Each surface gen-
erated in this way is differently oriented in the plan
view as a function of the
particular season chosen.

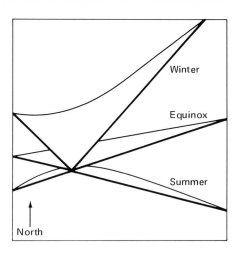

Winter

Equinox

Summer

North

At this point in the procedure the surface has no volume but receives energy
and can be evaluated as a function of the
degree to which it mitigates seasonal
variations in the energy profile. Such differences occur with slope, orientation,
and the season at which the surface is
generated.

A surface that is generated during the
winter solstice is more horizontal and receives much more incident energy in the
summer than it does in the winter. This
difference tends to diminish on more vertical surfaces generated at seasons closer
to the summer solstice (fig. 7.3). This
fact was recognized especially in the forms
of Acoma and Bonito. (For reference,
E_W/E_S = 0.33 for a cube oriented on the
cardinal points; fig. 7.4.)

Winter incident energy tends to be less
on all surfaces generated in this way on
north, east, and west slopes but more on
south slopes. The effect of slope and
orientation is reduced as the steepness of
the slope reduces, and on a horizontal
site, a surface generated during the summer solstice has a seasonal energy ratio,
E_W/E_S = 1.0. This ratio was used in Chapter 6 as a case-study standard for seasonal
insolation on a building increment.

Faceting
The energy ratio can also be systematically controlled by varying the precision
with which the original surface is defined.
This second part in the procedure is a
function of the number of facets used in
the definition.

Starting with a smooth, curved surface,
E_W/E_S increases as faceting decreases
(fig. 7.5). In the case of a single-facet
approximation of a surface generated
with the summer solstice rays, the ratio
shifts beyond the standard 1.0. This larger
winter insolation occurs generally on all
slopes but again tends to be less on north,
east, and west slopes, and more on south
slopes. In addition, the effect of the varying degrees of refinement of faceting is
less consequential for the surfaces generated at the winter solstice than at the
summer solstice (fig. 7.6).

Altitude
The third part of the procedure to modify
seasonal insolation involves the altitude
angle of surfaces and is a function of adding volume to the original reference
plane. In the process of adding volume,
a change in the altitude angle of the containing surface is the primary factor in
modifying the seasonal energy ratios, but
in addition, a useful correlation with S/V
can be made that allows the generation
of form to occur within the planning context of earlier discussions (see chap. 6).
In this last of the three steps, there is an
evident advantage in beginning from an
original reference plan with an initially
high E_W/E_S (fig. 7.7). Increasing volume
always decreases the ratio. Increasing volume to the north of the original reference lowers the ratio more than increasing
volume to the south, proving again the
advantage the pueblos gained by terracing
or adding volume to the south of a vertical plane or reference (fig. 7.8). Also,
the larger insolation ratio on the original
reference plane allows a greater range of
S/V, which is a significant advantage in
meeting site specifications.

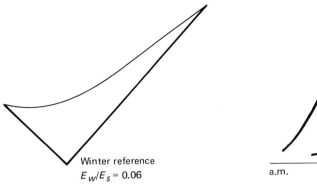

Winter reference
$E_W/E_S = 0.06$

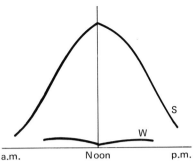

a.m.   Noon   p.m.

S
W

Fig. 7.3
A surface that is generated during the winter solstice has a much higher incident energy gain in the summer than it does in the winter $(E_W/E_S = 1/17.8 = 0.06)$; while as surfaces are generated at seasons closer to summer solstice $(E_W/E_S = 1/1.2 = 0.83)$, this difference tends to be reduced in favor of winter.

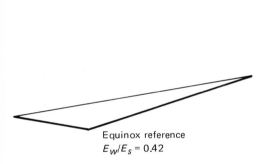

Equinox reference
$E_W/E_S = 0.42$

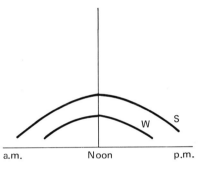

a.m.   Noon   p.m.

S
W

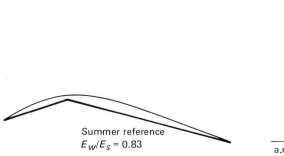

Summer reference
$E_W/E_S = 0.83$

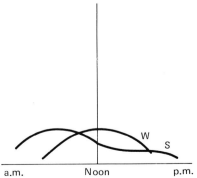

a.m.   Noon   p.m.

W
S

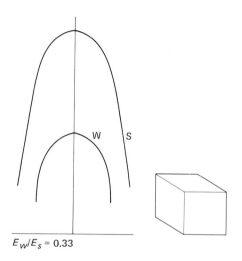

E_W/E_S = 0.33

Structure

By definition, form is a function of the regularities imposed by structure as well as a geometric or spatial function of shape. For example, pure shapes can be generated in relation to the geometry of earth and sun without reference to structure; that is, without reference to the ordering principles of construction or the scale implications of use. The mode of construction and the additional requirements of community activity both determine the size relation between a pure shape and the increments of its functional development.

Limits of Incrementation

Two related aspects of the structure of shapes result from the scalar effects of their incremental development: the definition of limits (the boundary of a shape), and the partitioning of space (the organization of its volume).

Consider a two-dimensional example in which a circle is generated out of squares that total the same area. Starting with a single square, systematic subdivisions will finally produce a square unit that can approximate the curving limits of the circle (fig. 7.9).

A three-dimensional example of the significance of increment size in defining a shape can be demonstrated with an oblate spheroid. When tilted to the south, at the altitude of the equinox sun at noon, this shape casts a shadow of nearly equal area upon a plane normal to the sun's rays, both summer and winter solstice. (This does not imply an equalization of seasonal energies because, in this demonstration, atmospheric effects are not considered.)

If hypothetical problems of construction require that the volume of the oblate spheriod be built of cubes and the smallest available cube happens to contain the needed volume the result is hardly recognizable as an oblate spheroid. But as the generating increment is systematically reduced in size and increased in number to maintain the required volume, an approximation of the pure shape is approached (fig. 7.10). A plot of volumetric subdivisions against the behavior of the form shows that beyond a certain level of incrementation there is no further advantage in using a smaller unit to define shape limits. This simple demonstration makes clear the scale relation between surface increment and overall shape. If the increments are thought of as useful building spaces, the implication is that the overall shape must be relatively large to gain the necessary shaping freedom.

Building domains. The structural definition of the boundary of a form has an aspect other than that of approximating the behavior of a pure shape. This is the aspect of surface variation which may be seen clearly when forms are simple. This was demonstrated in 1962-63, when architecture students at Auburn University, Alabama, working under the author's direction, varied the surface treatment on relatively conventional building shapes in response to insolation. The problem involved the use of a structural system comprised of planes that varied in their size and configuration. In general, the system varied from top to bottom of the building in response to increasing floor loads and from one orientation to another in response to insolation (figs. 7.11, 7.12). (There was a further user requirement in the program. The building was to house public spaces on its top and ground floors and private, office spaces in between.)

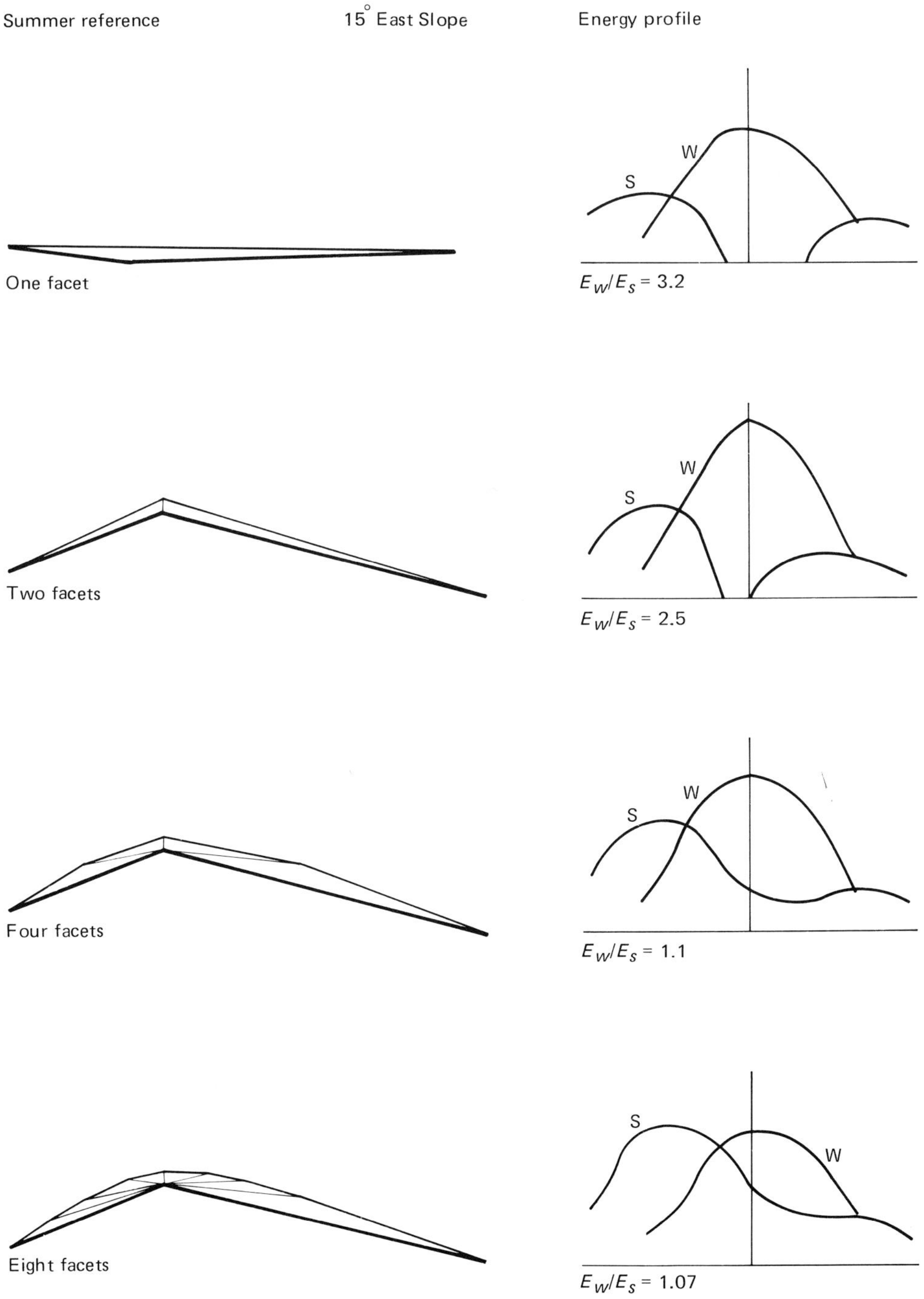
Summer reference
15° East Slope
Energy profile
One facet
W
S
E_W/E_S = 3.2
Two facets
W
S
E_W/E_S = 2.5
Four facets
W
S
E_W/E_S = 1.1
Eight facets
S
W
E_W/E_S = 1.07

Fig. 7.5
Faceting. The energy ratio (E_W/E_S) changes in favor of larger winter energy gains as faceting decreases.

Fig. 7.6
The effect of varying degrees of refinement of faceting is less consequential for the surfaces generated at the winter solstice than during the summer solstice; one facet (dotted line), two facets (solid line), four facets (dashed line).

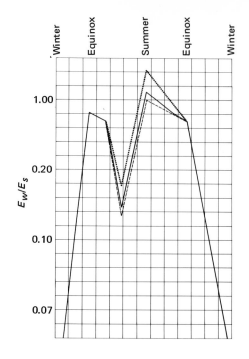

Fig. 7.7
There is an obvious advantage in beginning from a reference plane with an initially high E_W/E_S. If the final objective is to produce an $E_W/E_S = 1.0$, beginning with a reference plane that has an initial energy ratio of 1.0 does not allow for the addition of volume since that added volume always increases summer insolation at a greater rate than winter. The curves demonstrate variations of S/V and E_W/E_S, which result from the addition of volume to basic references of one, two, and eight facets.

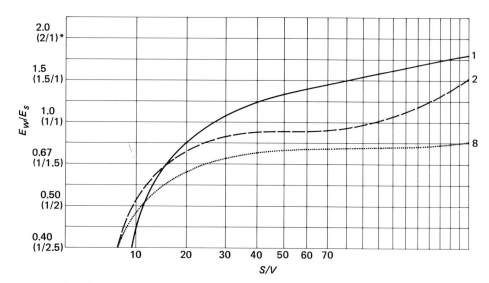

*In all graphs that follow, the ratio E_W/E_S will be shown as a single number.

The results of the program were unlike those of a conventional office building, which exhibits a uniform surface treatment. In order to relieve some of the energy requirements involved in machine responses to insolation, the different sets of conditions resulting from orientation were handled by varying the surface structure of the building (fig. 7.13, 7.14). This study demonstrated that different orientations of building surfaces produce distinguishable sets of environmental conditions, just as the later study of Owens Valley's varied topography produced different conditions of recurring force effect (fig. 7.15). On the building as well as in the valley, sets of conditions could be defined as force domains and could be responded to with an array of adaptive responses. Later, at the University of Southern California, generated shapes became more complex, requiring a further development of the notion of force domains on built forms. During these studies different techniques of generation were used to produce a variety of forms with predictable characteristics of insolation (figs. 7.16-7.26). Today's technology allows larger scale construction and greater shaping freedom (cantilevered surfaces for example) not available to the pueblo builders. With these advantages we should be able to extend the use of form as an adaptive mechanism.

The procedure illustrated in fig. 7.16 is used to produce an insolation ratio $E_W/E_S = 1.0$, as follows.

Three source points are chosen:
O_S = ½ dia. on summer hemisphere 1;
O_W = ½ dia. on winter hemisphere;
$O_{S'}$ = ½ dia. on summer hemisphere 2.

Curves traced: S_1, W, S_2 (in that order).

Procedure: The first summer sun-cone is inscribed in summer hemisphere 1. The end of the generator tracks from point A at dawn to a point O_W at sunset. O_W becomes the winter source point. Due to the nature of the earth-sun geometry construct, the first summer sunset generator $O_S O_W$ is parallel to the winter dawn generator. Because they share point O_W, they are colinear.

(Text continues on p.155.)

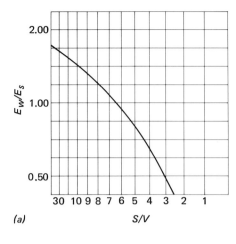

(a)

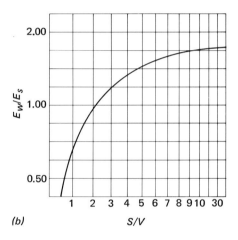

(b)

Fig. 7.8
S/V decreases as volume is added to the north or south of the original reference. But increasing volume to the north (a) is less advantageous for E_W/E_S than increasing it to the south (b).

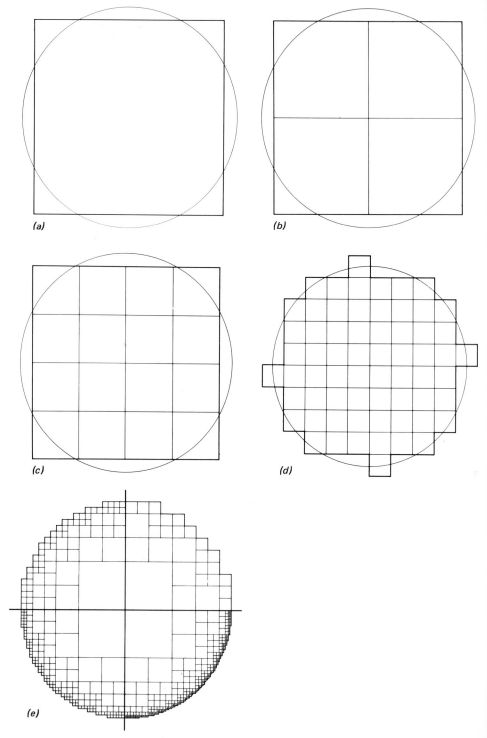

Fig. 7.9
The limits of a circle are progressively refined by decreasing the size of a descriptive increment. Since the information circle is carried at the periphery or limits, the increment requires a greater degree of refinement at the edge than toward the center. (The total area of squares is equal to the area of the circle.)

(a)

(b)

(c)

(d)

(e)

Fig. 7.10
(a) An oblate spheroid made of cubes. As the cube size decreases and the number increases to maintain a constant volume, an approximation of the pure shape is approached. (The total volume of the cubes is equal to the volume of the oblate-spheroid.) *(b)* A plot of volumetric subdivisions (incrementation) against the behavior of the form (optimization) shows that the curve of optimization stabilizes and no further incrementation is needed.

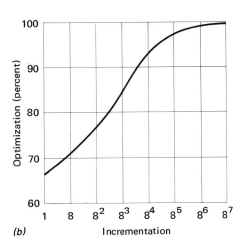

(b)

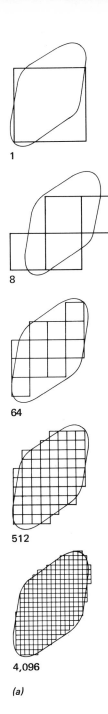

1

8

64

512

4,096

(a)

Fig. 7.11
A graph of gravitational forces acting upon the mass of the cube indicates a vertical differentiation of force effect without the differences from side to side characteristic of the sun responses. (Light, gravity and building studies of the cube were made at Auburn University in 1962 by C. Boutwell, W. Brown, R. Freeman, G. Oldham, J. Smith, and C. Snook.)

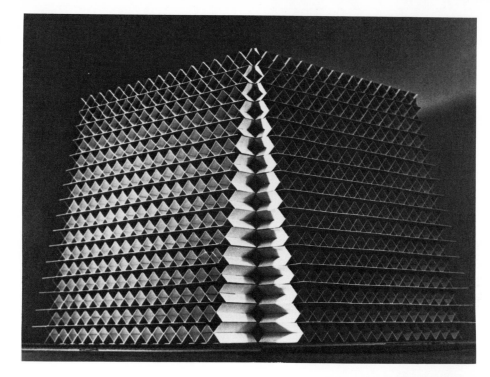

Fig. 7.12
A detail of the sun response at the upper southwest corner of the cube shows that while the basic spacing of the planes is orderly, i.e., regular and undifferentiated, the planes themselves exhibit different depths from the surface of the cube and different shapes from one orientation to another.

Fig. 7.13
The southeast corner of an office building based on the cube. The structure of the building is comprised of planes that control sunlight. The planes change vertically in response to gravity and from one orientation to another in response to sun.

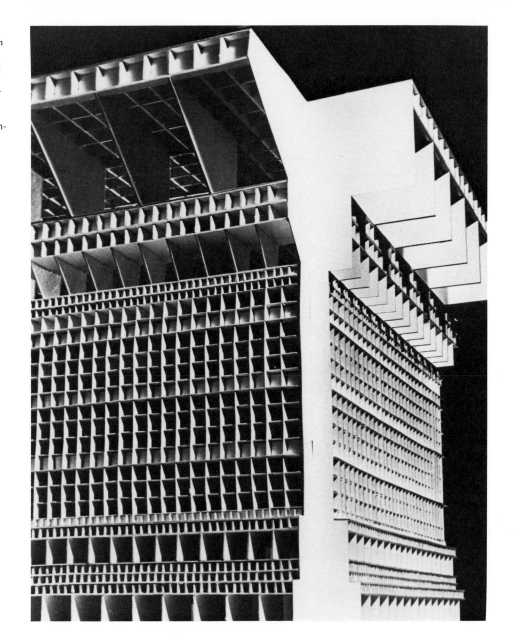

Fig. 7.14
Southeast corner of an office building based on the tetrahedron; the upturned surface faces south. (Studies of the tetrahedron were made at Auburn University in 1962 by R. Biggers, J. Coykendall, D. Egger, B. Hagler, J. Regan and W. Savage.)

Fig. 7.15
Insolation varies with orientation and season. Two curves are shown on each graph. The inner curve is corrected for atmosphere at sea level.

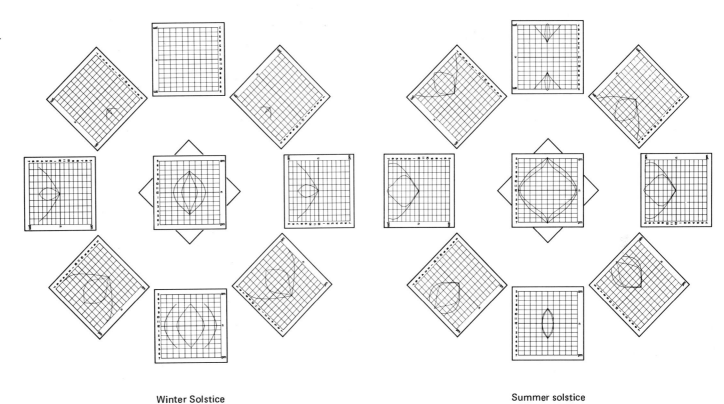

Winter Solstice   Summer solstice

Fig. 7.16
Diagram illustrating the
generation of a form of
predictable insolation characteristics. The form generated here has an insolation
ratio $E_W/E_S = 1$ (see text).

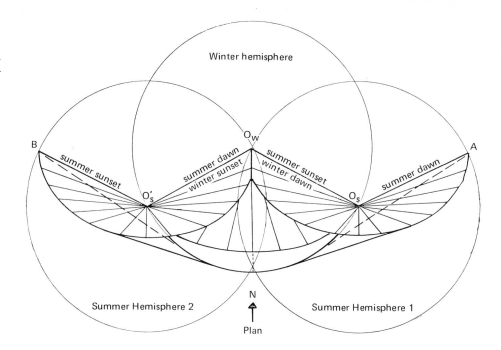

Fig. 7.17
Base plan.

Fig. 7.18
Aerial view from east
showing linear generators.

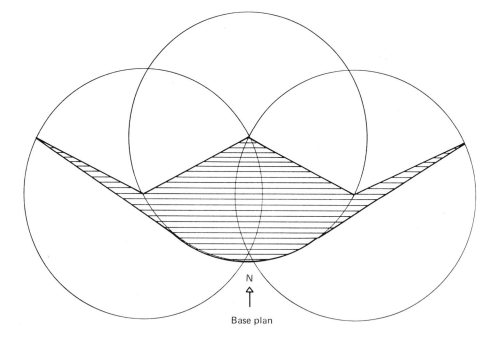

Fig. 7.19
Aerial view of pure shape from east.

Fig. 7.20
View from southwest of incremented model.

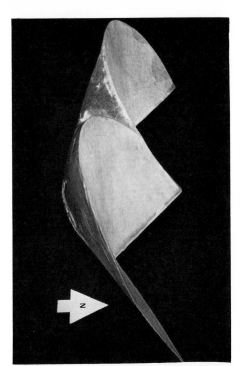

Fig. 7.21
Top view of incremented model.

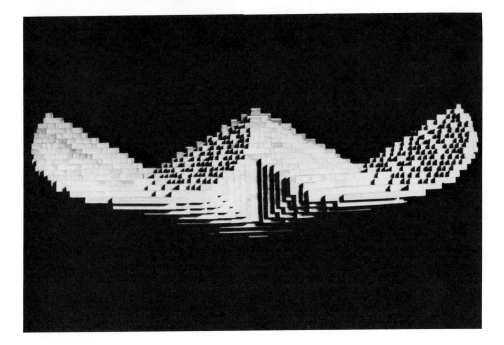

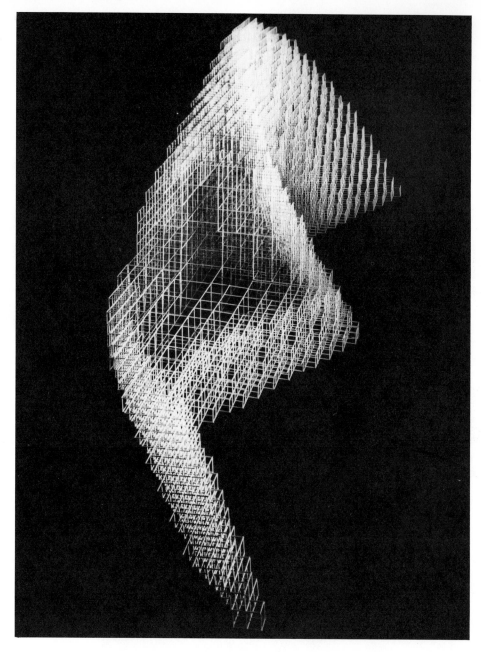

Fig. 7.22
View from east of cutaway
structured, large-scale model.

Fig. 7.23
View from the southwest of structured, large-scale model.

Fig. 7.24
View from west.

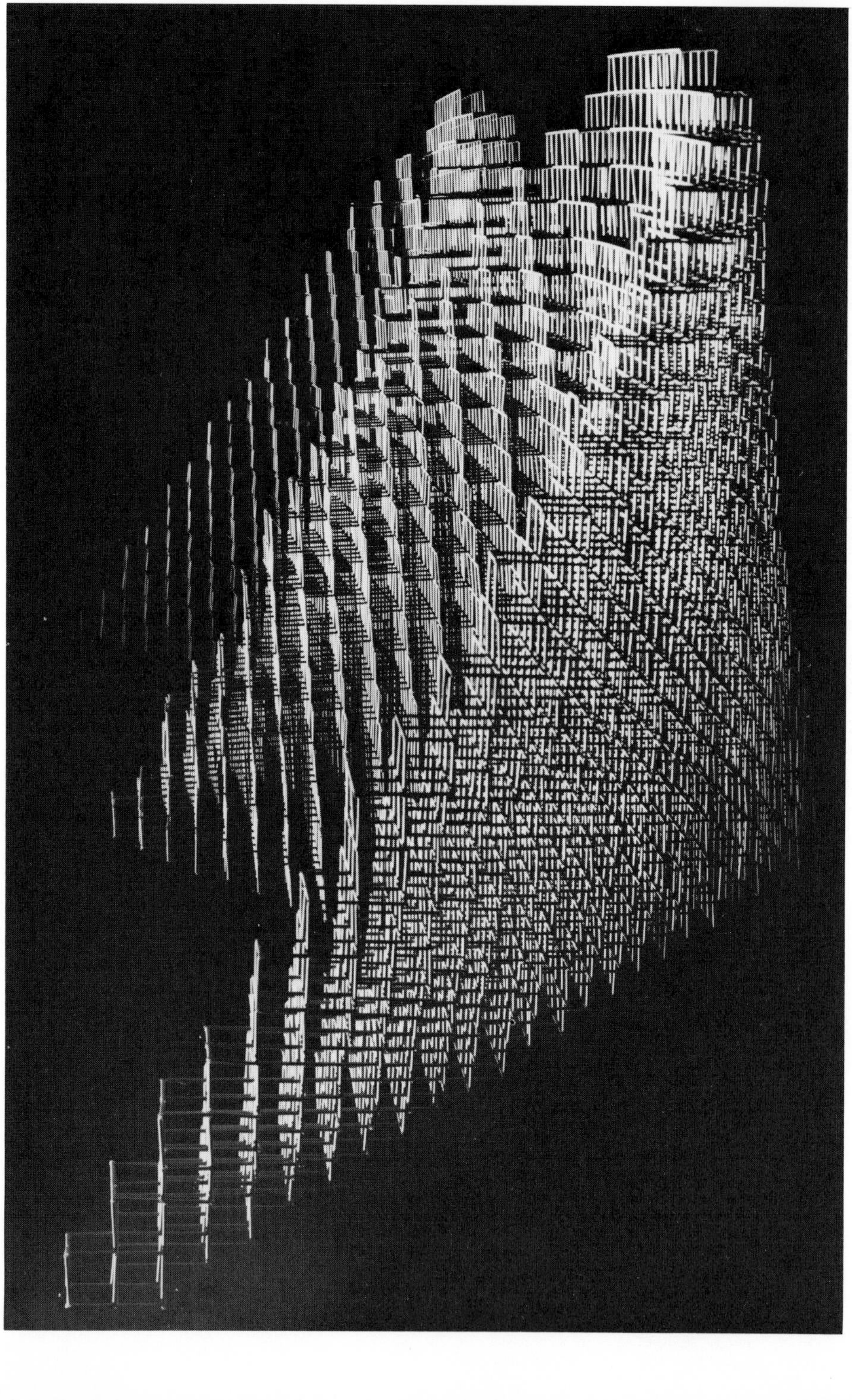

Fig. 7.25
Aerial view from southwest.

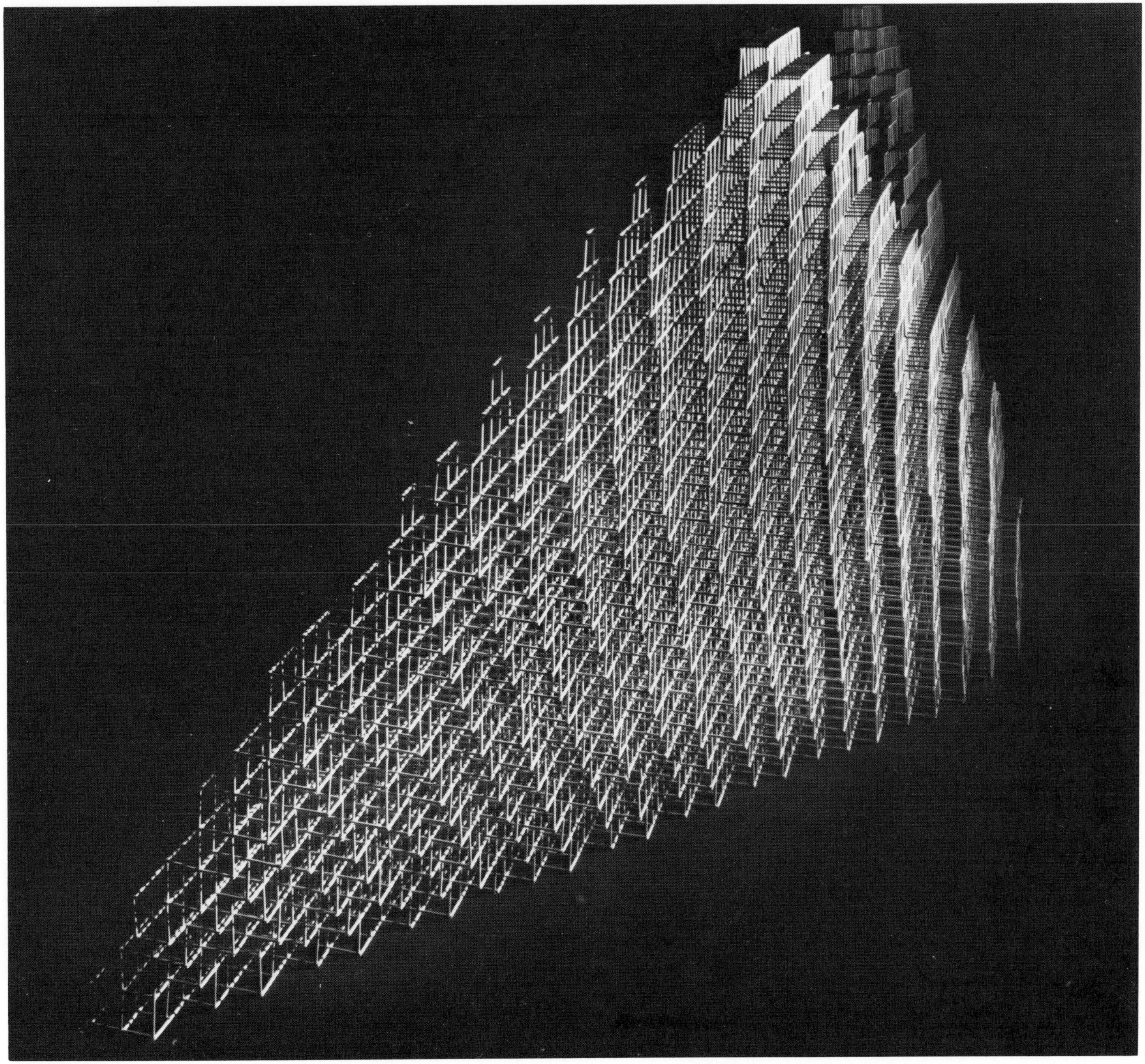

Fig. 7.26
View from southwest.

The winter sun-cone is generated from point O_S at dawn to a point O_S' at sunset. O_S' becomes the second summer source point. Note again the colinearity of the winter sunset generator and the second summer dawn generator.

The second summer sun-cone is inscribed in summer hemisphere 2. The end of the generator tracks from point O_W at dawn to a point B at sunset. This completes one generation cycle.

Clearly the method could be continued ad infinitum, taking point B as a second winter source point, and so on. Further studies are required. Of particular interest would be the obverse form of this one, i. e., a W-S-W sequence instead of the S-W-S sequence.

In this method, simple sun-cones are generated. Normally, volume would only result where the cones intersect at the center of the form, but an added set of tangents to the cones produces a physical form having volume at all points.

All forms generated in these studies have exhibited a differentiation of their surfaces as a result of the application of a descriptive increment. This differentiation naturally occurs even when the space-filling increment is maintained constant in size as it was for all the exercises. The result is a useful three-dimensional contouring that supplies both a visual description of the form and a variety of spatial conditions. (Method of generation developed by G. Togawa at the University of Southern California, 1967. Models built by P. Ohannesian, G. Shigamura, and J. Talski.)

Up to now in the studies at USC, principal concern has been for the control of insolation by learning the techniques of shaping an overall building framework. But there are structuring possibilities that involve the use of materials and methods of construction yet to be explored within the context of generated forms. It is possible to imagine, for example, that such forms might be made of earth (the original site or a modification with today's large earth-moving equipment) or buildings or any combination of the two. In any case, the overall forms could have desirable insolation properties, and areas on the forms could have predictable attributes, with one area having a predictable relationship to another. Such areas may be thought of as force domains subject to the same sort of analysis for development as Owens Valley.

In studies of incremented forms, force domains are manifested by a differentiation of the surface geometry (figs. 7.27-7.33). This differentiation naturally occurs even when the space-filling increment remains constant in size. The result is a useful three-dimensional description of a building framework. If the framework were actually developed, the addition of other criteria would probably result in variations of increment size and configuration, providing that such variations took place without modifying the overall shape to the point of changing its insolation ratio.

In the studies described here, such a change was evaluated in terms of insolation on single, isolated forms. In the context of Owens Valley, however, groups of forms were used to satisfy several criteria, and the scale relation between shape and structure, as well as absolute size, determines our ability to simultaneously meet those criteria.

Since the topography of the valley is not the same from place to place and is a strong determinant of building size, incremental development of the building may present a problem of scale on some sites. When site conditions require a small building, the size of the unit used to generate space may hinder shaping freedom. For example, assume a minimum dimension for a cubical, spatial increment to be 12.5 feet (a convenient dimension derived from successive subdivisions of the smallest square unit used to describe the topography of Owens Valley, fig. 7.34). The height of a building determines how close this increment can approximate the slope of a surface with good insolation properties (fig. 7.35). If the building is not only higher but also deeper, thus decreasing S/V, incremented forms can more easily approximate the insolation properties of pure shapes. Conversely, a high S/V can be correlated with small size and therefore with an inability to match the behavior of a pure shape with an incremented form (fig. 7.36).

The application of a fixed increment size to different building heights demonstrates the scale phenomenon that distinguishes large from small forms (fig. 7.37). The 12.5 foot minimum increment is too large to approximate the pure shape on the lowest reference (*One;* derived in chap. 6) nor can such forms meet the criteria set. On the other hand, the increment is sufficiently small to produce a very close approximation of the highest reference (*Sixteen*) and its ability to meet the specifications is correspondingly high.

(Text continues on p.163.)

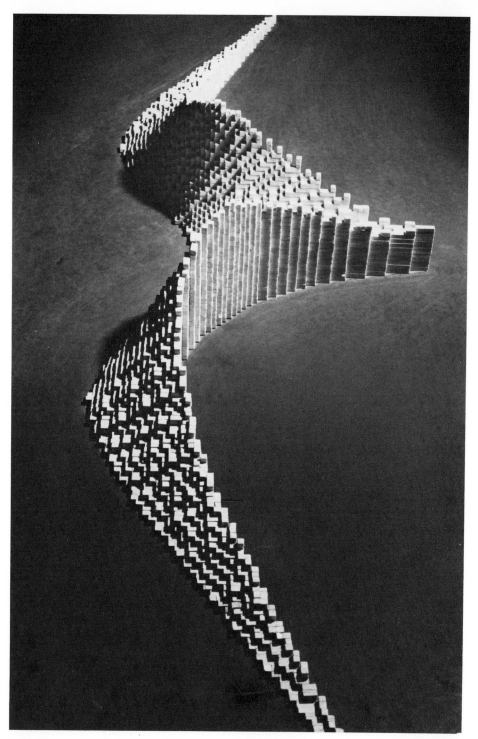

Fig. 7.27
Aerial view from the west.
(Figs. 7.27-7.29 are of models
generated and built by M.
Klingerman, D. Moser, and
R. Selvidge.)

Fig. 7.28
Aerial view from the north.

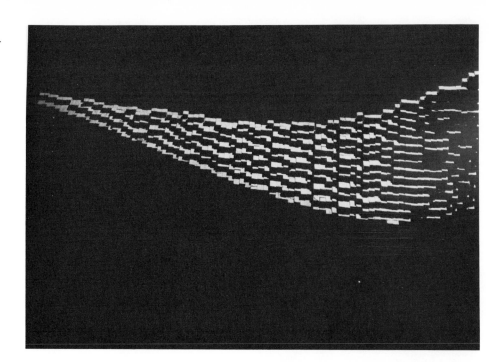

Fig. 7.29
Aerial view from the north.

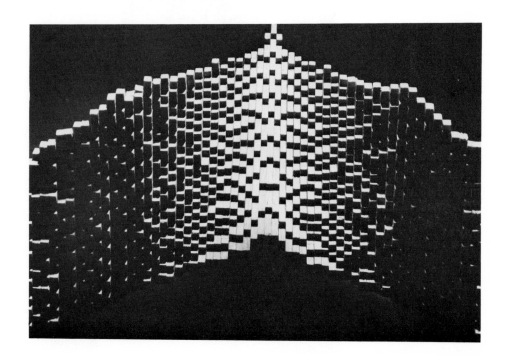

Fig. 7.30
Top view from the north.
(figs. 7.30-7.32 are of models
generated and built by G.
Freedman, S. Panja, and R.
Yanagawa.)

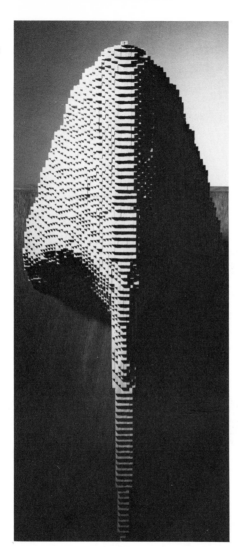

Fig. 7.31
View from the northwest.

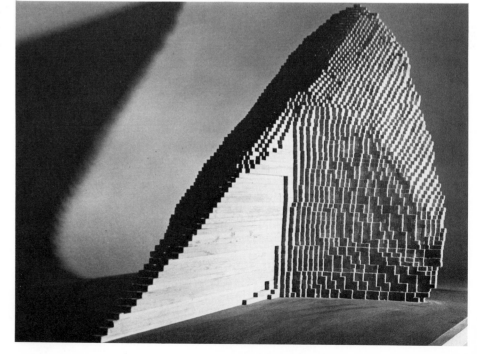

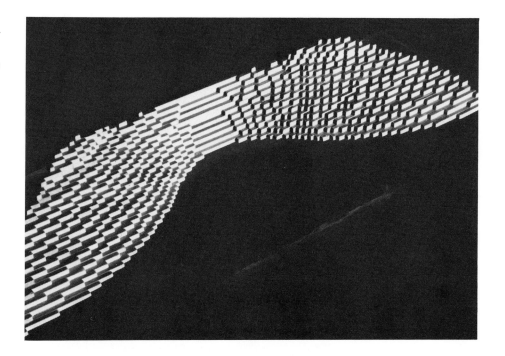

Fig. 7.34
Geometric subdivision of a
land increment (100′ X 100′)
brought a useful minimum
dimension of 12.5 feet for
containing and generating
space.

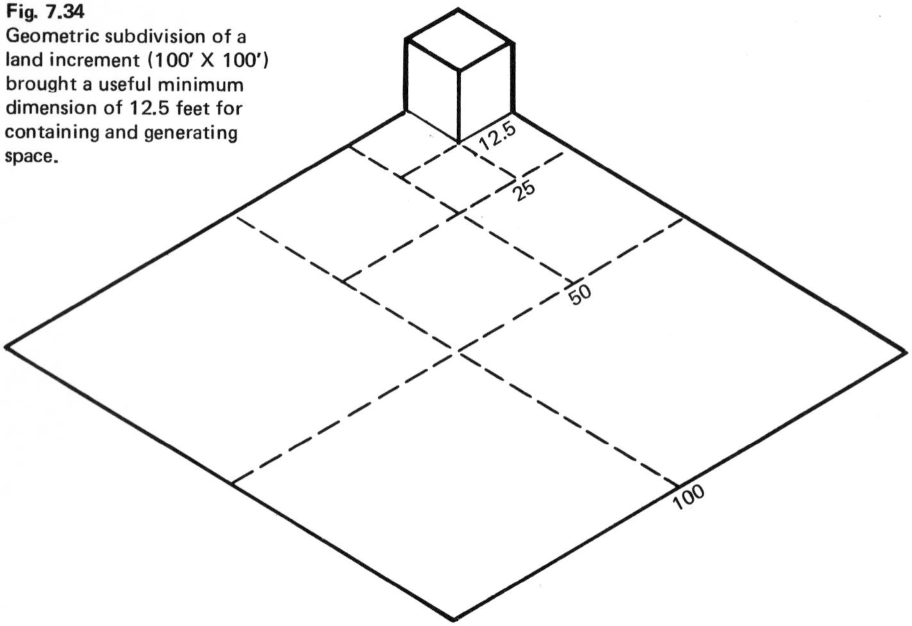

12.5
25
50
100

Fig. 7.35
When an attempt is made
to approximate the original
reference plane, a *Sixteen*
(organizational level) will
come closer than a *One*.
This is due to the increased
allowable height and shaping freedom.

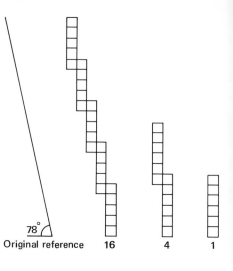

78°
Original reference   16   4   1

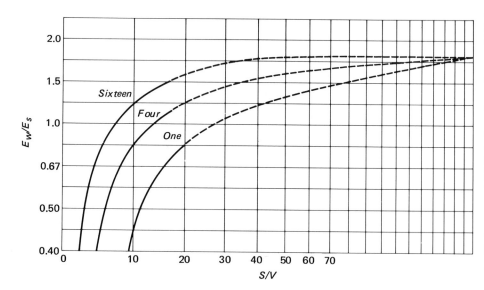

Fig. 7.36
Incremented forms can be
found that act analogously
(up to a certain *S/V* limit)
for all height references
shown representing three
different levels of organization. The curves demon-
strate pure forms as they
vary in surface-to-volume
ratio and insolation. The
solid line represents the extent of incremented forms
that duplicate pure form
response. Incremented
forms can be found to a-
chieve a seasonal insolation
ratio (E_w/E_s) greater than
1.0 at the *Four* and *Sixteen*
levels of organization. The
Sixteen represents potentially the highest reference
and the largest diversity of
forms.

Fig. 7.37
The application of a fixed increment size demonstrates the scale phenomenon that distinguishes large from small forms.

One

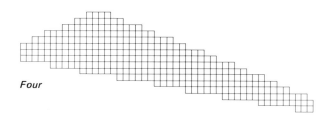

Four

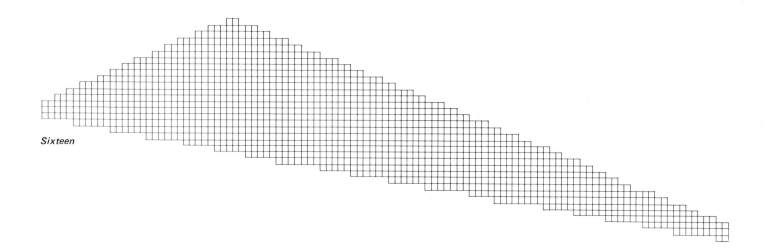

Sixteen

Fig. 7.38
(a) It is useful to consider what might happen had the networks shown that the domain was more critical because of a low contact diversity with adjacent domains and that its *S/V* range was necessarily smaller, perhaps 10 to 13 instead of 5 to 18. In such a case, the only reference that could have matched the narrow *S/V* range and still attained an energy ratio of 1.0 (or more) would have been the *Sixteen*. (b) Another possibility to consider is a shift in the stress range up or down the scale requiring a different *S/V* response. If the domain were not very critical (because of high contact diversity with adjacent domains), the range of *S/V* would have remained broad but would have shifted down (to the left on the graph) if the stress were greater and up (to the right on the graph) if the stress were lower. If the shift had been downward on the *S/V* scale to accommodate a higher stress coefficient range of 6 to 9, the result would have been no solution since even the *Sixteen* would not produce a low enough *S/V* ratio to match the high stress condition. On the other hand, a smaller stress coefficient (2) would still find acceptable solutions at the *Four* and *Sixteen*. (There is a theoretical but not practical solution at the *One* because of the method of incrementally reproducing shapes.)

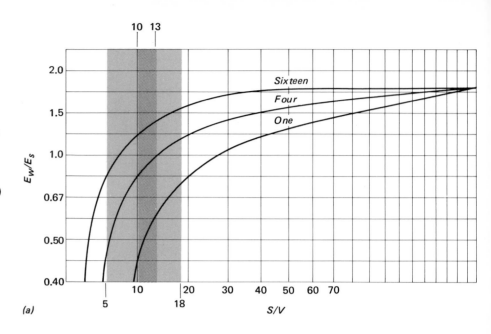

(a)

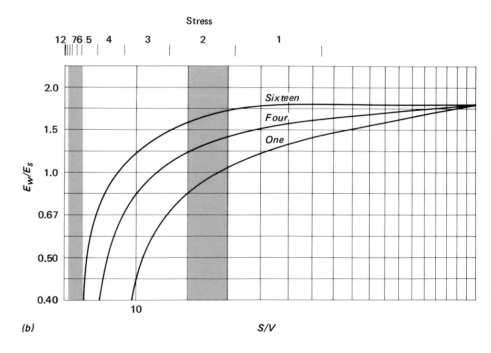

(b)

In between lies the mid-height reference (*Four*) which is barely defined by the 12.5 foot increment and, insofar as its capacity to meet the criteria, it lies on the borderline. In this height range, the procedure of incrementally building up a form of 12.5-foot increments sets an upper limit on the S/V ratio while still meeting the required energy ratio (fig. 7.38). Increasing S/V in this manner does not, however, indefinitely continue the significant increase of E_W/E_S and, beyond a certain point, reducing a building's depth in relation to height obviously minimizes its usefulness.

The incrementation or structuring procedures used in this study are quite limited. All solutions involve a face-to-face connection of space-filling increments forming a total closure upon the building surface and thus setting an upper limit on S/V. A technique for increasing S/V beyond these limits would involve building forms that, rather than having simple slab-like properties, may have perforations made in a systematic way to increase the S/V ratio, thereby accommodating the lower end of the stress scale.

Another possibility would involve frameworks similar to trusses, to approximate the shape required to mitigate variations of insolation. Within this framework, building components may be assembled in a wide variety of ways that may be complex in their external shapes and fitted together in loose organizational arrangements within the more rigid limits of the framework. Such assemblages would not only extend the S/V range upward to accommodate the low end of the stress scale in large buildings, but would accommodate a high degree of flexibility over time within the limits of the framework.

Interconnecting forms. One technique for lowering the ratio of susceptibility (S/V) while at the same time increasing the insolation ratio (E_W/E_S) is by interconnecting buildings so that broad surfaces are oriented to the south, as at Acoma. In the case of a basic building increment, only one reference height can be connected (fig. 7.39). As basic increments are clustered to produce more diversified groupings including larger buildings, the advantages of interconnection increase (fig. 7.40). But as at Acoma, the advantage of interconnection drops off beyond a certain number of increments. The advantage gained by interconnecting large buildings drops off before that gained by small ones, but then the larger building has an intially greater capacity to achieve a high E_W/E_S with a low S/V (fig. 7.41).

Incrementation of Volume
The discussion of structure has dealt with incrementing the functional limits of form that govern interaction with environmental forces. Seasonal insolation has been of particular concern and has been met with a specification expressed as $E_W/E_S = 1.0$. Beyond this, S/V and H/A have been met within tolerances established by a planning framework. The ability to meet these specifications is conditioned by the precision with which a particular shape can be described; that precision is a function of scale, of the size relation between a generating increment and the final form.

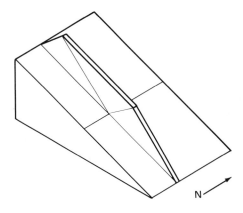

Fig. 7.39
One technique for extending the capacity of a building form to withstand environmental stress is by interconnecting the original references. This procedure lowers S/V and increases the possibility of improving winter insolation with a southern exposure.

Fig. 7.40
Interconnection lowers
the *S/V* ratio and at the
same time increases the
winter energy gain. (*S/V*
range is 5 to 18.) Interconnection of the *One* does
not achieve an energy ratio
of 1.0 within the required
S/V range (5 to 18), but
both the *Four* and the *Sixteen* have picked up capacity to add volume while
maintaining an energy
ratio of 1.0 or higher.
Even if the tolerable range
of *S/V* had been reduced
because of a more critical
(less diverse) domain, a
Four as well as a *Sixteen*
could have been built
within tolerable limits.

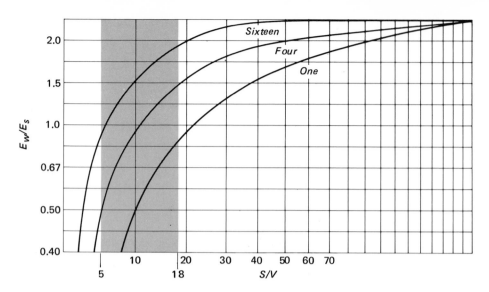

A second aspect of structure pertains to incrementation of a building's volume— the partitioning of its interior space. The partitioning of space is usually considered in relation to internal function and often without regard to external, natural forces. But partitioning may be thought of as a descriptive process in which the atten- uated effect of external forces is graphed in relation to increasing building depth. If the outside boundaries of a form are specifically shaped and structured in re- sponse to force in the environment, the form becomes what Sir D'Arcy Thomp- son suggested it would, "a diagram of force action."[1] Thompson's observations were made on natural forms, but they hold for buildings as well. If boundaries are not structured carefully, if the de- fining increments are too large, the build- ing diagram, as well as its purpose, is mod- ified. The diagram does not stop at the building's surface, however. As we move inward and away from that boundary, the descriptive increment used to diagram force action need not be so refined. More freedom may be taken with its size in de- scribing external influences (fig. 7.42).

Spaces deeper within a building experience less variation in their condition or state due to outside variations than do spaces near the surface. Consequently the larger and deeper a building, the more of its volume tends toward a steady state; the smaller or more shallow a building, the less of its volume can attain a steady state. This difference has already been generally pointed to as a function of the *S/V* ratio, which describes susceptibility to the composite of cyclic forces (chap. 4).

1. Sir D'Arcy Wentworth Thompson, *On Growth and Form* (London: Cambridge Uni- versity Press, 1961).

Lag time in buildings. The internal state of a small, one-room building changes in direct response to external variations. When the sun rises the outside temperatures go up; and temperatures inside the simple structure start to rise with the outside temperatures. The reason, of course, is the close proximity of the internal volume to the containing walls.

If the one-room building is made deeper, the delay in its change of state becomes greater. Inside exceedingly large buildings such as enclosed sports arenas or airplane hangars, the lag is so great that variations in conditions that recur at an interval of one day may have very little effect upon the internal volume.

This condition of internal lag is accentuated by the subdivision of volume or the partitioning of the volume into separate spaces. A variation in the thermal coefficients of such partitions and variations in the sizes of the contained volumes are useful tools in controlling what percentage of the total volume will be responsive to external variations. It is possible to imagine a solution in which large percentages of the volume do not respond to daily variations but would in fact respond to seasonal variations. Then, theoretically, if the building gets deep enough, there may be portions inside which do not even respond to seasonal variations, and maintain a steady state while the seasons come and go. Deep caves or mines do not vary more than a few degrees in temperature from one season to another.

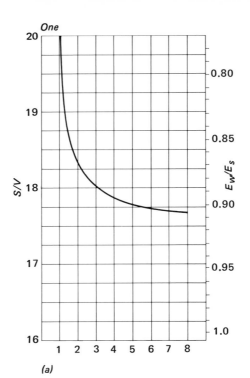

(a)

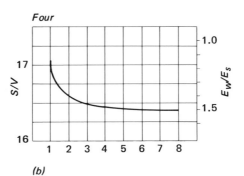

(b)

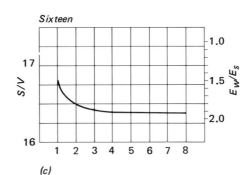

(c)

Fig. 7.41
S/V plotted against the interconnection of *Ones*, *Fours*, and *Sixteens* indicates that, as at Acoma, the advantage of interconnection is lost beyond a certain point. The number of attached elements that produced a benefit in meeting S/V and E_w/E_s varies with their size: (a) S/V modified by interconnection of *Ones*; advantage of interconnection is lost beyond eight increments. (b) S/V modified by interconnection of *Fours*; advantage of interconnection is lost beyond six increments. (c) S/V modified by interconnection of *Sixteens*; advantage of interconnection is lost beyond four increments.

Fig. 7.42
As we move away from the edge of any boundary separating two diverse states, the information that defines boundary, that edge, diminishes. In this case, running out of information is symbolized by making the descriptive increment larger. The example is a sand shape generated in a low-velocity wind tunnel. (Based on work done by Pierre Koenig at the University of Southern California, 1966.)

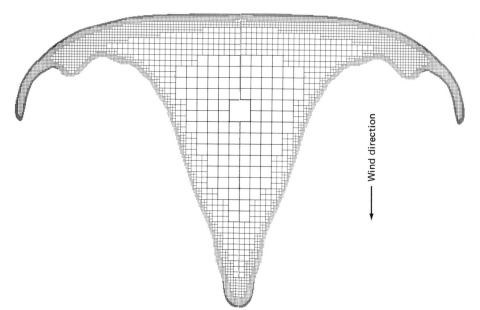

— Wind direction

Generally, the magnitude of external variation determines how much volume will be affected in a given building situation. The amount of volume affected by ambient air temperature tends to vary symmetrically throughout the entire day (fig. 7.43). The directional effect of insolation only occurs during the daylight hours. The combined effect of ambient air temperature and insolation affects some portion of the building volume throughout the entire day, leaving some part with a relatively steady state at the daily interval. Deeper buildings with many intervening partitions have the greatest portion of their volume unaffected by variations at a daily interval. In every case, the overriding factor in producing variation is direct insolation from the sun rather than ambient air temperature. This is especially true on the east and west orientations. The west orientation receives its maximum insolation during the afternoon when ambient air temperatures are highest. Recalling the Piutes, who used this phenomenon to their advantage, it would seem that we could learn from their example.

Not only is there a tendency for daily variations inside a building to reduce toward its center, but the time lag increases as well (fig. 7.44). Curve A represents the variation within a space adjacent to the external surface; B, C, and D are successively deeper into the building, with E representing the centermost space before the progression returns out the other side. Only ambient air temperature is considered here but it is clear that A has the most direct response to external variation and the least lag while E approaches a steady state and has the greatest lag. This picture can be modified by varying the U coefficients of partitions, and by varying the size of spaces (figs. 7.45, 7.46); but the general case holds that the conditions in the central portions of buildings, depending on the factors just discussed, might not fluctuate in direct response to external variations.

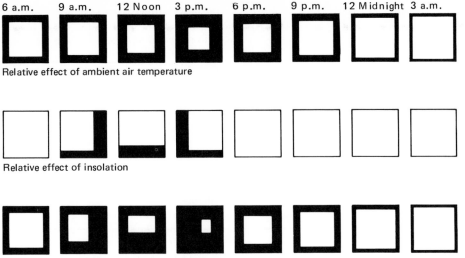

6 a.m. 9 a.m. 12 Noon 3 p.m. 6 p.m. 9 p.m. 12 Midnight 3 a.m.

Relative effect of ambient air temperature

Relative effect of insolation

Combined effect of ambient air temperature and insolation

(a)

Fig. 7.43
(a) Relative effects of ambient air temperature and insolation on a form, shown in plan, with north at the top. (Based on work done by J. Meisenhelder at the University of Southern California, 1971.) (b) The overriding factor in producing variation of heat flow through walls is insolation rather than ambient air temperature; this is especially true on the east and west orientation. (Based on a drawing in *Design with Climate* by Victor Olgay (Princeton N.J.: Princeton University Press, 1963), p. 148.)

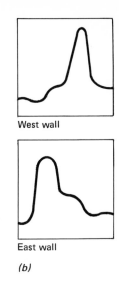

West wall

East wall

(b)

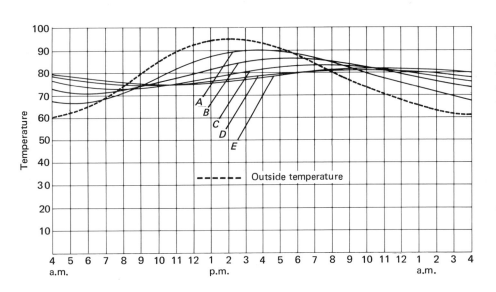

Temperature

100
90
80
70
60
50
40
30
20
10

A
B
C
D
E

- - - - - Outside temperature

4 5 6 7 8 9 10 11 12 1 2 3 4 5 6 7 8 9 10 11 12 1 2 3 4
a.m.   p.m.   a.m.

Fig. 7.44
The graph represents the temperature variation over a day for spaces within a form. *A* is the variation of a space next to the surface; *B, C, D,* and *E* are deeper, *E* being in the center of the form. Not only is there a tendency for daily variations inside a building to reduce toward its center, but there is an increasing time lag. (Based on work done by J. Meisenhelder at the University of Southern California, 1971.)

Fig. 7.45
Modifying the *U* coeffi-
cients of partitions separating spaces modifies the extent of internal variations.
0-2° F variation, 2-4° F variation, and 4-8° F variation.
(Based on work done by
J. Meisenhelder at the University of Southern California, 1971.)

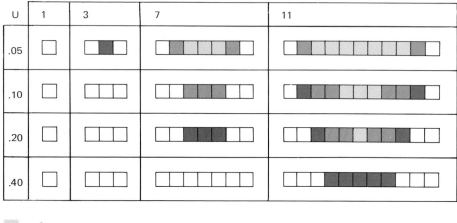

- 0-2° F variation
- 2-4° F variation
- 4-8° F variation

From such observations certain conclusions can be drawn, First, spaces deep
within a building experience less variation
in their states due to external variation
than do spaces near the surface. Second,
low *U* coefficient (low heat transfer) materials used in partitions cause less of the
volume of a form to be greatly affected
by varying outside conditions. High *U*
coefficients (high heat transfer) cause
greater portions of the volume to experience high temperature fluctuations.
Third, the depth of penetration from the
influence of external variation is less when
the size of contained spaces comprising
the volume is large.

These rather general comments can be
made clearer by graphing the amount of
variation per space against the number of
spaces. Assuming all partitions have the
same *U* coefficient and that all spaces
are the same size, the magnitude of variation from one space to the next becomes
smaller toward the inside (fig. 7.47). This
suggests that more responsive control is
necessary at the outside than toward the
center. It is reminiscent of a situation
described earlier in the sand and stream-
action studies. When the form of a system is not differentiated in response to
force action, there is a high degree of
variation in force effect, i.e., stress.

The difference in the magnitude of variation or the difference in state from space
to space amounts to an information asymmetry across an edge.[2] However, this differential or stress can be reduced by differentiating the form of the arrangement.

2. Kurt Lewin, *Principles of Topological Psy-
chology* (New York: McGraw-Hill Book Company, 1936).

The objective would be to reduce control problems by reducing the uncertainty from space to space, i.e., by equalizing the amount of variation in each space. Wall materials can be differentiated from outside to inside the building in order to eliminate the information drop from space to space, but a more graphic response would involve the differentiation of the spaces themselves.

When the compartmentalization of the volume of the shape is differentiated from outside to inside, information drop from space to space may be reduced. The uncertainty that leads to control problems is reduced. Following the example of a sandpile that increases in size toward its base while the load from above increases, thus maintaining a constant force per unit area throughout, a differentiated compartmentalization can maintain a nearly constant amount of thermal variation throughout (fig. 7.48).

Near the outside wall, where variation of temperature is inclined to be great within a space, the spaces are smaller; toward the center, where the temperature drop is inclined to be in smaller increments, the descriptive increment itself becomes larger, thus attaining approximately the same temperature drop per increment. Again, with the differentiation of form, the variation of force effect is minimized. Such a differentiation of the structure of a form tends to be most useful in mitigating daily variations in force effect.

This is a clear role for the structural component of form as distinguished from the shape component, which has been used primarily to mitigate seasonal variations. The two in combination, shape and structure, can produce a building that tends to maintain equilibrium by virtue of its form. The need to rely upon vast energy expenditures is reduced and some part of the energy crisis is relieved.

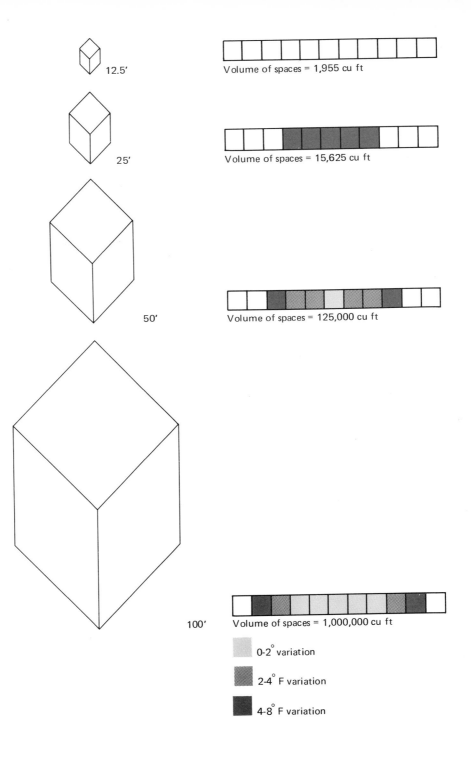

12.5'

25'

50'

100'

Volume of spaces = 1,955 cu ft

Volume of spaces = 15,625 cu ft

Volume of spaces = 125,000 cu ft

Volume of spaces = 1,000,000 cu ft

0-2° variation

2-4° F variation

4-8° F variation

Fig. 7.46
Modifying the size of spaces also affects the extent of internal variations. Each arrangement contains 11 identical cubical volumes separated by partitions. All partitions have the same U coefficients ($U = 0.40$). 0-2° F variation, 2-4° F variation, and 4-8° F variation. (Based on work done by J. Meisenhelder at the University of Southern California, 1971.)

Fig. 7.47
Assuming all partitions have the same *U* coefficient and that all spaces are the same size, the magnitude of variation from one space to the next becomes smaller toward the inside.

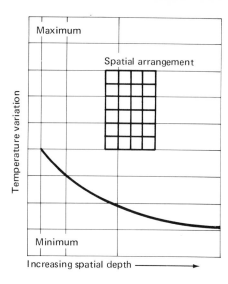

Fig. 7.48
When the compartmentalization of the volume of the shape is differentiated from outside to inside, the magnitude of temperature variation from one space to the next can be held constant.

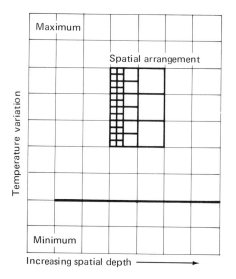

Of course, it would not be possible to eliminate all mechanical devices. Even in nature, with the vast array of form responses to environmental stress, metabolism is still a required mode of response. What shaping and structuring do is to produce a more predictable situation by reducing the amount of variation in the demand put upon mechanical systems.

Mechanical systems have been designed to handle uncertainty in the way forces act from place to place upon a form and over time as recurring force action produces a variation in energy demand. Such uncertainties in time and space are the real province of mechanical systems, which act as the equivalent of metabolism in nature. The question being raised by these studies does not have to do with the need for mechanical systems as such; it has to do with a reliance upon them as an exclusive mode of response to environmental stress.

Can we in fact reduce the degree of uncertainty attending the use of our mechanical systems? Can we, by form and location, minimize both the differentiation of force effect from place to place within the system and from time to time during the **course of a recurring interval?** If the answer is yes, then there are alternatives available to solve the critical energy supply questions of our time. While the search for cleaner and more efficient energy supply systems must continue, the need for energy can be lessened by the way we "grow" our urban arrangements; and at this point it seems that all reasonable alternatives must be considered.

One alternative, a logical extension of the form studies discussed in this chapter, lies in using the building itself as a solar energy collector. The energy could be stored for later use or it could be converted to electricity. Such conversion procedures are already used on a relatively small scale for heating and cooling houses and for such purposes as pumping irrigation water in hot, sunny climates. The conversion of sun energy to electricity is presently common practice in the space industry.

If we can begin to see the building form as an adaptive mechanism, the basic technology exists to use the form to mitigate daily and seasonal variation and to use it as a converter of solar energy for our own purposes. The advantages to be gained from such an approach are very great indeed.

First, using the sun's energy directly does not add more heat to the biosphere than is already being received daily. If the sun's energy is stored by buildings in order to be used at times when there is no insolation, the energy is being redistributed in time but the residual heat is not greater than what is being received directly from the sun in the short term. Second, when electrical power is produced it not only adds heat to the biosphere but it does so by converting materials that have been stored over millions of years. The offense to the environment is compounded: Air and water are overheated; the land is scarred and depleted.

Throughout this discussion of form as an adaptive response to environmental variation and as an alternative to high-energy mechanical responses, size has appeared to be a critical factor. There are two obvious advantages to large size: The first is lower susceptibility to the composite of cyclic forces that comprise a building's environment; the second is a favorable seasonal insolation ratio that is possible because of a shaping freedom evident in the earlier examples of large, generated forms. An obvious question follows then: If large buildings are so desirable, why not use them everywhere? There are two answers to that question. The first derives from our earlier site description of Owens Valley: Both topography and the natural environment vary with location. If building size is to be a sensitive measure of site conditions, it must vary and cannot, therefore, always be large. The second answer has not been so thoroughly discussed up to this point: There are criteria of community development that would discourage advocacy of an exclusive use of large structures. The most important of these are related to the fact that large developments are not made overnight. It takes time to build a megastructure.

In order for a built arrangement to function as a community, a variety of building sizes and types is needed from the beginning. And if the arrangement is to conserve energy, from the beginning, it must have the attributes of form that will allow it to function in equilibrium with nature. We saw, in the example of Bonito, that a high level of optimization was attained with the completion of the arrangement. Before completion, optimization was not achieved.

A more realistic view of community development would take time into account and would recognize the need for a step-by-step building process that provides a variety of size and complexity as the community need for diversity increases. Large size should not be devalued in the scheme of things but it may not be the first priority in community development and it may not be the first requirement in a successional development in which energy conservation is a continuing, governing criterion.

Fig. 8.1
Carcassonne, France. During
the Middle Ages, the gentle
pressure of accumulated
experience allowed by a
slower rate of growth foretold a result that was a
purposeful adaptation.

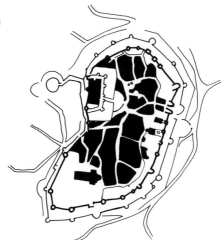

The full environmental potential of built form cannot be developed unless form is viewed as a dynamic as well as a static phenomenon. This is certainly true with regard to the user, who must be able to perceive the form of his environment before he can function in it. He must construct a useful environmental image based on a sequence of perceptual events over time. A larger and more complex environment requires more time for the user to adjust his many images so that he can better develop his own potentials.

More to the immediate point, the construction of the buildings that comprise the environment requires a sequence of events that take time and involve adjustment. When such events occur slowly, the adjustment period coincides with the time of growth.

A process that combines growth with adjustment may be usefully called self-organizing or adaptive. Adaptive behavior is exhibited in the development of many towns of the Middle Ages. While there were exceptions, in which plans were made for rapid growth, it was generally a time when the sequences of events that led to a functioning urban arrangement took place slowly and deliberately. Decisions about the placement and the form of a building were made at a leisurely pace by people who were intimately involved with the building process. Their cues came from direct perceptions of a sequence of events that occurred at a slow enough rate to be evaluated both as individual events and as occurrences in context.

Progressive development, whether of images or of buildings, can be reduced to simple relational terms of hot-to-cold, wet-to-dry, light-to-dark, sweet-to-acrid, and so on, describing the minimal structural statement of a phenomenon. The most basic environmental problems can be stated in those terms for purposes of analysis. The builders of the Middle Ages may not have been analytical or scientific in the modern sense but they were concerned with the feeling of the sun's warming rays on a bitter cold winter day. In such a milieu the gentle pressure of accumulated experience foretold a result that was a purposeful adaptation (fig. 8.1).

Today, when events occur in more rapid succession, when there is no time for the accumulation of experience that ties the builder intimately to the site, growth must be controlled if the results are not to be chaotic and unstable. For this we have some precedents, albeit not very encouraging ones.

Example include the hastily constructed workmen's town of Kahun, Egypt (fig. 8.2) and the Roman military camps laid out in a few days on a square grid as at Silchester, England (fig. 8.3); more recent examples include the grid plans that accommodated rapid westward expansion in the United States (figs. 8.4-8.6). Such schemes are made for expediency and have little ability to adapt to unique sets of conditions. It is possible to imagine the poor Roman soldier who finds that his predetermined spot in the grid is occupied by a creek-bed. What a predicament that must have been for someone trained to "fill the gaps" regardless of the consequences. There was little time or space to adjust, to adapt, to organize the situation through one's own efforts.

Our problem today is that we must build rapidly but without such repressive control. This requires an adaptive capacity to build continuities from one state to another without too great reliance upon either redundancy or insufficiency; there must be some kind of anticipatory mechanism at work. Some control is required over the sequence of constructive events if the result is to be an arrangement in equilibrium with nature at every stage of its growth.

A planning framework that specifically provides for the control of the sequence of development was first described in Chapter 6. It was the most highly organized of three planning frameworks that developed different levels of control. Only the size of a basic building increment was established in the first framework (*order* level, fig. 6.4). The framework was a completely regular grid. No differentiation appeared among building increments. The small and simple building increments from this first framework were merged in the second framework allowing transformation to higher levels of organization. (*structure* level, fig. 6.7). Increment size could vary. The basic increment presented here was purposely maintained on the periphery of the framework to recognize the special nature of the edge of a force domain; but larger and potentially more complex building increments appeared toward its center. Building increments of different size and complexity were joined in the third and last framework to allow the possibility of interconnecting buildings for purposes of energy conservation (*system* level, fig. 6.10). At this highest of the described levels of planning, control over the sequence of building can produce the best results if certain simple rules are followed. Adherence to them must be deliberate and consistent if the resulting arrangement is to be self-regulating and adaptive.

Fig. 8.2
Kahun, Egypt. This hastily constructed workmen's town bears the regular imprint of predetermined geometry. (Drawing by D. Hockett, Auburn University, 1962.)

N

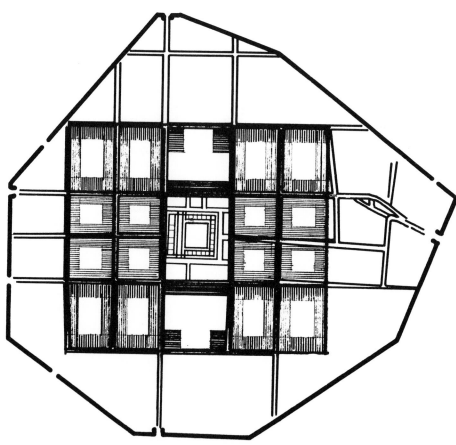

Fig. 8.3
Silchester, England. Such town plans as this one based on an early Roman military camp have little ability to adapt to unique sets of conditions. (Drawing by B. Hagler, Auburn University, 1962.)

Fig. 8.4
Far West, Missouri. An example of an undifferentiated framework developed by the Mormon leader Joseph Smith for expansion offers no clues to where different parts of a development might be placed or in what sequence.

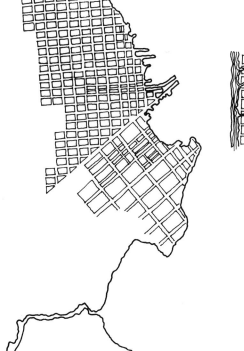

Fig. 8.5
San Francisco. This plan sought a simple, highly uniform framework to accommodate rapid growth. The grid was applied with minimal regard for the site's significant topography.

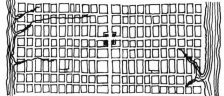

Fig. 8.6
Philadelphia. William Penn's scheme was made to accommodate expansionary growth with almost no recognition of natural limits.

The first and most general rule to follow is that a building increment must be viewed as a whole and any condition pertaining to it must be satisfied at every phase of its growth. The second rule is that redundancy (beyond controlled tolerances, which are a function of contact diversity; see chaps. 5 and 6) will never be built into the system at any phase of growth, i.e., the system will not be overdesigned to anticipate future insufficiencies; and the third rule is that the system will not be allowed to act insufficiently (again, beyond controlled tolerances) at any phase of its growth, i.e., it will not be underdesigned in anticipation of future redundancies.

While adhering to these general rules, the particular building increment used in the following discussions must satisfy a range of S/V and H/A (derived from Owens Valley site conditions) and it must function as a whole with an energy ratio E_W/E_S = 1.0. In other words, what will be discussed is a strategy of succession toward maximum built volume maintained in equilibrium with nature at minimum energy cost. When viewed in this way, a building increment of the *system* level framework becomes a successional unit with innate properties that are known and can be developed by the planner as community need for space arises.

The Development of a Successional Unit

The first successional unit selected for this discussion has been isolated from the final planning framework developed in Chapter 6 (fig. 8.7). It contains twenty-eight original building increments called *Ones* that comprised the total *order* level framework (fig. 6.4). These *Ones* were merged into seven more complex increments called *Fours*, which appeared in some portions of the *structure* level framework (fig. 6.7). Finally, the *Fours* were joined into a single, potentially interconnected successional unit that was selected for this discussion from among many units comprising the *system* level framework (fig. 6.10). Within this unit, interconnection may occur at two different building heights (fig. 8.8). It must occur in a controlled sequence that satisfies all three previously described specifications at every stage of the sequence.

Some parts of this case study progressed simultaneously rather than sequentially. For example, studies of building form and studies of networks were going on at the same time. Since the maximum building height of a basic increment (referred to earlier as a *One*) on a 15° east slope is only 21 feet (fig. 4.10), the building-form studies were carried out on a 10° east slope that allowed a height of 65 feet and some shaping freedom. There was little possibility for the work to proceed on the steeper site. At the same time, a particular slope-orientation domain was selected by those students investigating networks because of the wide range of study conditions it represented. In order to make use of all the building studies, within a slope-orientation domain that had already been analyzed the 15° slope was shifted to 10°.

The shift had two simple consequences. First was an increase in the dimension of a building increment because of the more gentle slope. The particular successional unit under discussion then is comprised of seven *Fours,* each *Four* approximately doubling in size to become 800 feet on a side (fig. 8.8). The second consequence was a modification of H/A because of the size increase, but this change did not affect the work because of the great tolerance in the H/A range derived from the original slope-orientation network (fig. 6.20). The study proceeded then on a hypothetical 10° slope using the tolerances for S/V and H/A derived for the real 15° slope. Except for this shift of slope, all procedures are unmodified.

All buildings in the plans that follow are indicated diagramatically by showing the basic planar reference to which volume would be added for community growth. Because of the vast array of possible building shapes and structures that might be generated over time from these basic references in response to real community need, the temptation to show one or more specific solutions has been avoided. Instead, the basic reference is shown. As community needs evolve, an array of future building solutions would evolve from it.

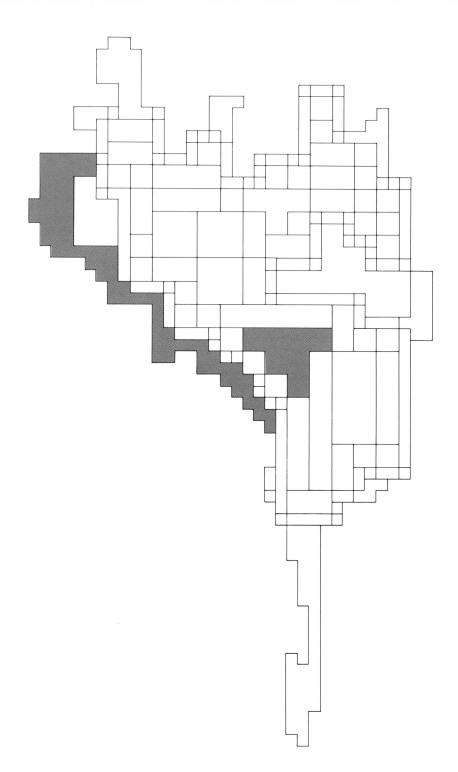

Fig. 8.7
This east-facing force domain contains a variety of energy increments, two of which are selected for case study. (See fig. 6.10.)

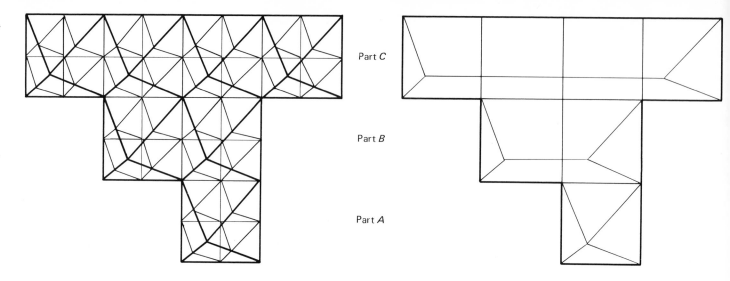

Fig. 8.8
Case study no. 1: The energy increment is comprised of seven *Fours*, each *Four* being 800 feet on a side.

Fig. 8.9
Case study no. 1: Within the energy increment Part *C* has the greatest capacity for interconnection in the east-west direction; Part *A* has the least capacity for interconnection.

Part *C*

Part *B*

Part *A*

The major advantage of planning at this level is that interconnection becomes a useful tool for energy conservation, but it must occur in the east-west direction. In our case study, the greatest potential for interconnection with that orientation appears in the northern part of the successional unit. There, Part C has the greatest capacity to meet both S/V and energy ratio requirements (fig. 8.9). By contrast, Part A, to the south, has the least capacity to achieve equilibrium and any degree by which it falls short of meeting requirements may be handled subsequently by parts with greater capacity as we develop to the north.

Beginning then with Part A, we go through a step-by-step process to determine the range of S/V that can be simultaneously developed with an energy ratio of 1.0. This would require us to know how many of the five potential components comprising Part A can act independently and how many must be interconnected to satisfy specifications. It would also require a determination of how many of the five components can be built to act interdependently during this phase of construction.

Generally alternative arrangements are available to meet energy and activity requirements at any phase of the sequence, with the larger and more highly connected building references allowing more alternatives. There is, however, a further limit upon the number of alternatives available, which limit occurs because of interaction among the several parts of a built arrangement. Interconnection increases interaction between buildings placed to the north and south of each other with a consequent decrease of E_W/E_S. If two interconnected Fours were shaped so that E_W/E_S = 1.0,

interaction would modify that ratio downward (fig. 8.10). The solution, of course, would be to build an initially higher energy ratio into the Fours so that interaction would not drop the energy ratio below 1.0.

It should also be noted here that S/V is being simultaneously modified and may become the controlling factor. Where it is not close to the limits, there is some opportunity to maneuver and to bring the energy ratio up to specification.

Increments of Fours
Part A: 1 Four. Theoretically, several alternatives are available for Part A. Most of these are eliminated either because of interaction or because of the incapacity of the arrangements to meet the criteria for S/V = (5.5 to 18.2), H/A = (1.2 - 5.4; already satisfied) and E_W/E_S = 1.0. Some solutions are insufficient either because S/V is too high or because E_W/E_S is too low (fig. 8.11). Other solutions are redundant because S/V is too low or because E_W/E_S is too high (fig. 8.12).

The theoretical alternatives would be four separately acting Ones or two sets of interconnected Ones; a singly acting Four, or a Four in any one of a number of combinations of singly acting or interconnected Ones. Of these possibilities, a single Four can be built by itself to meet the necessary criteria (figs. 8.13, 8.14). Sufficient capacity can be built into that Four to

support one or two independently acting Ones (fig. 8.15); a single Four can also support two interconnected Ones located to avoid adverse interaction (fig. 8.16) but that is its limit set by the maximum available S/V for an incremented (structured) Four (fig. 8.17). There remain two Ones unbuilt, either connected or unconnected. Those that cannot be built at this phase of the sequence must wait for a subsequent phase in which sufficient capacity can be built to allow the unbuilt Ones in Part A to be placed.

Referring to the general rules, only that portion of an arrangement can be built that operates sufficiently; nor may it carry too much redundancy with it while waiting for a subsequent phase of building to take place. Part A would be operating insufficiently if it fell below the criteria set; it would be redundant if it more than met those criteria. Specifically, the arrangement would be operating insufficiently if S/V > 18.2, and E_W/E_S < 1.0; the arrangement would be redundant if S/V < 5.5, and E_W/E_S > 1.0.

Part B: 2 Fours. Moving north, the options available for Part A are also available for Part B. In addition, a greater range of alternatives becomes possible because of the advantage gained by interconnecting two Fours. The least advantage that could be taken of the interconnection allows the building of four separately acting Ones (fig. 8.18). This combination achieves an energy ratio of 1.0; S/V is 17.35, just within the tolerable limit. There is no additional capacity to help Part A.

Fig. 8.10
Interconnection increases interaction between buildings placed to the north and south of each other. If two interconnected *Fours* were initially shaped so that $E_W/E_S = 1.0$, interaction would modify that ratio downward. The advantage of interconnection is outweighed by disadvantageous interaction in this case.

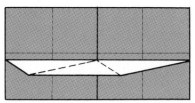

$E_W/E_S = 1.0$

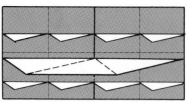

$E_W/E_S = 0.96$

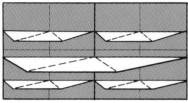

$E_W/E_S = 0.90$

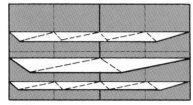

$E_W/E_S = 0.82$

Fig. 8.11
Part *A*, theoretical alternatives: S/V too high; E_W/E_S too low.

Insufficient solutions

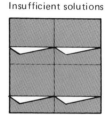

$S/V = 20.00$
$E_W/E_S = 0.77$

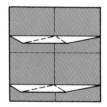

$S/V = 18.30$
$E_W/E_S = 0.87$

Fig. 8.12
Part *A*, theoretical alternatives: S/V meets specifications; E_W/E_S higher than required by specification.

Fig. 8.13
Part *A*, real alternative; both S/V and E_W/E_S meet specifications.

Redundant solution

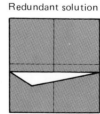

$S/V = 17.10$
$E_W/E_S = 1.15$

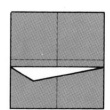

$S/V = 14.0$
$E_W/E_S = 1.0$

Fig. 8.14
By building enough capacity into a *Four* or a *Sixteen*, it is possible to support elements of a lower reference level (a *Four* supports *Ones*, a *Sixteen* supports *Fours*) and still maintain the required S/V and E_W/E_S. The energy ratio may not be modified below our specification ($E_W/E_S = 1$) by the addition of independently acting lower references. The ranges on the graph result from the addition or subtraction of volume to the original reference plane.

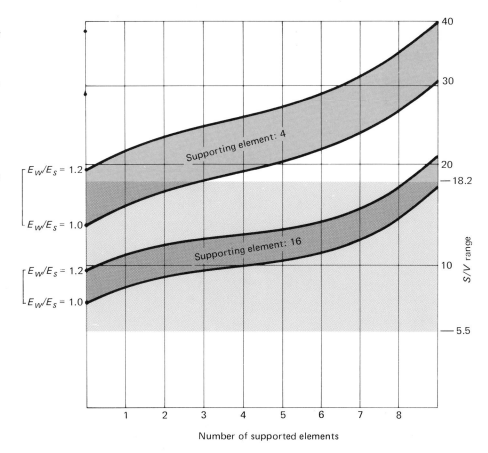

$E_W/E_S = 1.2$
$E_W/E_S = 1.0$
$E_W/E_S = 1.2$
$E_W/E_S = 1.0$

Supporting element: 4
Supporting element: 16

40
30
20
—18.2
10
—5.5

S/V range

1 2 3 4 5 6 7 8
Number of supported elements

Fig. 8.15
Part *A*, real alternative: sufficient capacity can be built into the *Four* to support one or two independently acting *Ones* (independently acting *Ones* can be placed to the north or south of a *Four* without adverse interaction).

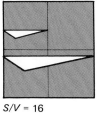
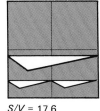
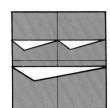

$S/V = 16$
$E_W/E_S = 1.0$

$S/V = 17.6$
$E_W/E_S = 1.0$

Fig. 8.16
Part *A,* real alternative: a single *Four* can support two interconnected *Ones* located to avoid adverse interaction. The north position for interconnected *Ones* provides less adverse interaction than a south position because of the greater spacing between elements and the triangular shape of the *Four* that casts a smaller shadow area than an interconnected reference.

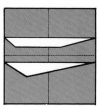

$S/V = 17.45$
$E_W/E_S = 1.0$

Fig. 8.17
The interconnection of references increases their capacity to support the addition of elements at a lower reference level. The supporting elements on this graph become two interconnected *Fours* and two interconnected *Sixteens.*

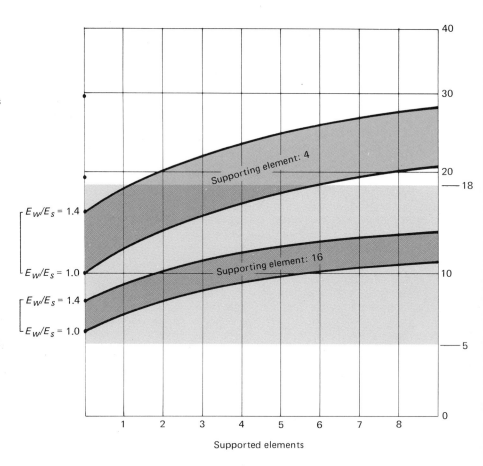

The maximum advantage is gained by increasing the amount of interconnection. In fact, the least amount of interconnection that would allow the completion of all components of *A* and *B* would produce an energy ratio of 1.0 and S/V = 17.6, very close to the tolerable limit (fig. 8.19). This solution also represents the maximum amount of interconnection possible because of two factors: First, greater interconnection increases interaction and reduces the energy ratio below 1.0; and second, the crudeness of incrementation takes its toll and finally eliminates the advantage of interconnection (fig. 8.20).

This solution represents a reduced S/V and theoretically greater capacity to achieve a higher energy ratio; but at the upper limit of S/V = 17.4, the lack of shaping freedom imposed by the structuring increment holds the solution down to an inadequate energy ratio.

Part C: 3 Fours. The final phase of building involves Part *C,* with still more alternatives that result from the interconnection of four *Fours.* It is possible to build combinations that range from no interconnected *Ones* (fig. 8.21) to total interconnection of all parts (fig. 8.22).

Part *C* has sufficient capacity to meet the criteria and offers a great range of alternatives to satisfy other functional requirements as well. Some successional units are more restrictive. They may not provide the higher degree of organization represented by a *Four* in contrast to a *One,* or they may not be capable of generating the east-west continuities essential for useful interconnection. They may not offer such a range of alternatives in sequencing or simply may not be buildable in part or in total.

The second unit selected for this discussion cannot meet the three specifications required for building. It lies at the western edge of the framework (fig. 8.7). It is quite small in the east-west direction, to allow minimal interconnection of *Ones,* which have a low capacity to meet the specifications.

In order to establish specification tolerances for this successional unit, we must refer back to the network of the *system* level planning framework. Here we can see that this second example has the most vectors (15) and the highest total vector value (13,500; fig. 6.15) of any successional unit in the domain. Such strength of associations suggests two things: First, the unit plays a potentially important role in the community because of the number of its associations. Special care must be taken to plan a use for the site in relation to a potential diversity of adjacent activities; second, specification tolerances can be broad because of the contact diversity of the force domain. These tolerances can be determined from an average vector value for the unit.

The average vector value representing the relative condition of the increment is 13,500/15 = 900.0 which was then used to determine what portion of the S/V and H/A ranges for the domain could be used by that increment in fulfilling its role. An average vector value of 900.0 for the increment produced a value of 2 percent for the required optimization (fig. 6.18). An optimization of 2 percent produces an S/V range from 3.9 to 19.9 and an H/A range from 0.1 to 5.4. Since the H/A for a *One* is 4.8, this particular requirement is met. Further consideration will be for S/V related to E_W/E_S. Even though the network indicates a greater S/V range (approximately 4 to 20; 2 per-

cent optimization) in contrast to the somewhat smaller range of the first successional unit (5.5 to 18.2; 23 percent optimization) the limits upon interconnection and transformation provide the greater and critical restriction upon this increment.

Increments of Ones
Part A: 1 One. As with the first example, parts of the unit are classified according to the amount of interconnection possible and consequently upon the number of alternatives possible (fig. 8.23). Parts labeled *A* represent a single basic building increment with no possibility for interconnection in the east-west direction. For those parts, the highest energy ratio attainable within the S/V restriction is less than required; E_W/E_S = 0.77 when S/V = 20.0 (fig. 7.25). This happens to be the upper S/V limit for a structured form without resorting to some technique of perforation or infilling of an open truss, a possibility previously suggested.

Part B: 2 Ones. This increment allows the east-west interconnection of 2 *Ones.* This interconnection improves the energy ratio to 0.87 while reducing the S/V ratio to 18.3; but the improvement in the energy ratio is not sufficient, and any modification of S/V by perforation or any other technique will not improve that energy ratio. So, like Part *A,* Part *B* does not allow a building solution that satisfies the criteria.

Fig. 8.18
Part *B,* the least advantage that could be taken of the interconnected *Fours* allows the building of four separately acting *Ones.*

Fig. 8.19
Parts *A* and *B,* real alternatives; the optimum amount of interconnection at both reference levels that will allow specifications to be met.

Fig. 8.20
Parts *A* and *B,* theoretical alternatives; too much interconnection reduces E_W/E_S because of adverse interaction.

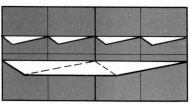

S/V = 17.35
E_W/E_S = 1.0

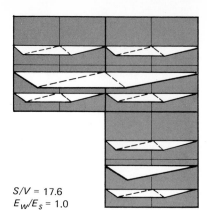

S/V = 17.6
E_W/E_S = 1.0

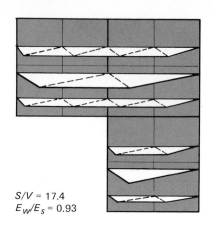

S/V = 17.4
E_W/E_S = 0.93

Fig. 8.21
Part *C,* real alternative; least interconnection that allows building all references and satisfying specifications.

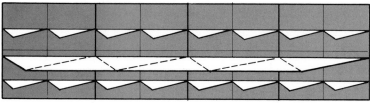

S/V = 15.4
E_W/E_S = 1.0

Fig. 8.22
Part *C,* real alternative: most interconnection that allows building all references and satisfying specifications.

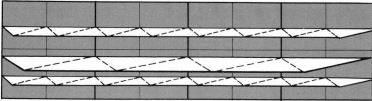

S/V = 17.0
E_W/E_S = 1.0

Part C: 3 Ones. The increment of 3 *Ones* reduces the S/V to 18.00, bringing it still further inside the range, but the energy ratio has increased only slightly ($E_W/E_S = 0.89$) and does not satisfy the criterion of equalizing summer and winter incident energies. In fact, a plot of growth by interconnection against S/V and E_W/E_S indicates that nowhere in this force domain can a successional unit comprised entirely of *Ones* meet specifications by interconnection (fig. 7.40). Within the limitations of size imposed by the single reference of a *One,* the criteria for building cannot be met.

This particular successional unit is so lacking in capacity to meet the energy balance requirements that would overcome the effects of peak loading caused by seasonal variation that no building solution is possible. Since transformation to higher levels of organization and higher reference levels is not tolerated by the control system, building cannot take place in this part of the domain unless there is a change in the specifications. This condition is typical of the entire periphery of the case study domain, but as the network suggests, special care must be taken in determining a community use for this particular segment of land where no major building can take place. The land must be left essentially open and useful to people who live and work nearby. It could best be put to use as recreational land.

Away from the edge of the domain, transformation to higher levels of organization along with east-west interconnections will produce an array of building options to satisfy the spatial needs of a growing community while meeting specifications for energy conservation.

Of course, all domains would not present a similar picture. Some would be more restrictive, some less. A more gentle slope, for example, that allowed a larger land increment, or an orientation that allowed greater height with less adverse interaction, or perhaps a different configuration for the domain as a whole that allowed different sets of associations to occur would tend to allow more of the domain to be built upon, even at the edge. An east-facing slope of 5 degrees, for instance, would contain 800-foot basic land increments with an increase of building height. This height increase would probably have allowed building to occur at certain places along the edge of the domain. On the other hand, steeper domains, especially on north slopes, would be more restrictive.

It might be argued that building could take place along the edge of the sample domain without resorting to transformation if the deficient successional unit were to share attributes with another, more capable one. This sharing would occur in such a way that the greater capacity of a unit comprised of *Fours* or *Sixteens* (especially if they were interconnected in an east-west direction) might support one of less capacity. The net result would be an interaction between units of different organizational levels based on an "energy trade." Redundancy would be built into one unit to make up for the insufficiencies of another. The redundant unit would overcompensate for seasonal variation allowing energies to flow to the unit that cannot compensate to the specified extent by the way it is grown and formed.

Fig. 8.23
Case study no. 2: Limits upon interconnection and transformation in this energy increment make a building solution impossible even though tolerances are great.

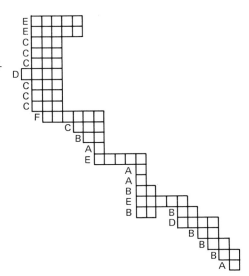

Although this requires further study, such interactions from one successional unit to another tend to blur distinctions and reduce diversity independently of the identity of the unit as established by the networks.

When the identity of a domain is high by virtue of high contact diversity, with adjacent and distinctive domains, it can be tolerant of building modes that tend to blur those distinctions. A simple example would be the intersection between flat land and exceedingly steep, high slopes where the distinction is so sharp that regardless of what is built there, the condition will persist. The information establishing the relationship between vertical and horizontal cannot easily be obliterated, nor can the attending ecological structure. Perceptually strong edges are more tolerant than weak edges of a growth mode that reduces distinctions. The networks have been used in a way that reflects this fact, but they have not been used to establish tolerance for maintenance energies to support otherwise unstable successional units. Each unit must meet the requirement of an established level of seasonal mitigation by sharing capacities among components within itself, not between itself and another successional unit.

The use of energy-supply systems to support building arrangements that cannot achieve proper energy balances themselves is a procedure which is now almost universally followed. Industrial societies take energy resources from one place and feed them to another in such magnitudes that low diversity growth can be supported over tremendous land areas. An analogous situation would have been for us to build

great capacity into the more highly organized and therefore more capable units toward the center of the domain. There would have been two consequences. First, because of their great capacity, a few large units might be used to support a great many independently acting elements representing low diversity over a relatively large land area. There would be *variety* but at two extreme ends of the scale. There would be a few large and highly organized parts related to many small and simpler ones. There would be nothing between to insure a continuity of scale, an evenness in apportionment, an *equitability* of parts comprising the domain from its edge to its center. The arrangement would be susceptible; its long-term equilibrium would depend upon a continued role being played by a few parts that have both the greatest capacity and tendency to transform and to change their attributes over time. Long-term community needs for diversity among building types would not seem to be satisfied by such an arrangement either.[1]

1. Variety and equitability are terms generally applied to the description of biological diversity. They are used here to describe analogous phenomena in building. Variety refers to the number of different kinds of parts in relation to the number of parts comprising a system. Equitability refers to the evenness of apportionment. The attitude taken here is that stability in a built arrangement results from diversity; the components of that diversity would be variety of parts and evenness in the apportionment so that some kinds of parts do not occur in critically small numbers making the system as a whole dependent on their survival. See E. P. Odum, "The Strategy of Eco-System Development," *Science,* 164 (1969), 262-270.

The second consequence would have to do with sequencing in which either the high capacity part would have to be built first, thus representing a high degree of redundancy until the low capacity and unstable portions would be completed, or the reverse would happen; the low capacity and unstable parts would operate insufficiently if built first while waiting for the large part to follow and complete the balanced energy system. The alternative would be to build a great portion of a system at one time so that a few large parts could interact with a great many small ones. While this is theoretically a possibility, aside from the previously mentioned susceptibility of such an inequitable arrangement, growth does not normally take place in such large steps. It tends rather to take place in a sequential way in which smaller parts are built and inhabited while the rest of the system is not yet begun. The parts first inhabited begin to mature into a community. Diversity is continuously developing in them while successive phases of building are still to be completed.

This diversity at every stage of growth, needed to maintain a balanced energy system, is also a condition for a balanced life. It provides variety and choice. The significance of this fact lies in what appears to be a fundamental purpose for the formation of communities; that purpose is to establish an environment in which the maximum number and variety of energy transactions between members or parts can take place. In general, the greater this number and variety, i.e., the greater this diversity, the greater is the stability of the arrangement as a whole. For human communities, the provision of an environment that allows for the widest choices would answer the question whether man can satisfy his own purposes while building in equilibrium with the natural environment.

Applying Successional Principles to Owens Valley

The implications of developing such an environment must be recognized: More control is required along lines described in Chapter 6. The large-scale land-use implications of applying such controls must be recognized as well. If the techniques described in Part 3 were to be applied to all of Owens Valley, settlement could not take place indiscriminately and could occur, with the described controls, only in certain places. Settlement is most likely to occur without offense to the land and without high maintenance costs at that intersection between the mountains and the valley floor, where the land is neither very steep nor very flat and where the Piutes, so long ago, built their permanent houses (fig. 8.24). In general, settlement could not take place either in the mountains or on the basin floor and be consistent with the described principles of energy conservation.

Steep slopes in the Sierra Nevada and Inyo-White mountains result in large areas of small building increments with high susceptibility to environmental perturbation. In such small increments, S/V is too high to accommodate the composite action of recurring, natural forces measured on the site. In addition to being highly susceptible to general environmental stress, small building increments do not allow the shaping freedom to handle the specific problem of insolation. Form cannot be effectively used as an adaptation mechanism. Such an insufficient arrangement of small increments would not be built if the governing criterion is to conserve energy while maintaining equilibrium.

Development could not take place on most of the valley floor either, not because the increments are generally insufficient, small, and incapable of being shaped, but because they are so large that they can accommodate a redundant building solution. A required match of building increment size and topography would not allow development on most parts of the basin. Environmental stress, as measured in the study of Owens Valley, is not high enough there to justify the low S/V resulting from large buildings. Where stress is high it makes sense to protect the contained spaces with a lower S/V; but if the stress is low and the S/V is low because of large size, the cost of maintaining a large volume is not compensated by the inertia such a large volume provides. The result is a high cost for the equipment to keep a large volume serviced with light, air, and water. The benefit of the large volume derives from its resistance to external fluctuations. When those fluctuations are relatively small, paying to support a large volume is not justified. Where large land increments occur in low-stress areas the result is a redundant solution on a scale measured in the valley.

Based solely on energy criteria, parts of Owens Valley are unbuildable. Development would be generally insufficient in the mountains and redundant in the basin. There would, of course, be other implications to such a conclusion that have to do with land use. The mountains are well suited for recreational purposes and could serve the Southern California region, which badly needs such areas. Some of the basin is well suited for agriculture and grazing and should not be covered over and scraped off—a fate that has befallen so much arable land.

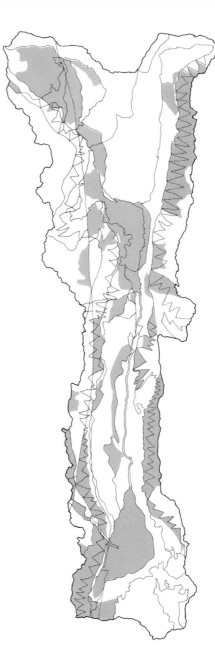

Fig. 8.24
In Owens Valley, areas that are considered unbuildable result from conditions of redundancy or insufficiency (in terms of the correlation made between slope, increment size, S/V, and stress). It is an interesting fact, although not one from which we have tried to draw specific conclusions, that all of the significant historical settlements, both Piute and modern, fall within the "buildable," (shaded) areas.

Owens Valley is a unique place, serving a larger region in several ways. While the techniques set forth here do allow a more responsive development of land resources, Owens Valley might better be preserved as a resource for many more people than could ever safely be permanently situated there. Beyond that, while tools developed in the Owens Valley study are generally valuable for raw land development, society is faced today with the serious question of the advisability of developing *any* new land resources. The potential of transforming our existing urban centers by reorganizing them and directing the change that characterizes them holds out a promise for the future.

While Owens Valley is relatively undeveloped, much that was learned about modes of growth and levels of control is general and can be applied both to raw land and to successive land-use development in existing cities. In an existing urban situation, domains may be defined in terms of historical development as well as the natural environment. For example, roads, population, land value, and buildings measured in time and space become necessary descriptors along with the cyclic forces of nature.

In the Los Angeles area, as in many other urban areas, construction on raw land has tended to generate a minimal diversity growth (*expansionary*) at a minimal control level (*order*). The result is a misuse of the land as a resource, accompanied by the high energy costs of successive and unplanned stages of growth as the development diversifies to survive. The result is a wasteland of unused and essentially open space; a cheap and uncontrolled growth mode that benefits the private sector of the economy becomes, in the end, a public liability as maintenance costs rise. The alternative is a different mode of growth involving differentiated levels of control in space and time.

Those poorly used areas within the city represent a significant land resource if growth can take place as transformation rather than primitive expansion and if the level of control can be differentiated to achieve higher diversity. Differentiating the level of control over growth, whether by expansion on raw land or transformation of the existing city, requires modeling the growth process before it takes place. A framework for growth would develop not the greatest number of parts but the greatest distinction among parts, the highest degree of diversity, and the greatest probability of associations among adjacent parts. This would be done with common regard for land resources and for the need not just to increase individual choice, but to provide a basis for that choice.

9
Toward a Synthesis

People have traditionally clustered together in communities in attempts to increase their own potentials. This has certainly been a fundamental purpose in the building of cities, but the rate and magnitude of urbanization makes our time unique. Some experts estimate that we must build in one decade the equivalent of all that has been built since this country began.

Unlike schools of fish and flocks of birds, cities of men, with the support of modern technology, are not limited in their growth by the availability of resources in the immediate environment. The modern city, by drawing upon world resources, can grow beyond an individual's ability to comprehend its structure and limits. But without such individual comprehension, the main purpose of clustering is defeated. If people are "lost" in the city, the possibility is not very great that they will realize their full potential as individuals or that they will increase the number and variety of their communications. If the modern city is to be comprehensible to the individual, if it is to serve its fundamental purpose for people, the increments of its growth as well as rate and direction must be reconsidered.

At one time the individual house was the largest increment of growth that needed to be considered. The rate and direction of its generation across the land were determined by the availability of resources that could be had by applying simple hand processes. A house was permanent. It sheltered a man and woman, children, grandparents, the dog, and a cow. A man would live all his life, his children all their lives, and his children's children all their lives in that house. Such a house accumulated the dust of generations and was important enough for the whole community to take part in determining its placement and its form.

The community no longer has time to seriously consider each house; nor do individuals possess the long-range interest. The possibility that one will live out even his own life in the same house is unlikely today. Any one of us will probably live in a minimum of three houses before he dies and possibly even ten or twelve. With such mobility, our concern for what lies beyond that single house becomes intensified. We are not self-sufficient; we depend increasingly upon the world outside. Our thoughts of the future are not limited to one place. We are forced to reconsider what would be a useful increment of growth and what determines its attributes if the city is to be richly diversified, yet comprehensible, and if the individual is to be able to orient himself properly for useful behavior.

At the scale of modern urban life, the ultimate constraints upon the system lie in nature. Energy-balanced development must derive from the main recurrences of heat, light, wind, and water. We must, for example, remember that shadows, representing differential heat gains, are not the same from one season to another. When it is necessary to place hundreds of buildings at a time, not just one, that kind of fact can be taken into consideration. If there is no choice in locating a building, if it must be only here or there, the location becomes a fact and accommodation to that fact takes place as a bigger heating or cooling unit. But if the building can be positioned, if it can be made taller or shorter and on this slope or that, if the packing can be denser on some slopes and sparser on others, a new design freedom can be created that does not totally depend upon the heater or cooler to provide a comfortable range of temperatures. Recognition can be taken of the fact that not only among seasons but at any given instant over the site, the energy gains from the sun are not the same.

Animals and plants have always taken into account such variations in nature. Can we, if we deal with large enough parts of the environment, make arrangements that are as subtly responsive? Once we overcome the attitude that all land increments must be the same size, there is no reason for increments on south slopes to be the same size as the increments on north slopes. In nature, north and south slopes look different, as do windward and lee slopes. These are lessons worth considering, but only if we are able to build in larger increments and only if there is control over more than what we have conventionally defined as a single building. With that lies the possibility of truly responsive form.

In the summer of 1964, I and five architecture students from the University of Southern California began to study a large site that would contain many buildings. The site was a hilly 1,200-acre section of the huge 85,000-acre Irvine Ranch property. The Irvine planners asked us to develop the site, primarily with single-family housing on the slopes.

As part of the project, we undertook heat and light studies of the site with the intention of differentiating single-house lot sizes from one orientation of slope to another. The object of these studies was a very simple one based on an equalization of amenity over a site with different conditions. The amenity was that a yard be in sunlight the majority of the day.

Our studies showed considerably more shadow on the site in winter than in summer, with related seasonal differences of insolation (fig. 9.1). The seasonal as well as daily differences in light and heat were most pronounced on north and south slopes. Our intent was to mitigate the effect of these differences by differentiating lot size.

Summer   Winter

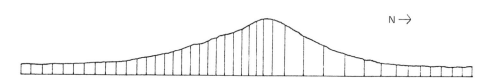

N →

Fig. 9.1
The plan of a 1,200 acre hilly site being developed in southern California demonstrates seasonal differences due to the effects of sun. Shadows at the same time of day (4 p.m.) vary from one season to another. This variation can become a determining factor in the establishment of house type and orientation, lot size and orientation, road orientation, and landscape type. Plans based on those for the Irvine Company, Irvine, California, by Ralph L. Knowles.

Fig. 9.2
A typical section of a hilly site near the coast of southern California demonstrates a differentiation of lot dimension from north to south slopes. This differentiation based upon orientation derives from the desirability of heat and light near the sea coast. In order to catch the sun on some part of the lot during the day, a north-facing slope must be developed with larger increments to allow more generous ground surface for alternative placements of a house within its lot limits. Section based on plans prepared for the Irvine Company, Irvine, California, by Ralph L. Knowles.

Let us assume, for example, two similar houses, one sited on a south slope, one on a north slope. Simple heliodon experiments or even one's own experiences with the differing lengths of shadow cast from objects of equal height will quickly show that houses might be more closely packed on south than on north slopes and still have equal yard areas in sunlight.

The Irvine Ranch studies produced the smallest lots on south slopes, the largest on north slopes, and moderate size lots on flat land. (Fig. 9.2; east and west slopes not shown in the section were also studied and also produced moderate size lots.) This simple example of differentiated lot size is introduced in the final chapter for two reasons. First, it demonstrates that even with small and conventional buildings, some component of the design can be made effectively responsive to natural variation. The result is an overall response at a larger scale than the small lot increments that are differentiated to make the final form. Such simple techniques can and should be employed today, not just to make sunny yards for greater recreational enjoyment, but to provide each dwelling unit with proper general exposure. Second, this simple example of differentiated lot size, while it comes nowhere near demonstrating the full potential of the techniques described in the text, does allow us to return to three points about economics, community, and aesthetics made in the introduction of the book.

The first point compared short and long-term views of the economics of development. The point has been made several times that we grow cheaply and maintain expensively. Using this approach, most developers would not take the time and additional expense to distinguish one orientation of slope from another. As a result, some lots have a higher amenity than others, yet all houses would initially be priced the same. Consequently, over time the property value is differentiated over the site with the introduction of attendant economic and probable social instability. Such failures to recognize the long-term economic implications of even the most basic aspects of orientation can be seen in almost every city.

During the late 1950s, I worked in downtown Boston and very often walked along Commonwealth Avenue near the Public Garden. Years later, I recalled the street as broad and separated by an island of large deciduous trees. What seemed incongruous in these recollections was the contrast between the condition of the houses on the two sides of the street.

The houses were all large and had evidently been designed for a gracious style of life, with the important living spaces facing the street, the service spaces in the back. Those houses on the south side of the street were generally run down and many had been converted to rooming houses. Some were vacant. By contrast, the houses on the north were generally well kept and, insofar as could be seen from the outside, were generally occupied by families. Reinforcing the contrast of condition and use was the quality of light on the house fronts. The houses on the south of the street fronted north and were generally dark. Those on the north fronted south and caught the rays of the sun. Not until several years after leaving Boston did the possible correlation between orientation and condition of the buildings occur to me. The sevice spaces had the desirable southerly orientation for houses on the south side of the street. The important living spaces received the south sun on on the north side of the street.

The correlation of economic and social change with orientation has been reinforced by observations made in Los Angeles where similar deterioration and ultimate change of function can be seen along segments of Wilshire Boulevard. Recent discussions with real-estate brokers who handle property along Wilshire support the observations in very real terms of leases and rents. The north side of Wilshire on which shops face south has the economic advantage. Over time, the tendency has been for the whole street to transform from a few stories to tall commercial structures, but the rate of transformation is usually greater on the side that fronts north. An obvious solution and a lesson for the future would involve the differentiation of building type and function to avoid deterioration and ultimate changes over time.

The second point concerned the importance of contact diversity in a community. The normal mode of development under similar circumstances often produces a near standardization of the house-lot-street relationship in which the whole combination of parts is made to look like all others in spite of differences in the shape and structure of the land and the differences that orientation can make. Tops of hills have been flattened, their sides terraced, and valleys filled, in an attempt to standardize building sites that cannot be standardized in a highly differentiated context. Very simply, flatland houses do not belong in the dimensional world of hills. Some of the functional consequences become obvious in places like Southern California where seasonal rains and unstable soil conditions can transform disrupted natural drainage systems into disaster areas.

Other functional consequences do not become so dramatically evident but still pressure for transformation in the long run. The likelihood that economic and social instability will ultimately result from an undifferentiated plan has already been mentioned. What is the meaning to the community of a differentiated plan? What are the advantages of a diversified physical environment in which, at the least, a functional distinction is made between different degrees of slope and orientation? The answer is that close-contact diversity of community functions would be provided where now we are more likely to find vast areas of low-diversity development. The critic who would remind us of the site with less pronounced slopes and change of orientation should be encouraged to look closer at changes of soil, the natural ambulation of streams, changes of wind direction, and building orientation to sun—all factors that would generate a diversified built arrangement.

In the case of the Irvine site, the choice is not between two similar houses, one with a generally pleasant orientation and one without. The choice is rather between two different kinds of arrangement in which the natural rhythms of light and dark, warm and cool find a correlation in the form of the arrangement. The choice can be immediately perceived and is reinforced over time as the two differently oriented houses change their character with the passing hours and the changing seasons. This leads directly to the last point about aesthetics.

The provision of diversity and choice in the built environment is not sufficient if the possibility of choice is not understood. This requires that people be able to comprehend their environment, to perceive the associations that comprise it, to orient themselves so that they may function within it. To understand in a general way that present urban environments do not provide useful clues to orientation, it is important to recognize that the original source of our perceptual abilities is the natural environment. Since man has survived, his perceptual abilities must have adequately adapted to the natural environment and been maintained and improved through countless generations.

Adequate adaptation of man's perceptual ability has led to ultimate dependence upon characteristics of those conditions in nature to which any organism may adapt, namely those congruent with recurrence. A primary characteristic of such conditions is functional differentiation; through the processes of adaptive evolution this characteristic has affected the essential scale range of man's senses. Within this range, phenomena may be perceived while any attempt to extend the range in magnitude, in time, or in direction may produce sensory discontinuities and subsequent disorientation; these may be used as the terms for stating fundamental problems since orientation is the essential condition for free choice.

In an environment of low built diversity, there is a lessened opportunity for orientation. Any built arrangement that correlates with natural diversity will itself exhibit diversity at a scale that reflects the sources of man's perceptions. It may be hypothesized for future testing that an artificial environment made in response to the recurrences of nature will exhibit functional differentiation that can act as an aid to orientation and to the subsequent useful behavior of man.

Whether this statement can be tested and proved remains to be seen. That people respond with pleasure to the variety of nature is not in doubt. To do such a simple and possible thing as differentiating the housing from one slope to another in response to the same forces that give rise to natural diversity is, indeed, to deal in a different aesthetic than we now accept. It might be called a natural aesthetic. If the basis for differentiation is energy conservation, as it has been discussed in this book, the term used in the introduction may be appropriate—an aesthetic for survival.

We have been discussing individual perceptions, but institutional man has requirements also. Not only has individual man's perceptual ability adaptively evolved out of the natural environment but his institutions bear the cyclic imprint of natural recurrence. The sun rises and sets, seasons come and go; their passage has always signaled repetitions of adaptive behavior in men. Repetition has led to reinforcement and on to institutionalization. This formal recognition that certain conditions could be met by the organized and anticipatory actions of a community has had many advantages. It provided a framework within which men could feel secure in their long-range plans. Not every man need be responsible for all his own needs. Needs could be anticipated within an institutional framework and planned for by diversifying the roles of individuals. With a diversity of roles came the possibility of choosing one's role; and so long as men lived in direct and evident balance with nature, the role of each individual had clear meaning and an obvious importance to the community. As societies could further remove themselves from a direct and obvious relation to nature, individuals and institutions seem to have lost meaning.

The process by which people have become less obviously related to nature can be described in three phases which are characterized by their achieved levels of technology.[1] The first is pre-urban and pre-literate and consists of small numbers of people gathered in self-sufficient homogeneous groups. In this situation primitive man was forced to improve the essential image of his environment by adapting his perception; such adaptation was naturally responsive to the primary, cyclic characteristics of the environment. The slow process of evolving into more complex societies through settlement in villages and through advances in technology gave rise to the second level, that of civilized pre-industrial or feudal society. It was in the context of this second type of society that the world's first cities developed; but though they provided environments very different from nature, their physical form and their institutions were usually constrained by the shape and scale of the land and by the cyclic forces of nature. The third phase in the development of man's artificial environment is represented by the modern industrial city; it is characterized by the tremendous technological breakthrough in new sources of inanimate energy that produced the industrial revolution. This industrial and technological revolution has had a profound effect on the natural environment. It has resulted in the superposition upon virtually all natural variations of an increasing range of man-made effects, multifolded in response to technology and independent of the community needs of people.

1. See Gideon Sjoberg, "The Origin and Evolution of Cities," *Scientific American,* 213 (September 1965), 55-63.

Only strong societies have the ability to shape the natural environment in opposition to individual mental and physical needs. It is done in the name of progress and in the context of the nineteenth-century industrial heritage that interprets efficiency in terms of mass production. Independently of what is being done with the land, modern procedures are based on the notion that the least expensive way to grow any system is through a process of low-diversity reproduction. Two primary examples are the way we build our urban arrangements and the way we grow our food and fiber. But the maintenance implication of this cheap mode of growth is neglected. For the built arrangement, that cost is usually a tremendously high level of fossil fuel conversion to maintain environmental equilibrium. In the case of the food and fiber industry, maintenance cost is that of artificial fertilizers and insecticides. We cannot live with these costs much longer. Present energy production systems are inadequate to the task and often have serious effects upon the environment, as do procedures for maintaining a biologically unstable agriculture. Concern is increasing about the long-term effects of residual heat buildup resulting from the combustion of fossil fuels and the cooling of nuclear reactors. There is as much concern over the long-term effects of wet farming and feed lots, of insecticides and chemical fertilizers.

Procedures for urban development and for agriculture, both of which tend to "grow" and sustain low diversity and unstable systems by the constant conversion of maintenance energy, stem from a primitive and overprolonged attitude about efficiency in essentially nineteenth-century industrial terms. This attitude, that it is cheaper to build if the same increment of building is reproduced over and over again, developed partly out of a

legitimate attempt to understand and to use a vastly expanding capacity to multifold standardized parts. While there are tremendous advantages to be gained from the industrialization of a building system that depends upon the mass production of items that can be assembled in a variety of unique combinations, the actual attitude that developed around simple multifolding allowed standardization in situations that derived little or no benefit from a powerful and useful tool.

Perhaps future urban growth can be generated independently of a fixed and repetitive increment. A single, fixed increment for growth, whether it be a repeated wall, floor, or whole building, should not constitute the urban design tools of the future. They are clearly not working today.

In the future, frameworks must be designed within which increments can fit. The framework will be a mechanism for control that is instructed by nature, anticipates change, and predicts the least susceptible type and size of development. It will be able to state if development can take place at all, and if so, in what sequence and at what rate.

The building of cities must be consciously organized and limited within the environmental capacity to transform energy and the human ability to comprehend such transformations. If the building process is clearly organized in relation to energy conservation, people will be able to read and understand their constructed environment. We have turned to nature to find those phenomena that man has used throughout history to organize his constructions. We have looked at the successful attempts of early man to build in response to natural recurrences. Those settlements offer much that is needed today: clarity, stability, relatively low maintenance cost, and symbolic importance.

Modern man, aided by technology, has been living in opposition to nature. His cities are distortions of the natural laws of energy conservation. They have lost their meaning in relation to his own biological nature. Now this period seems to be coming to a close, exposing a basic flaw in our contemporary attitudes about the uses of energy for purposes of growth and maintenance of our cities. For that reason, we must look for an approach that will lower these energy costs. In order to avoid waste, the city system must be made more responsive to environmental stimuli. Whether or not ecological stability and human choice in settlement are mutually exclusive objectives, and whether or not they lie in opposition to one another are critical questions. These studies suggest that, on the contrary, they are one and the same. Ecological stability depends upon a natural model whose most distinguishable attribute is diversity. Without diversity, there can be no choice. Therefore, the basic intent of this work has been to generate frameworks for settlement that maintain a stable relationship with nature and in so doing exhibit the diversity essential to human choice.

The basic structure for all problems dealing with society, its institutions, and the freedom of the individual to function within those institutions must be made with final reference to both man and nature. Man-made arrangements that lie in some balanced response to nature can provide the combined benefit of a trajectory toward stability over the long term and of a continuing diversity essential to choice. It is the intent of this work to make such balanced arrangments. The alternative is unacceptable.

Bibliography

Abrams, Charles. *The City Is the Frontier*. New York: Harper & Row, 1965.

Aginsky, B. W., and Aginsky, E. G. *Deep Valley*. New York: Stein & Day, 1967.

Alexandroff, Paul. *Elementary Concepts of Topology*. Translated by Alan E. Farley. New York: Dover Books, 1961 (Moscow: 1932).

Allport, Floyd H. *Theories of Perception and the Concept of Structure*. New York: John Wiley & Sons, 1955.

Ashby, W. Ross. *Introduction to Cybernetics*. New York: John Wiley & Sons, 1956.

—— *Design for a Brain*. New York: John Wiley & Sons, 1960.

Bagnold, Ralph A. *The Physics of Blown Sand and Desert Dunes*. New York: William Morrow and Company, 1941.

Barnum, J. D. "Development of Water Resources Is Not an End in Itself." Transcript of a lecture presented to Senate-Assembly Water Committee Hearing, 17 October 1968, at Sacramento, California.

Bates, Marston. *The Forest and the Sea*. New York: Random House, 1960.

Bavelas, Alex. "A Mathematical Model for Group Structures." *Applied Anthropology* 7 (1948): 16-30.

Beer, Stafford. *Cybernetics and Management*. New York: John Wiley & Sons, 1967.

Bellman, Richard. "Control Theory." *Scientific American* 221 (1964): 186-190.

Bertalanffy, Ludwig von. *General Systems Theory*. New York: George Braziller, 1968.

Bonner, J. T. "The Size of Life." *Natural History* 78 (1969): 40-45.

Boulding, K. E. "Toward a General Theory of Growth." *Canadian Journal of Economics and Political Science* 19 (1953): 326-340.

Brody, Samuel. *Biogenetics and Growth*. New York: Reinhold Publishing, 1945 .

Brooks, Norman. "Energy and the Environment." *Engineering and Science* (California Institute of Technology) 34 (1971): 20-23.

Buettner, Konrad J. K., and Thayer, Norman. *On Valley and Mountain Winds*. (Vols. I, II) Seattle: Department of Meteorology and Climatology, University of Washington, 1956, 1961.

—— *On Valley and Mountain Winds III and Valley Wind Theory*. Seattle: Department of Atmospheric Sciences, University of Washington, 1962.

Busacker, Robert G., and Saaty, Thomas L. *Finite Graphs and Networks*. New York: McGraw-Hill Book Company, 1965.

Carson, Rachel L. *The Edge of the Sea*. Boston: Houghton Mifflin Company, 1955.

Chalfant, W. A. *The Story of Inyo*. Stanford, Calif.: Stanford University Press, 1933.

Chase, Richard Allen. "Biological Aspects of Environmental Design." *Clinical Pediatrics* 8 (1969): 268-273.

Clausen, V. C. *Report of the Owens Valley*. Los Angeles: Los Angeles Department of Water and Power, 1964.

Dubos, Rene. *So Human an Animal*. New York: Charles Scribner's Sons, 1968.

Eberhard, John P. "Man Centered Standards for Technology." *Technology Review* 71 (1969): 50-55.

Festiger, Leon. *Social Pressures in Informal Groups*. New York: Harper & Bros, 1950.

—— *Changing Attitudes Through Social Contact*. Ann Arbor: University of Michigan Press, 1951.

Fitch, James Marston. 1965. "The Aesthetics of Function." *Annals of the New York Academy of Sciences* 128: 709-710.

—— *American Building*. Boston: Houghton Mifflin Company, 1972.

Frisch, Karl von. *Man and the Living World*. New York: Time, Inc, 1962.

—— *Dance Language and Orientation of Bees*. Cambridge, Mass.: Harvard University Press, 1967.

Galbraith, J. K. *The New Industrial State*. Boston: Houghton Mifflin Company, 1967.

Geiger, Rudolph. *The Climate Near the Ground*. Cambridge, Mass.: Harvard University Press, 1965.

Grobstein, Clifford. *The Strategy of Life*. San Francisco: W. H. Freeman & Company, 1964.

Gutkind, E. A. *Our World From the Air*. Garden City, N. Y.: Doubleday, 1952.

Hall, A. D., and Fagen, R. E. "Definition of System." *General Systems* 1 (1956): 18-28.

Harary, Frank, and Norman, R. Z. *Graph Theory as a Mathematical Model in Social Science*. Ann Arbor: Institute for Social Research, University of Michigan, 1951.

Harrington, Michael. *The Other America*. New York: Macmillan, 1962.

—— *The Accidental Century*. New York: Macmillan, 1966.

Jackson, W. H. *Structural Geology and Volcanism of Owens Valley Region, California: A Geophysical Study*. California Division of Mines and Geology. Washington, D.C.: U.S. Government Printing Office, 1964.

Judd, Neil M. *The Material Culture of Pueblo Bonito*. Washington D.C.: Smithsonian Institution, 1954.

—— *The Architecture of Pueblo Bonito*. Washington, D.C.: Smithsonian Institution, 1964.

Kansky, K. D. *Department of Geography Research Paper No. 84*. Chicago: University of Chicago Press, 1963.

Kemeny, John G., and Snell, J. Laurie. *Mathematical Models in the Social Sciences*. Boston: Ginn and Company, 1962.

—— , and Thompson, Gerald L. 1957. *Introduction to Finite Mathematics*. Englewood Cliffs, N.J.: Prentice-Hall, 1957.

Knopg, Adolph. *A Geologic Reconnaissance of the Inyo Range and the Eastern Slope of the Southern Sierra Nevada, California.* U.S. Geological Survey. Washington, D.C.: U.S. Government Printing Office, 1918.

Knowles, R.L. "The Derivation of Surface Responses to Selected Environmental Forces." *Arts and Architecture* 81 (1964): 21-23.

—— Form and Stability. Paper read at Building Research Insititute, at Washington, D.C., April 23, 1968.

Kormondy, E. J. *Readings in Ecology.* Englewood Cliffs, N.J.: Prentice-Hall, 1965.

——*Concepts of Ecology.* Englewood Cliffs, N.J.: Prentice-Hall, 1969.

Lapp, Ralph, and Dietsch, Robert. "Burning Up Resources." *New Republic,* June 26, 1971, pp. 14-17.

Lee, Charles H. *An Intensive Study of the Water Resources of a Part of the Owens Valley, California.* Washington, D.C.: U.S. Government Printing Office, 1912.

Lynch, Kevin. *The Image of the City.* Cambridge, Mass.: MIT Press, 1960.

Margalef, Ramon. *Perspectives in Ecological Theory.* Chicago: University of Chicago Press, 1968.

Matthiessen, Peter. *Wildlife in America.* New York: Viking Press, 1969.

Mayo, Elton. *Social Problems of an Industrial Civilization.* Boston: Division of Research, Graduate School of Business Administration, Harvard University, 1945.

McGregor, John C. *Southwestern Archaeology.* New York: John Wiley & Sons, 1941.

McHarg, Ian. *Design With Nature.* Garden City, N.Y.: Natural History Press, 1969.

Mooney, H. A. "Influence of Soil Type on the Distribution of Two Closely Related Species of *Erigeron.*" *Ecology* 47 (1966): 950-958.

——, St. Andre, G., and Wright, R. P. "Alpine and Subalpine Vegetation Patterns in the White Mountains of California." *The American Midland Naturalist* 68 (1962): 257-273.

Morowitz, Harold J. *Energy in Biology.* New York: Academic Press, 1968.

Odum, E. P. *Fundamentals of Ecology.* 2d ed. Philadelphia: W.B. Saunders Company, 1959.

——"The Strategy of Eco-System Development." *Science* 164 (1969): 262-270.

Olgyay, Victor. *Design With Climate.* Princeton University Press, 1963.

Palmer, John D. "How a Bird Tells the Time of Day." *Natural History* 75 (1966): 48-53.

Parr, A. E. "Mind and Milieu: A Scientific Approach to Environment." *Arts and Architecture* 80 (1963): 21.

Rand, Christopher. *Los Angeles: The Ultimate City.* New York: Oxford University Press, 1967.

Rasmussen, Steen Eiler. *Towns and Buildings Described in Drawings and Words.* Cambridge: Harvard University Press, 1951.

Rensch, H. E. *Historic Spots in California.* Stanford, Calif.: Stanford University Press, 1948.

Reps, John W. *The Making of Urban America: A History of City Planning in the United States.* Princeton, N.J.: Princeton University Press, 1965.

Robinson, David M., and Graham, J. Walter. *Excavations at Olynthus: The Hellenic House.* Baltimore: Johns Hopkins Press, 1938.

Robinson, Nathaniel. *Solar Radiation.* Amsterdam: Elsevier Publishing Company, 1966.

Rudofsky, Bernard. *Architecture Without Architects.* New York: Doubleday and Company, 1964.

Rush, Philip S. *Historical Sketches of the Californias: Spanish and Mexican Periods.* San Diego: 1953.

Schumacher, Genny. *The Mammoth Lake Sierra.* San Francisco: Sierra Club, 1961.

Sedgwick, Mrs. William T. *Acoma, the Sky City.* Cambridge, Mass.: Harvard University Press, 1926.

Sharp, Thomas. *The Anatomy of the Village.* Harmondsworth, Middlesex, England: Penguin Books, 1946.

Shepard, Paul. *The Subversive Science: Essays Towards an Ecology of Man.* Boston: Houghton Mifflin Company, 1969.

Shibutani, Tamotsu. *Society and Personality.* Englewood Cliffs, N.J.: Prentice-Hall, 1962.

Sjoberg, Gideon. "The Origin and Evolution of Cities." *Scientific American* 213 (1965): 55-63.

Smithsonian Institution. *Annual Report of the Smithsonian Institution.* Washington, D.C.: Smithsonian Institution Press, 1945, pp. 379-86.

Sowers, G. N. *Introduction to Soil Mechanics and Foundations.* New York: Macmillan, 1965.

Spicer, Edward H. *Human Problems in Technological Change.* New York: John Wiley & Sons, 1965.

St. Andre, G., Mooney, H. A., and Wright, R. D. "The Pinyon Woodland Zone in the White Mountains of California." *American Midland Naturalist* 73 (1965): 225-239.

Steward, J. H. *Petroglyphs of California.* Berkeley, Calif.: University of California Press, 1929.

——*Ethnography of the Owens Valley Piute.* Berkeley, Calif.: University of California Press, 1933.

—— *Myths of the Owens Valley Piute.* Berkeley, Calif.: University of California Press, 1936.

——*Nevada Shoshoni.* Berkeley, Calif.: University of California Press, 1941.

——*Northern and Gosiute Shoshoni.* Berkeley, Calif.: University of California Press, 1943.

—— *Basin-Plateau Socio-Political Groups.* Washington, D.C.: U.S. Government Printing Office, 1958.

Stubbs, Stanley A. *A Bird's Eye View of the Pueblos.* Norman, Okla.: University of Oklahoma Press, 1950.

Thompson, Sir D'Arcy Wentworth. *On Growth and Form.* London: Cambridge University Press, 1961.

Vickers, Geoffrey. "Control, Stability and Choice." *General System* 2 (1957): 1-8.

Watson, E.B., and Storie, R.E. *Soil Survey: Bishop Area California.* Washington, D.C.: U.S. Government Printing Office, 1928.

Webber, Melvin. *Explorations into Urban Structure.* Philadelphia: University of Pennsylvania Press, 1964.

Weil, Simone. *Need for Roots.* Boston: Beacon Press, 1948.

Weiner, Norbert. *The Human Use of Human Beings: Cybernetics and Society.* New York: Doubleday & Company, 1954.

Von Werlhop, J. C. *Rock Art of the Owens Valley.* U.S. Archeological Survey. Berkeley, Calif.: University of California, 1965.

Whitehead, Alfred North. *Science and the Modern World.* New York: Macmillan, 1967.

Wing, Kittridge. *Bandelier National Monument.* Washington, D.C.: National Park Service Handbook No. 23, 1955.

Wright, R. D., and Mooney, H. A. "Substrate-oriented Distribution of Bristle-cone Pine in the White Mountains of California." *American Midland Naturalist* 73 (1965): 257-284.

Wynne-Edwards, V. C. "Population Control in Animals." *Scientific American* 211 (1964): 68-74.

Index

Date Due